BUILD AN eBAY® BUSINESS

QuickSteps

Second Edition

JOHN CRONAN

CAROLE MATTHEWS

McGraw Hill

New York Chicago San Francisco
Lisbon London Madrid Mexico City
Milan New Delhi San Juan
Seoul Singapore Sydney Toronto

DISCARDED

The McGraw·Hill Companies

Cataloging-in-Publication Data is on file with the Library of Congress

McGraw-Hill books are available at special quantity discounts to use as premiums and sales promotions, or for use in corporate training programs. To contact a special sales representative, please visit the Contact Us page at www.mhprofessional.com.

eBay® is a registered trademark of eBay, Inc.

Adobe® and Photoshop® are registered trademarks of Adobe Systems Incorporated.

Microsoft®, Excel®, Expression®, and Windows® are either registered trademarks or trademarks of Microsoft Corporation in the United States and/or other countries.

This book was composed with Adobe® InDesign.

Information has been obtained by McGraw-Hill from sources believed to be reliable. However, because of the possibility of human or mechanical error by our sources, McGraw-Hill, or others, McGraw-Hill does not guarantee the accuracy, adequacy, or completeness of any information and is not responsible for any errors or omissions or the results obtained from the use of such information.

1234567890   CCI CCI   0198

ISBN   978-0-07-160145-0
MHID   0-07-160145-7

SPONSORING EDITOR / Roger Stewart

EDITORIAL SUPERVISOR / Jody McKenzie

PROJECT MANAGER / Vasundhara Sawhney (International Typesetting and Composition)

ACQUISITIONS COORDINATOR / Carly Stapleton

SERIES CREATORS AND EDITORS / Marty and Carole Matthews

COPY EDITOR / Lisa McCoy

PROOFREADER / Julie M. Smith

INDEXER / Valerie Perry

PRODUCTION SUPERVISOR / George Anderson

COMPOSITION / International Typesetting and Composition

ILLUSTRATION / International Typesetting and Composition

ART DIRECTOR, COVER / Jeff Weeks

COVER DESIGN / Pattie Lee

SERIES DESIGN / Bailey Cunningham

As we have used eBay and focused our attention on the vast community it serves, we have become aware of the profound changes in how we buy and sell in the global economy. eBay represents a shift in tangible and intangible ways. Not only are millions of people conducting business at some level (from online garage sales to huge, global companies), but also we are thinking about the world in a very different way. No longer is that buyer in England a stranger or that seller of silk in Cambodia an unattainable source. We might not know whether our seller is tall, male or female, color-blind, or a soccer fan, but we do know whether he or she conducts business in an honorable way. What is this thing that combines materialism with such a sense of the essence of who we are? With that question mark, we would like to dedicate this book to the millions of eBay users who have helped to transform the age-old practices of buying and selling into this vital and dynamic global economy.

John Cronan and Carole Matthews

About the Authors

John Cronan has over 28 years of computer experience and has been writing and editing computer-related books for over 13 years. His recent books include *eBay QuickSteps Second Edition, Microsoft Office Excel 2007 QuickSteps*, and *Microsoft Office Access 2007 QuickSteps*. John and his wife Faye operate an antiques business in Washington state and frequent area auctions and sales in search of merchandise they can "bring back to life." An eBay member since 1999, John couples his in-depth experience in writing books on software products with his antiques familiarity and eBay use to bring a unique perspective to *Build an eBay Business QuickSteps, Second Edition*. John and Faye (and cat Little Buddy) reside in Everett, WA.

Carole Boggs Matthews has more than 30 years of computing experience. She has authored or co-authored more than 90 books, including *eBay QuickSteps, PhotoShop CS4 QuickSteps, Photoshop Elements 3 QuickSteps, Microsoft Office PowerPoint 2007 QuickSteps*, and *Microsoft Office 2007 QuickSteps*. Prior to her writing career, she co-founded and operated a computer business, developing tools to help others use computers in their businesses. An eBay user since 1998, Carole now applies that experience and many years of writing to *Build an eBay Business QuickSteps, Second Edition*, bringing both business and computer knowledge to the book. Carole lives in Washington state with her husband Marty, son Michael, and family cat and dog.

Contents at a Glance

1
2
3
4
5
6
7
8
9
10

Contents

Chapter 4 | **Creating Super Listings** 67

Chapter 5 | **Managing Your eBay Business** 91

Acknowledgments

As it takes a village to raise a child, so it takes a talented and dedicated team to produce a book. In fact, to create a book on eBay, it actually takes two teams:

Comprising the first team, there are the publishing professionals that work behind the scenes, nurturing our concept for the book from its proposal to the finished product. We wish to thank Roger Stewart as our acquisitions editor, Carly Stapleton for overall project coordination, Valerie Perry for indexing, Lisa McCoy for copy editing, and Vasundhara Sawhney for project management.

The second team consists of the dozens of eBay users, businesses, and government entities that offered their time, expertise, listing data, and materials to us. Though we cannot acknowledge all of you here for your efforts, we extend our appreciation for your contributions in making this a better book. We would like to recognize our PowerSeller advisor, Vicki Detwiler (dvdet), eBay PowerSeller, eBay Store owner, and Registered eBay Trading Assistant, for her time and the use of her facility to educate us on many of the finer points related to selling on eBay as a business. We'd also like to recognize Carol R. McGeehan (luvantiqs), another accomplished PowerSeller, eBay Store owner, and Registered eBay Trading Assistant, for her generous support of this book.

Thanks to all!

Introduction

QuickSteps books are recipe books for computer users. They answer the question "How do I...?" by providing a quick set of steps to accomplish the most common tasks with a particular program. The sets of steps are the central focus of the book. Sidebar QuickSteps provide information on how to do quickly many small functions or tasks that are in support of the primary functions. Sidebar QuickFacts supply information that you need to know about a subject. Notes, Tips, and Cautions augment the steps, but they are presented in a separate column so as to not interrupt the flow. Brief introductions are present, but there is minimal narrative otherwise. Many illustrations and figures, a number with callouts, are also included where they support the steps.

eBay characters, such as PowerSeller Sally, Newbie Sally, Nonprofit Sally, Professor Polly, Buyer Bob, and Browser Earl, each add a unique perspective to the main topic being described.

QuickSteps books are organized by function and the tasks needed to perform those functions. Each function is a chapter. Each task, or "How To," contains the steps needed for its accomplishment, along with the relevant Notes, Tips, Cautions, and screenshots. Tasks are easy to find through:

- The Table of Contents, which lists the functional areas (chapters) and tasks in the order they are presented

- A How To list of tasks on the opening page of each chapter

- The index, which provides an alphabetical list of the terms that are used to describe the functions and tasks

- Color-coded tabs for each chapter or functional area, with an index to the tabs in the Contents at a Glance (just before the Table of Contents)

Conventions Used in This Book

Build an eBay Business QuickSteps uses several conventions designed to make the book easier for you to follow. Conventions used include:

- An icon in the Table of Contents and in the How To list in each chapter references a QuickSteps 🔍 or QuickFacts 🪐 sidebar in a chapter.

- **Bold type** is used for words or objects on the screen that you are to do something with, like click **Save As**, open **File**, and click **Close**.

- *Italic type* is used for a word or phrase that is being defined or otherwise deserves special emphasis.

- <u>Underlined type</u> is used for text that you are to type from the keyboard.

- SMALL CAPITAL LETTERS are used for keys on the keyboard, such as **ENTER** and **SHIFT**.

- When you are expected to enter a command, you are told to press the key(s). If you are to enter text or numbers, you are told to type them.

How to...

Chapter 1

Planning Your eBay Business

In this chapter you will learn what it takes to structure your selling on eBay so that it conforms to generally accepted good business practices. You will also learn what is necessary to be considered a legal business in the eyes of local, state, and federal authorities.

It doesn't really matter how you find yourself in the position to build an eBay business—whether you started as most eBay sellers do, selling household or easily acquired merchandise part-time or as a hobby to make a few bucks; or if you are trying to sell items online from your traditional storefront ("brick and mortar") business; or if you are starting from scratch with the idea of building a new eBay business. In all cases, to reach the level of an eBay PowerSeller (a designation by eBay of high-volume sellers), you will need to plan for and

BUILDING AN eBAY BUSINESS

The list of eBay success stories is endless. If you need a reason to build an eBay business (probably not, since you purchased this book), see if any of the following rationales pertain to you:

- Increase the sales of your current business
- Close your current business storefront and operate a virtual business
- Close your independent Web storefront and open an eBay Store
- Gain financial independence by running an eBay business as a full-time career

Once you've decided to build an eBay business, you can profit (or nonprofit, in the case of authorized charitable organizations) from this online phenomenon in several ways:

- Sell merchandise and services on eBay and in eBay Stores (see Chapter 2 for information on selling tactics and Chapter 6 for information on creating an eBay Store)
- Become a trading assistant (see Chapter 7)
- Find consignment goods and sell using a registered eBay drop-off locations (see Chapter 7)
- Sell on specialty sites (see Chapter 8)
- Sell to promote nonprofit charitable causes (see Chapter 9)

execute standard business practices if you are to be trusted by customers, lenders, suppliers, and others who are key to your financial success. This chapter covers common business-planning resources and tax, legal, and financial considerations that help you ensure a smooth transition into using eBay as a full-fledged business. To help you start or improve your eBay business, this chapter also explores assistance available from eBay and from professional resources.

Develop a Business Plan

You don't have to hire a $250-an-hour consultant to create a business plan for you. Unless you are seeking funding from financial institutions (in which case, see the "Getting Professional Help" QuickFacts later in the chapter), a business plan can be simply a written statement, coalescing your vision and goals, financial resources, and a description of the products you want to sell and the customers you want to reach. Many experts today think that spending much time on a business plan instead of getting in and experiencing what is needed to sell your product is counterproductive; that is, the plan itself is not the real value. Rather the planning itself—finding and working through potential problems and obstacles you may encounter is the value of a business plan. That said, the plan offers a sanctuary to return to when you find yourself buried in the trenches of day-to-day eBay selling. When time is of the essence and decisions that affect the long-term success of your business come up, it's nice to be able to dust off that business plan and refer to the principles that got you going in the first place.

Professor Polly says: "It pays to plan ahead. It wasn't raining when Noah built the ark."

TIP

A business plan can be seen as an "umbrella" document that contains several sub-plans, as shown in Figure 1-1. For example, within your eBay business plan, you could include a *marketing* plan (see "Market Your Business" later in the chapter), an *operating* plan (to outline the process that controls how your business runs), a *technology* plan (to identify computer, other hardware, software, and telecommunication needs you anticipate), and a *financial* plan (to identify the finances needed to implement the other plans and provide the foundation for a budget).

Figure 1-1: **A business plan is typically a container vehicle for other documents, or plans, that define your business goals, processes, and finances.**

TIP

A popular mnemonic to help write "smart" objectives is, well, SMART—*Specific, Measurable, Achievable, Realistic, and Time-Bound.*

Create a Business Plan

If you've never created a business plan before and are daunted by the prospect, don't let that stop you. Like many other first-time endeavors, the hardest part is just starting. Start by creating broad strokes, and then fill in the details as required by external sources (such as loan officers and vendors) and by your own needs.

OUTLINE YOUR EBAY BUSINESS

So what are you really trying to accomplish by ramping up your current eBay sales or moving your current traditional business to eBay? Three common tools that businesses use to help clarify their raison d'être (reason to be) and where they see themselves in the future can help you focus your ideas for a business plan. In fact, coalescing your ideas into a few categories may be all you need for a business plan that doesn't require external financing. In *The One Page Business Plan* by Jim Horan, these categories, along with a few others, could comprise your business plan:

- The **Vision Statement** lets you dream on paper. Place your idealistic thoughts as to what you want your business to be into words, for example, "to create a presence on eBay recognized as the go-to seller for vintage women's clothing."

- The **Mission Statement**, at its core, describes the purpose of your business, for example, "to provide quality, interesting, and functional articles of vintage clothing."

QUICKSTEPS

BECOMING A POWERSELLER

So you've been selling a lot of items on eBay and covet that slick PowerSeller icon you see next to some sellers' User IDs. Becoming a big eBay seller is not a trivial matter, however, and eBay only hands out these PowerSeller icons after you've earned your eBay stripes. (You are invited to join when eBay determines you've met their criteria.) To check to see if you qualify to become a PowerSeller:

1. Click **Site Map** on the eBay header.

2. Under Selling Resources, click **PowerSellers**. Under Choose A Topic on the sidebar:

   - Click **Requirements** to find out how you will qualify to be a PowerSeller.

   - Click **Program Benefits** to find out why you might want to be one.

BE A PROLIFIC SELLER

- Start now and keep selling for at least 90 days.

- Sell a minimum number of items: at least two items a month for the three months prior to your consideration for PowerSeller status or two items per month for 12 months.

  –And–

- Sell a minimum sales amount: at least $1,000 per month in average gross sales or 100 items for three consecutive months for entry-level PowerSeller status (Bronze). Or, sell annually a minimum of $12,000 or 1,200 items for the past 12 months.

Continued . . .

- **Goals and Objectives** list what you want your business to accomplish in specific, measurable terms, for example:

  - Maintain a minimum of 100 items for sale on my eBay Store and 25 auction listings at all times.

  - Reach PowerSeller sales volume within one year (see the "Becoming a PowerSeller" QuickSteps).

  - Reduce returned items by 20 percent.

  - Become a trading assistant in six months.

  - Attend eBay Live!

Browser Earl says: "Once you have 10 DSRs, you can check your Seller Dashboard to see how close you are to being a PowerSeller."

Newbie Sally dreams of the day she will become a PowerSeller.

INVESTIGATE RESOURCES

- Learn as much as you can from free resources, such as the library and government or business Web sites. The Small Business Administration (SBA) (www.sba.gov) and Entrepreneur.com, Inc. (www.entrepreneur.com) offer a plethora of information on starting a business and creating business plans and include links to supporting resources.

- Practice writing a business plan by using tutorials. CIT Small Business Lending Corporation (www.smallbizlending.com/resources/workshop/sba.htm), an SBA lender, provides a two-part tutorial.

- Purchase business plan software or templates. Sample plans get you going, and most packages provide supporting documents and other assistance. Business Resources Software, Inc. (www.businessplans.org) is a popular choice.

- Gather all required documents and data.

Browser Earl says: "Access links to the SBA at pages.ebay.com/ education/advanced/byb.html."

QUICKSTEPS

BECOMING A POWERSELLER
(Continued)

- Keep selling and increase your three-month average gross sales to achieve higher PowerSeller levels: $3,000 (Silver), $10,000 (Gold), $25,000 (Platinum), $150,000 (Titanium).

BE A GOOD EBAY CITIZEN

- Maintain outstanding feedback, with at least 100 entries at a 98 percent positive rating.

- Maintain a rating of at least 4.5 over 12 months for the Detailed Seller Ratings (DSRs), which evaluates feedback from buyers on your performance in four categories: item as described, shipping time, communications, and shipping and handling charges.

- Do not run afoul of eBay policies.

- Pay your eBay bills on time.

TIP

Don't dwell on perfection—in many cases, the business plan is only for your benefit: to quantify and document your thoughts and plans. "A good battle plan that you act on today can be better than a perfect one tomorrow." (General George S. Patton)

Implement Your Business Plan

The business plan is a living document. You cannot simply click Save and place the file four layers deep in your Documents folder, or pull the final draft from the printer and file it away in the back of a file cabinet drawer. For the document to be effective, it needs to be presented to others, periodically reviewed by you, and assessments turned into actionable changes.

1. Review the plan internally and externally, with business professionals, such as loan officers, SBA online counselors, and SCORE (Service Corps of Retired Executives) volunteers, taking a look at it.

2. Before providing the plan to others whose money, resources, or assistance you seek, create a professional presentation package:

   - Create a **cover letter** to introduce the business plan to the recipient. Summarize any prior communications and the purpose of your proposal.

   - Create a **title page** that provides key information about your eBay business (see Figure 1-2). Also, if your plan includes any information you consider proprietary, add a confidentiality or copyright notice.

   - Include a **table of contents** to help readers understand the scope of your plan and assist them in navigating through it.

3. Post elements of the plan where you and your employees will be constantly reminded of its underlying principles.

4. Update the plan whenever major changes occur or new ideas are brought forth.

5. Review the plan periodically to measure how close you are toward reaching your goals and objectives.

Market Your Business

As part of the business plan, or as its own plan, a marketing plan, along with a timetable to carry it out, clarifies your big-picture marketing strategy, identifies your target market (or audience), and helps you match your product to that audience.

QUICKFACTS

DESIGNING A BUSINESS PLAN

The basic sections of a business plan are:

- The **Business** includes a description of your eBay business, marketing plans (see "Market Your Business" earlier in the chapter), your competition, operating procedures, personnel, and business insurance.

- **Financial Data** describes any loan applications, capital equipment and supply lists, a break-even analysis, and financial statements, such as a balance sheet, profit and loss projections (out to three years; by month the first year, by quarter for years two and three), budgets, and a cash flow report, as shown in Figure 1-3.

- **Supporting Documents** includes copies of a franchise (for example, Worldwide Brands X, an eBay drop-ship wholesaler), leases or purchase agreements for building space, licenses and other legal documents, letters of intent from suppliers, and résumés and personal financial data on all partners.

(source: United States Small Business Administration)

WORLDWIDE BRANDS X *The What To Sell and Where To Get It Experts!*

Business Plan
For

Acme Antiques
1234 Main St.
Anywhere, WA 98000
(206) 555-1212

Prepared by:
John Smith
President Acme Antiques
jsmith@acme-antiques.com

This content in this plan is confidential, copyrighted, and is the sole property of Acme Antiques. No copying, reproduction, reuse, or disclosure of this material is allowed unless written permission is obtained from Acme Antiques.

Figure 1-2: A good title page includes your eBay business' basic demographics and any confidentiality caveats.

	A	B	C	D	E	F	G
1		Superior Office Supplies					
2		2010 Budget					
3	Superior Office Supplies	1st Qtr	2nd Qtr	3rd Qtr	4th Qtr	Total Yr.	
4	Revenue						
5	Paper Supplies	$23,456	$35,938	$38,210	$39,876	$137,591	
6	Writing Instruments	$5,437	$5,834	$5,923	$6,082	$23,276	
7	Cards and Books	$14,986	$15,043	$16,975	$16,983	$63,987	
8	Other Items	$25,897	$26,729	$27,983	$28,721	$109,330	
9	*Total Revenue*	*$69,887*	*$83,544*	*$89,091*	*$91,662*	*$334,184*	
10							
11	Expenses						
12	Wages	$8,345	$8,598	$9,110	$91,662	$35,354	
13	Income Tax	$1,252.00	$1,290.00	$1,367.00	$1,395.00	$5,303.00	
14	Social Security	$1,035.00	$1,066.00	$1,130.00	$1,153.00	$4,384.00	
15	Medicare	$242.00	$249.00	$264.00	$270.00	$1,025.00	
16	*Total Expenses*	*$10,874.00*	*$11,203.00*	*$11,870.00*	*$12,119.00*	*$46,066.00*	
17							
18							

Figure 1-3: Having accurate financial data is vital to the success of any startup business.

TIP

Your vision statement, mission statement, goals, and objectives make great motivational and inspiration taglines for you and your employees, and provide a sense of your business professionalism to your customers. Post them where you create listings, package items, and greet customers; add them to screen savers; and include them on your invoices to buyers.

NOTE

On December 2 and 3, 2007, there were 32 million unique visitors to eBay. On December 10, 2007, $880 million was logged—the highest online retail sales for one day ever. (Source is an eBay online workshop, "Unlocking the Potential of Your Business on eBay," in 2008.)

Fortunately, eBay does a great deal to help its sellers make buyers aware of the products and services they offer. You can distinguish your business by using the tools provided by eBay, using third-party tools and services, and harnessing your own creative efforts summarized in a marketing plan (see Chapter 2 for specific selling strategies).

Apply a Marketing Strategy

The foundation of any marketing strategy is known as The Four Ps. The following sections describe how to apply these to a potential eBay business.

DEVELOP YOUR PRODUCT

It's always best to sell a product that people want. (It tends to increase sales!) In order to determine what to sell:

1. Research your customer base (eBay members) and see what people are buying:
   - View **Completed Listings** for products you're thinking about selling.
   - Check out What's Hot on eBay (click **Site Map**; under Selling Resources, click **What's Hot**). You'll see the categories of merchandise that will be promoted by eBay on the home page and via e-mails, as seen in Figure 1-4.

2. Sell what you understand. Become knowledgeable about a product line so people come to rely on you as a source of expertise.

3. Sell what interests you. The passion for your product line will become evident in every facet of your business.

4. Sell what makes you money. The purpose of a for-profit business is just that, making a profit. If you run the numbers and determine you cannot sell the product for more than your acquisition, shipping, and overhead costs, it's time to change products.

Search Options
Location
Worldwide ▼
Items within 200 ▼
miles of 98260
Show only
Items listed with PayPal
Buying Options
Auctions ▼
Free Shipping
✓ Completed listings
🎁 Gift items

What's Hot for Spring

The eBay merchandising team combs trade magazines, gathers predictions from respected industry experts, and looks at eBay sales data to determine what's in demand. Here's the scoop on which hot products will be promoted on the home page, emails, and buyer catalog this season.

ART, ANTIQUES, COLLECTIBLES

Pop Art Print
Buddha Statue
Cuckoo Clock
Retro Ball Clock
Roman Numerals Clock
George Nelson Clock
Vintage Schwinn Bike
Vintage Lone Ranger Comic Book
Vintage Belt Buckle
Indian Moccasins
Marilyn Monroe Doll
Vintage Guitar

Vintage Hot Wheels
Radio Flyer Tricycle
LEGO Wild West
Toy Story Woody
Elvis Cookbook
Beatles Yellow Submarine Figure
Johnny Cash Signed Photo
Grateful Dead Poster
Kiss Doll
John Wayne Movie Poster
Saturday Night Fever Record

TECHNOLOGY

Bushnell Digital Binoculars
Canon PowerShot SD1000
Blackberry Pearl Unlocked
Nokia N95 Cell Phone Unlocked
Motorola H700 Bluetooth Headset
Motorola RAZR2 V8 Unlocked
Apple iMac
Garmin nuvi 660
TomTom One
Sling Media Slingbox
Sony Bravia 46" LCD HDTV

Apple iPod touch 4GB
Garmin Forerunner 305
iPod Shuffle
Kicker Amplifier
JL Subwoofer
Classic Movie DVD
Tiger Woods PGA Tour 08 Video Game
Nintendo Wii Remote Controller
Guitar Hero III
Rock Band Video Game Bundle
Sony PSP 2000

FASHION

Figure 1-4: eBay lists categories that will be promoted either on the home page or by e-mails for the current season.

PLACE YOUR PRODUCT

eBay defines your primary sales channel, but there are several ways you can leverage your eBay business with other selling venues. Developing synergy between your eBay business and a traditional retail business, for example, allows you to combine the two separate sales channels into a common profit-generator.

NOTE

If you can find something to sell that is unique or that you have a unique knowledge of, your chances of success will be greatly improved. It is important to know what the hot items are, but it is also imperative to remember that many items will get cold more quickly than they got hot. You don't want to be stuck with merchandise that has gone out of favor. When you are looking for merchandise to sell on eBay, always think about Beanie Babies before you lay out your cash. Beanies were on fire some years ago, but they sell so slowly now that the eBay staff has deep concerns about the future of the Collectibles category where Beanie Babies are sold. Many Beanies now will sell for only a small fraction of their original cost.

PROMOTE YOUR PRODUCT

Promotion gets the word out about your product to your target audience. In eBay, you have several promotional upgrades and features you can apply to your listings (see Chapter 4 for general information and Chapter 10 for eBay Store promotions). Examples of other promotional actions you can explore include:

● **Use the cross-promotional feature** available in eBay Stores to promote your auction listings along with your Store inventory items as a PowerSeller (see the "Becoming a PowerSeller" QuickSteps).

• **Use eBay's Marketing Tools** found in My eBay to customize your responses to buyers, such as Customize End Of Auction Emails or Custom Invoice.

• **Enhance your About Me page**, an example of which is in Figure 1-5, to provide in-depth information about you, your company, and your product (see Chapter 10 for information on creating an About Me page).

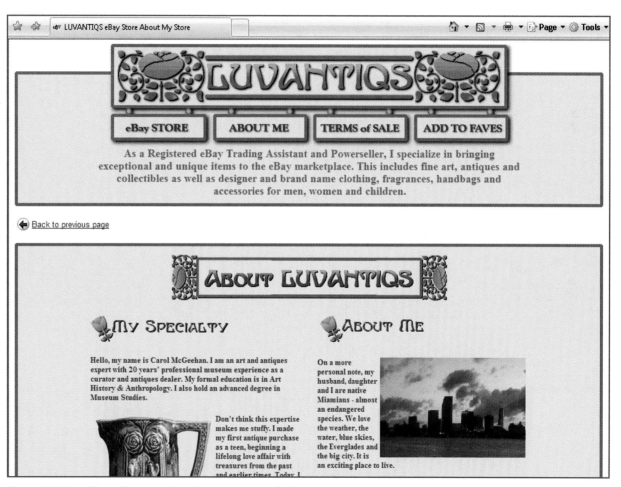

Figure 1-5: Your About Me page gives buyers a sense of who you are.

QUICK**FACTS**

UNDERSTANDING MARKETING

Ask most people to define "marketing," and you get answers like "a fancy word for sales," "it's advertising, you know, Madison Avenue and all that," and "getting people to buy something they might not necessarily want." Marketing has elements of those definitions, but the main thrust of *micro-marketing* (those activities performed by a single business, as opposed to *macro-marketing,* which looks at the entire economy) is to identify the needs of your buyers and then meet those needs. A fledgling eBay business is no different from a Fortune 500 company in this regard.

Unlike conventional businesses, most eBay businesses are not committed to selling a particular product (unless you are using eBay as just another sales channel for your product). You have the luxury of scouring the entire marketplace to find the product or products that are in demand and then offer them to the eBay buying population (see "Develop Your Product").

Instead of hiring a marketing manager, use eBay to help you decide whether to sell an item or product line and, if you do, how to do it. Table 1-1 describes common marketing considerations, questions, and eBay solutions (marketing considerations extracted from *Basic Marketing* by E. Jerome McCarthy and William D. Perreault, Jr.).

MARKETING CONSIDERATIONS	QUESTIONS TO ASK YOURSELF	POTENTIAL SOLUTIONS PROVIDED BY eBAY TOOLS AND FEATURES (EACH IS DESCRIBED IN THIS BOOK)
Analyze the needs of the potential buyers for your product.	Do buyers want more of them or a variation?	What's Hot, Sell By Category, Want It Now listings (see Figure 1-6)
Predict the **types** of the product buyers will want.	What colors, sizes, and materials are selling?	What's Hot, Sell By Category, Want It Now listings
Estimate the **pool of potential buyers** and how long they will be buying your items.	Is the item more of a fad or a commodity?	eBay statistics and demographics, eBay Live!
Predict **when** buyers will be buying your items.	Are your items seasonal?	What's Hot, Completed Items (auctions and Buy It Now items)
Figure out **where** your customer base is located.	Will shipping costs become onerous (to you or your buyers), or do you need to limit shipping by geographic boundaries?	Shipping Center
Estimate the **item's pricing** so you make an acceptable profit.	Should you establish a reserve, how much of a Buy It Now discount should be offered, or should you let the auction process determine the item's value?	Completed Items (auctions and Buy It Now items), Marketplace Research
Choose **promotions** to better make potential buyers aware of your product.	eBay provides a plethora of fee-based listing enhancements—which provide the best sales-versus-cost ratio?	Listing upgrades, cross-promotions, shipping flyers, eBay Store sales, free shipping
Determine the **level of competition**.	How many, what type, and for how much are others selling items similar to yours?	Completed Items (auctions and Buy It Now items)

*Table 1-1: **Marketing Considerations and eBay Solutions***

Figure 1-6: **Want It Now listings provide a glimpse into what buyers want.**

PRICE YOUR PRODUCT

Pricing strategies are not unknown to an eBay seller. Most of the same considerations apply to selling an occasional item as to selling many. Whether to set a reserve price, where to start a bid price, and whether to add a Buy It Now option are familiar to anyone who has climbed the eBay selling ladder. And, as we all know, there is no perfect answer—if there were, we'd all be doing it.

2

3

4

5

6

7

8

9

10

NOTE

When pricing your product pay particular attention to the shipping price. eBay is offering incentives for sellers to have free shipping for the products they sell. Also, some products, such as books, CDs, DVDs, video games and similar products are limited in how much the seller can charge the buyer for shipping. Investigate this thoroughly.

TIP

To really dig deep into selling trends for a particular product, such as patterns, market size, competition, pricing and profit margins, and other marketing research, consider subscribing to eBay Marketplace Research, a market research company that provides advanced data on market opportunities (see Figure 1-7).

TIP

The About Me page is like free advertising for you as a seller—an opportunity not to be missed. You have a chance to give potential buyers information about you and your business, your products, your policies, and other selling information. You can even have a link to your Web site on the About Me page (with several eBay policy caveats). Chapter 10 describes how to create an About Me page.

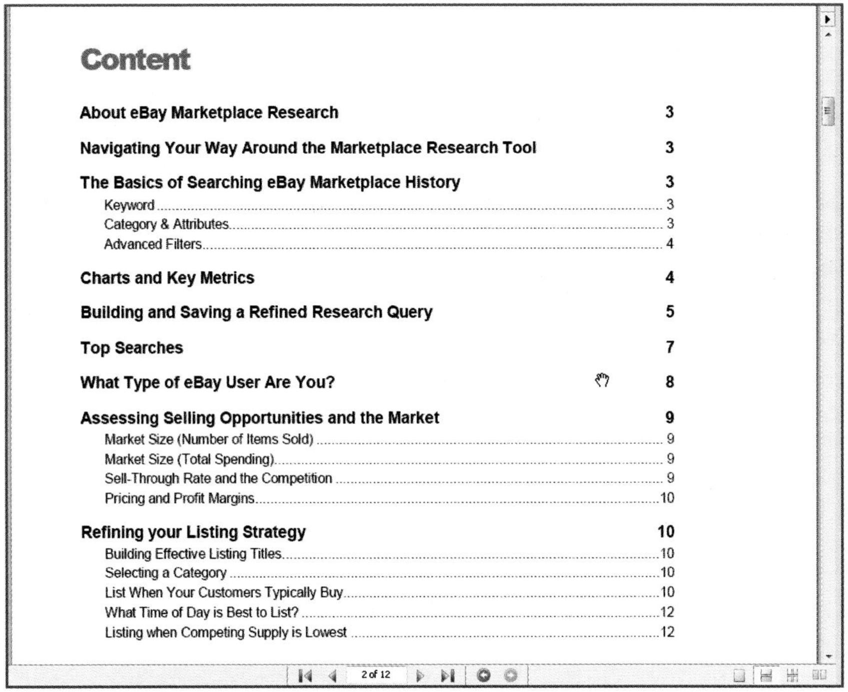

Content

Figure 1-7: This table of contents for the 12-page eBay Marketplace Research manual provides a glimpse of the possibilities in using that tool to help define and clarify your target market.

Create a Marketing Plan

The marketing plan combines your product analysis and research into a document that provides a road map you can use to implement actions, schedule events, and quantify costs.

1. Target the plan to its audience. With a marketing plan used to procure financing, an executive summary covering your marketing strategy should suffice. A more detailed plan is needed for internal use and decision making.

2. Start with a narrative overview of your plan. Include a summary, a market overview as you see it, your marketing strategy, and goals and objectives (see "Create A Business Plan" earlier in the chapter).

3. Develop a marketing budget.

4. Set up a system to evaluate the effectiveness of the plan.

QUICKFACTS

UNDERSTANDING BUSINESS ENTITIES

The typical business entities recognized by local, state, and federal authorities include the following.

SOLE PROPRIETORSHIP

This is the simplest entity to establish for a single owner, typically requiring only state fees to obtain a business license to get a business started and few, if any, recurring fees. Tax preparation is relatively easy, as all income is treated as personal income. Easy setup and maintenance is offset, however, by lack of special business income tax benefits and exposure of personal assets to business liabilities—for example, if your company is sued, so are you.

PARTNERSHIP

Easy to set up and maintain, a partnership agreement should be crafted to consider all eventualities, including dissolution, departure of a partner (this can be tricky; it's good to think things through early), and management control. The main difference between general and limited partnerships is the classification and liability of members:

- **General partnerships** are comprised of two or more members who share individual responsibility for taxes and liability of the business concern.

- **Limited partnerships** provide for two classes of partners: general and limited. General partners share similar responsibilities to those in a general partnership. Limited partners do not share in the management of the partnership and are not personally liable for any more than their individual investments in the company.

Continued . . .

Choose a Business Entity

When you establish a business, government entities at all levels will want to share in your success, from the $10 local municipality business license to the double hit the federal government imposes on collecting Social Security tax. The type of entity you choose will have serious tax, reporting, and legal consequences, so take the time to consult with professionals and business people to see what makes the most sense for you.

Establish Your Business Entity

Key steps in setting up your business entity are:

1. Choose a business entity based on several factors, including:
   - Tax considerations
   - Legal protections/liabilities
   - Ownership issues
   - Time involvement
   a. (See the "Understanding Business Entities" QuickFacts for information on how these factors are incorporated into various entities.)

2. Obtain an EIN (Employer Identification Number) or federal Tax ID number for your entity by submitting an IRS Form SS-4. (Sole proprietors use their Social Security numbers.)

3. Register your entity with your state department of revenue or analogous office. This will also get you on board with state unemployment and Labor & Industries (L&I) offices. (Sole proprietors don't have to worry about unemployment and L&I.)

4. Understand the taxes and reporting required of your business entity—for example, payroll (FICA, FUTA, and Medicare), federal and state income, state unemployment, and sales. Know when each is due, and do not fail to file on time. (Corporate filings are taken quite seriously by the IRS and other affected offices.)

5. Obtain city or other local municipality business licenses. Consider zoning laws—for example, if you sell large items that require shipping trucks to pick up and deliver goods.

QUICK**FACTS**

UNDERSTANDING BUSINESS ENTITIES *(Continued)*

CORPORATION

Corporations are the most expensive entities to create and maintain (think board meetings, minutes, issuance of stock, and so on), but can be bought and sold, either privately or publicly (although this is not really practical for an S corporation due to a limit on the number of stockholders), and enjoy some favorable tax treatment. Corporations are a separate legal entity and generally shield owners (called *shareholders*) from personal liability:

- **C corporations** are what govern the largest companies in corporate America. Not generally associated with small startups, these corporations are taxed at the entity level, and shareholders are also individually taxed on dividends.

- **S corporations** provide the personal liability protection of a C corporation but "pass through" the corporation's income to the shareholders' personal tax obligation, avoiding the "double-tax" issue. This is usually a better option for most smaller businesses.

LIMITED LIABILITY COMPANY

A limited liability company (LLC) combines many of the favorable tax treatments of a corporation with personal liability protection and the management structure of a partnership. The rules governing LLCs vary state to state, so check with a tax or business professional in your area to see if an LLC might be a better option in your case than an S corporation. Key differences between the two are that an LLC can be owned by non-U.S. citizens and nonresident aliens, while an S corporation can be owned only by U.S. citizens or permanent resident aliens; and an LLC may have any number of shareholders, while an S corporation is limited to 75.

TIP

The letters "C" and "S" used to distinguish corporations are derived from the subchapters of the Internal Revenue Code that govern each. S corporations, in particular, are frequently referred to as "subchapter S corporations."

6. Set up business financial accounts, such as a checking account and credit/debit cards.

7. Join or subscribe to associations or other business societies to be recognized as a viable business in that industry.

Professor Polly says: "Obtain vendor accreditations or ratings—for example, become a certified appraiser through the International Society of Appraisers (ISA)."

Solicit Help

Everyone who started an eBay business was at one point an eBay "clueless newbie." For those who persisted to reach PowerSeller status, a great deal of time, effort, and probably some money was expended to make that transition. The experience of those who have traded before you is a great resource to utilize, especially since much of it is free. To avoid many of the pitfalls of setting up a business, consider free sources of professional assistance, but don't totally dismiss hiring paid professionals when needed to fill in any coverage gaps.

Tap into the eBay Community

Don't be afraid to ask questions and get advice from other eBay business people.

JOIN DISCUSSION BOARDS AND GROUPS

Online discussion boards and groups provide focused topics that you can join to communicate with others and share selling and business ideas.

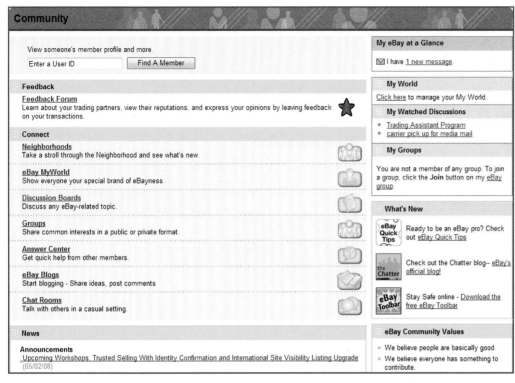

Figure 1-8: *You can join newsgroup-like discussion boards or more interactive groups to discuss your new eBay business.*

1. Click **Community** on the eBay header.

2. On the Community Hub, shown in Figure 1-8:

   • Click **Discussion Boards**, under Connect, to view threads of conversations on several topics, organized into *boards*. Click a board to view a list of links to related topics. (You will need to register to start your own topic or to reply to others.)

Connect
Neighborhoods
Take a stroll through the Neighborhood and see what's new.
eBay MyWorld
Show everyone your special brand of eBayness.
Discussion Boards
Discuss any eBay-related topic.
Groups
Share common interests in a public or private format.

   • Click **Groups** to join or start a group that provides a forum to discuss topics on a common theme and allows members to participate in polls, view or post related pictures, and maintain a group calendar.

TIP

Many banks will provide a business account for you and will also provide you with credit card processing services. Prices for these services can vary widely, so check all costs and fees before opening an account for your business. It is not widely known, but many banks will negotiate some of the credit card processing costs, and in some cases, you can get them to provide the necessary equipment at no cost. Also, check out aggregators, such as Costco Business.

2

3

4

5

6

7

8

9

10

FUNDING YOUR eBAY BUSINESS

There's nothing terribly unique about funding an eBay business as compared to other businesses. Some of the types of equipment you use will be particular to selling online (for example, computer equipment and auction-management software), and possibly your inventory will be unique to the types of items you sell.

FUNDING OUTLAYS

Where your startup money's going to go:

- Equipment (computer system, camera/mini-studio, auction-related software)
- Inventory (merchandise and items to sell)
- Operating capital (rents, payroll, phone, utilities, professional fees, shipping fees, listing fees)

FUNDING SOURCES

Where your startup money's coming from:

- Self-financing
- Investors
- Borrowing

Browser Earl says: "At pages.ebay .com/sellercentral/resources.html, you can find lists of resources for selling on eBay, such as Building Your Business, Seller Community, Best Practices, and many others."

ATTEND WORKSHOPS

Workshops are a special form of a discussion board that covers a particular eBay topic during a scheduled time. If you cannot be at your computer during a workshop, not to worry—workshops are archived for several weeks.

1. Click **Community** on the Bay header.

2. On the Community Hub page, under News, see the workshops that are being scheduled. Under Education, click **Workshops** and click the link to join a workshop in progress.

   –Or–

   On the Workshop Calendar page, click Archives on the sidebar to view a listing of past workshops.

> **Choose A Topic**
>
> About
>
> **Current Calendar**
>
> Archives - 2007
>
> Archives - 2006
>
> Archives - 2005
>
> Archives - 2004

–Or–

On the Workshop Calendar page, click **Host Your Own Workshop** on the right sidebar to e-mail a request to the eBay staff to run your own workshop.

ATTEND EBAY LIVE!

eBay Live! (see Figure 1-9) is the love-event for all things eBay. The convention lets you access eBay staff; attend classes, lectures, and forums; visit vendors and

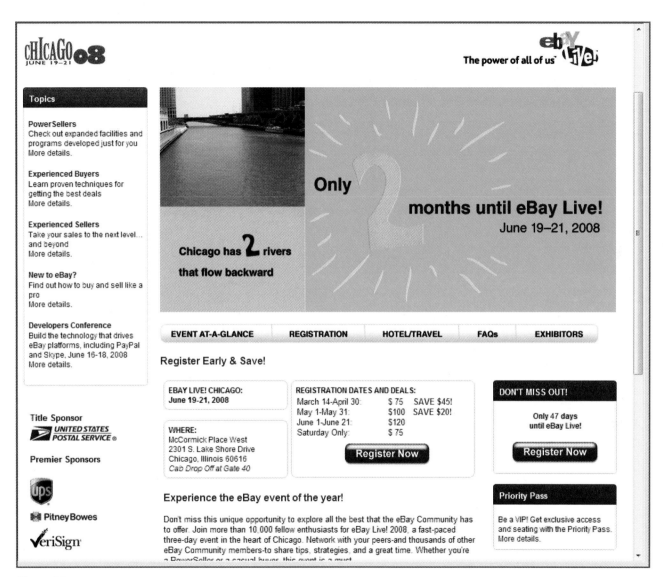

Figure 1-9: eBay Live! is a three-day conference on all things eBay.

UICK**STEPS**

FINDING POWERSELLERS

Seek out those eBay sellers who have proven their effectiveness by attaining PowerSeller status. You can identify whether members you meet in discussion boards and other community areas are PowerSellers by the presence of the PowerSeller icon in their listings (under Meet The Seller in listings) and contact them by searching for a member's User ID or looking up a member's profile.

SEARCH FOR A MEMBER

1. Click **Advanced Search** on the top of any eBay page.

2. On the Search: Find Items page, click **Find A Member** on the left sidebar.

3. On the Search: Find A Member page, type the member's User ID or e-mail address, and click **Search**. Provide the security code, and click **Continue**. You will see a one-line summary of the exact member's information, plus a listing of closely matching member IDs.

eBay Stores provide a virtual storefront for listing several items for sale.

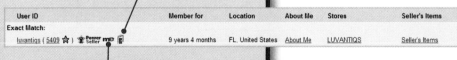

About Me provides a page where you can describe your business.

LOOK UP A MEMBER'S PROFILE

Get the most information about a member by viewing his or her profile and feedback data (see Chapter 5 for more information on receiving and providing feedback).

1. Click **Site Map** on the eBay header, and, under Feedback, click **View A Member's Feedback**.

Continued . . .

Sign Up for Your Complimentary eBay Seller OnRamp Consultation

Seller OnRamp is eBay's official phone consulting program offered at no cost to qualified business sellers. OnRamp consultants help new business sellers with best practices and tips to start and grow their business on eBay.

Select a date and time for your scheduled consultation. An eBay advisor will contact you during your scheduled time to help you get your business started on eBay.

DATE (mm/dd/yyyy)   TIME (All Appointment Times Are Pacific Time)

Select Time ▾   Check for Availability

Your advisor will call you within your scheduled hour. Appointments generally last 15-20 minutes.

*Figure 1-10: **The Seller OnRamp provides a live consultant who can help guide you towards your selling and business goals.***

exhibitors; and rub elbows with others in the biz. Attendees at eBay Live! are eager to share their experiences with other sellers. This is your chance to get information that will not be available again on a face-to-face basis until the next event.

Get Personal, Free Consulting

The Seller OnRamp feature within eBay provides a great free consultation service for those who do not have much eBay selling experience. Simply call a toll-free number during normal business hours, and speak with a live Seller OnRamp marketing consultant. Once you explain your situation, the consultant will start you on a program to reach your immediate goals.

1. Click **Site Map** on the eBay header; under Selling Resources, click **Seller Central**.

2. On the Seller Central page, click **Advanced Selling**. Under Seller OnRamp in Business Solutions, click **Schedule Your Appointment**. The Seller OnRamp page displays, as shown in Figure 1-10.

QUICKSTEPS

FINDING POWERSELLERS *(Continued)*

2. On the Feedback Forum: Find Member page, type the member's User ID, and click **Find Member**. The good, bad, and ugly of a member's eBay history is displayed, as shown in Figure 1-11.

E-MAIL A MEMBER

1. On the member's profile/feedback page, click **Contact Member**.

2. Type your message and click **Send Message**.

> **Member Quick Links**
>
> Contact member
> View items for sale
> View seller's Store
> View more options ▼

TIP

You can keep abreast of the most current trends and activities on eBay by simply listening to eBay Radio a few hours every week (see in Figure 1-12). Using the multimedia equipment on your computer (speakers, soundboard, and media player), you can listen to the live show with "Griff," the dean of eBay University, or play back a show from the archives. The live show is broadcast Tuesdays from 11 A.M. to 1 P.M. PST. This is followed from 1 to 2 P.M. by an "eBay Radio PowerSeller Show." Then, too, there is an "eBay Radio Ask Griff" every Thursday from 5 to 7 P.M. PST. To attend the live shows or to listen to past shows, check the Calendar Events on the Community Hub to access a link to the site.

Browser Earl says: "Listen to eBay Radio at www.wsradio.com/ebayradio."

Member Details

luvantiqs (5409 ☆) 🏆 Power Seller m🅱 📓
Member since Dec-14-98 in United States

Lifetime Summary: Positives: 5409   Negatives: 0 | Positive Feedback: 100%

Click to contact member

Feedback scores

Recent Feedback Ratings (last 12 months) ⓘ

	1 month	6 months	12 months
➕ Positive	29	210	539
◐ Neutral	0	0	1
➖ Negative	0	0	0

Detailed Seller Ratings (since May 2007) ⓘ

Criteria	Average rating	Number of ratings
Item as described	★★★★★	354
Communication	★★★★★	352
Shipping time	★★★★★	353
Shipping and handling charges	★★★★☆	348

Member Quick Links

Contact member
View items for sale
View seller's Store
View more options ▼

Detailed Seller Ratings (DSRs) rates how the seller performs

| Feedback as a seller | Feedback as a buyer | All Feedback | Feedback left for others |

6,408 Feedback received (viewing 1-25)

Ratings mutually withdrawn: 3

Comments provided by other eBay members

Feedback	From / Price	Date / Time
➕ Excellent Ebayer...Great communication. Would definitely buy from again. A+++++	Buyer: firebird219 (174 ☆)	May-03-08 16:20
4X CLINIQUE GLOSSWEAR FOR LIPS 06 MYSTIC (#360044988000)	US $18.50	View Item

Figure 1-11: *Everyone's buying and selling history and eBay persona is available from their profile.*

Figure 1-12: *Listen live to discussions on eBay Radio, and call in with your questions.*

GETTING PROFESSIONAL HELP

Much like building a house, starting and building a business requires a firm foundation to get things going:

- **A Certified Public Accountant (CPA)** is vital in helping you set up your business entity, establishing a bookkeeping system, and ensuring you collect and pay all required federal, state, and local taxes. Get referrals from other business owners in your area.

- **Business mentors** provide valuable advice to avoid pitfalls and help you execute your business and marketing plans. Visit the SCORE Web site (www.score.org) to find a counselor near you.

- **Legal work** may be required over and above what a CPA provides if you are setting up a larger operation or involving multiple owners or partners and employees. At a minimum, consider having a tax and business lawyer review your business documents, partnership agreements, vendor contracts, and employee-hiring practices. Many areas have a discount legal services program for initial consultations. Contact your state bar association for more information.

- **Computer consultation** may be needed to help you expand beyond the single desktop computer you've been using to post listings. A network specialist can help you craft a system to integrate multiple computers, printers, scanners, and broadband Internet connectivity to extract more from the sum of your hardware investment. A software guru can help you install and optimize the various software packages you will be using: auction management, photo organization and enhancement, scanning, accounting, inventory control, and any specialty programs for your product lines.

Continued . . .

TIP

eBay has category research and marketing information to help you succeed in selling through their categories. eBay wants you to be successful and will share ideas with you. Click **Site Map** on the eBay header, click **Seller Central** (under Selling Resources), and then click **Category Tips** on the sidebar. Scroll down to the category that interests you, and click the link to learn a great deal about your category.

Antiques
Seller's Edge
Seller Profiles
In Demand
Discussion Board
Seller Guide

**Browser
Earl**

Browser Earl says:
"Find the category centers at http://pages .ebay.com/sellercentral/ sellbycategory.html."

3. Call 1-866-325-EBAY (3229) to speak with a consultant and receive follow-up advice and suggestions via e-mail. As you progress in your eBay-manship, you can call back and get further guidance.

**Browser
Earl**

Browser Earl says:
"Check out eBay Live!, a must-do event for the serious eBay business person, at www.ebay .com/ebaylive."

Browser Earl says:
"Get on the Seller OnRamp at http:// pages.ebay.com/ startselling."

GETTING PROFESSIONAL HELP
(Continued)

- **eBay training** provides two classes called Selling Basics and Beyond the Basics of Selling. These classes may be presented in your town or neighborhood, or you can buy a CD or DVD to view in classes in your home. The eBay University page is shown in Figure 1-13.

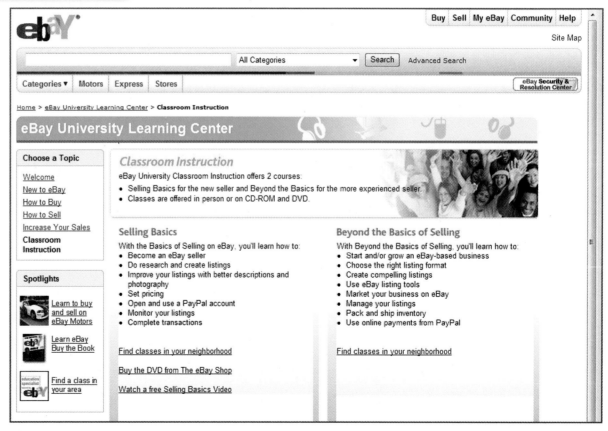

Figure 1-13: eBay University Learning Center offers live classes or CD/DVD classes for the new and more experienced eBay seller.

How to...

Chapter 2

Developing Selling Strategies and Inventory

To operate a successful business on eBay, you need to consistently offer items for sale that buyers are interested in purchasing. The key to consistent selling is to have a steady stream of product available to list and to develop selling strategies that keep you one step ahead of the eBay competition. These concepts are true whether you sell unique and hard-to-find items or if you volume-sell a single product.

In this chapter you will learn how to develop and apply strategies to help you sell your product and stand out from the competition, and how to become a good buyer *(or purchaser)* and procure items *(or inventory)* to sell beyond the yard sales and thrift stores where many of us started finding items to sell.

Develop Sales Strategies

Two basic sales strategies are employed on eBay, although there are an infinite number of variations on these two central themes:

- **Sell fewer, more expensive items**, where each sale provides the opportunity for a high profit.

  –Or–

- **Sell more, less expensive items**, with each sale providing a small profit.

For example, you can sell one antique Oriental rug and retain a profit of hundreds of dollars, or you can sell hundreds of battery-operated bug swatters and net $1.50 per sale. From a profit standpoint, the businesses are a wash, but there are other factors to consider:

- Selling unique items requires you to be a specialist in that genre, or at least highly knowledgeable. eBay buyers want reliable and accurate information on items, and your inexperience with an item will be obvious to an informed pool of bidders. Also, there is typically a smaller pool of buyers for unique items than for mass-market items. If you are a specialist in a specific area, you are more likely to develop repeat customers. If you want to be a specialist in one area, you should be flexible enough to consider other types of merchandise outside your current area of expertise.

- Volume selling can be labor-intensive. Each transaction requires time to process, ship, respond to inquiries, deal with buyers who don't pay, and all the other details involved in completing a sale on eBay. You can use certain techniques to minimize time spent on a transaction (see "Use Drop-Shipping" later in the chapter and Chapters 4 and 5 for information on using software tools, such as Turbo Lister and Selling Manager/ Selling Manager Pro), but many charge a fee for the services provided.

Ultimately, there is no right or wrong, better or worse, sales strategy to pursue. Depending on your interests, merchandise availability, and the time you have to devote to the eBay business, you can successfully employ either strategy or a blend of the two.

TIP

Of course, there's that universal sales strategy that should not be a tree lost among the forest of business school research, eBay University courses, and the opinions of eBay pundits (just about anyone with an eBay User ID)—that is, buy low and sell high!

Newbie Sally and Buyer Bob say: "Whether you are buying or selling, persistence is extremely important. To make a success of your eBay business, you must treat it like a job. It is work, but you will receive a payoff in the end. This is an important part of establishing your presence on eBay."

MAKING THE eBAY SELLING TRANSITION

There's a fairly common hierarchy of sales maturity seen in eBay, from the type, sources, and quantity of items sold to the profit realized by the seller. Figure 2-1 shows the progression of the typically maturing eBay business, from the selling of garage sale items to the PowerSeller:

- Merchandise is first procured from an across-the-board selection of eBay categories.

- As the seller experiments with selling different items in several categories and gauges the success and profitability of each, the range of items begins to focus.

- Top success is reached when merchandise is limited to a few merchandising lines; suppliers are few, but reliable; and an eBay presence or brand is established (see "Establish an eBay Brand" later in the chapter).

NOTE

At some point as your volume increases, you might be able to go directly to the manufacturer, thereby cutting out one middleman. This will give you an opportunity to increase profits and possibly increase your buyers, as you would be in a position to offer a lower price than a competing seller who has to buy through a middleman. See "Acquire Wholesale Sources" later in the chapter for information on direct-buying from wholesalers.

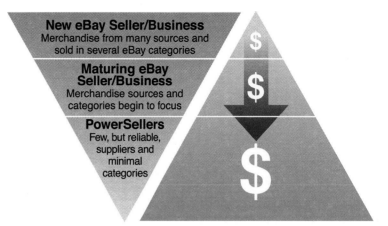

Figure 2-1: *As an eBay business matures, merchandise is sold in fewer eBay categories, fewer suppliers are needed, and profits grow.*

Sell by Volume

Volume sales concentrate on selling a lot of a few items. You can achieve several economies of scale by selling more and more of the same item:

- **Negotiate better prices with your supplier.** The price per item you pay is lower if you buy in bulk.

- **Listings are similar, if not the same.** You can leverage the work you do creating a listing, thereby lowering your transaction costs per item.

- **Packaging becomes cookie-cutter.** The item's weight, dimensions, insurance, and other packaging considerations are static and allow you to obtain quantities of packaging material at a lower cost. Labor time and cost are also reduced as the process becomes rote and more efficient.

eBay offers several features that help you sell similar or multiple items (see "Acquire Inventory" later in the chapter for information on finding multiple items to sell).

TIP

If you have multiples of the same item to sell, you can create the listing once and set it to launch over and over—for instance, once a week. All you have to do is collect the money, pack, and ship. The listing lives as long as you have merchandise. See Chapter 4 for more information on creating listings.

NOTE

Dutch auctions (a type of multiple-item auction) are only available if the number of items times the price is less than $100,000.

USE DUTCH AUCTIONS

In a Dutch auction, multiple items are sold at the same price, but with a couple of differences. An example of a Dutch auction is shown in Figure 2-2. A Dutch auction is conducted as follows:

● The seller lists the items, giving a minimum acceptable price.

● Bidders bid on the number of items they want and at what price.

● The winners pay the lowest acceptable price made by a bidder, who is assured of getting at least one item; his or her bid will zero out the total of the quantities available.

● The highest bidders will win first and get the quantities they want, even if the quantity is oversold.

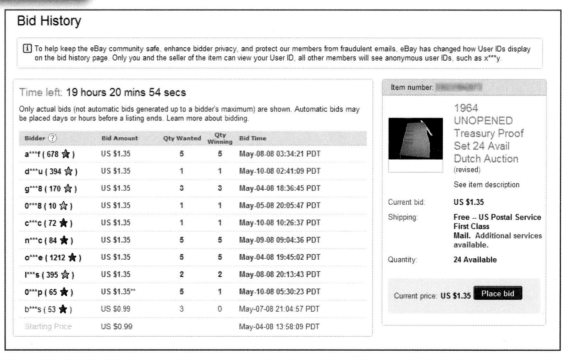

Figure 2-2: Multiple bids from one bidder help ensure that he or she gets the quantity desired.

For example, a seller offers ten copper spoons at $10 each:

- Bidder A bids $10 for three spoons.
- Bidder B bids $10.50 for five spoons.
- Bidder C bids $12.00 for eight spoons.
- Bidders B and C will both pay $10.50 for the spoons.
- Bidder B will only get two spoons.
- Bidder C will get eight spoons.
- Bidder A will get no spoons since Bidders B and C zeroed out the quantities available.

SELL MULTIPLE ITEMS AT A FIXED PRICE

In a fixed-price listing, you sell all items for a fixed price. Bidders enter the number of items they want at your fixed price. After each sale, the quantity of items is reduced by the number sold in that particular auction. The listing remains active as long as there are items to sell; it closes when the quantity of items is zero.

SELL LOTS

Lots are packages, groups, or collections of the same or similar items.

For example, you could sell 200 scarves in groups of ten. You can choose to sell items at a fixed price, such as $8.99 per lot, or you can list them as auction items. Enter the number of lots and the number of items per lot in the Quantity area of the Sell Your Item form.

Newbie Sally says: "In order to sell multiple items, you need to be ID Verified or be registered on eBay for 14 days or more and have a feedback rating greater than or equal to 30. If you accept PayPal as payment for the listing, however, you can list with a feedback rating of 15."

You may need to click the Add Or Remove Options link to find the Lots entry box. Some pointers to consider when selling lots:

- Don't add too many items per lot. Although people like buying in Costco-sized quantities, there is a point of diminishing returns. For example, in the field of collectible magazines, you often see a single issue sell for $15. At the same time, another seller will offer a lot of 20 similar issues that only sells for $25. Typically, the buyers of such lots are dealers, who break the lots up and sell them individually.

- Keep the lot starting price low to attract bidders.

- Add the number of items per lot and the most commonly searched keyword for bulk items—"lot"—to the listing's title. For example, "Entire Lot Gone to Dogs—50 Brand New Nylabones."

- Package lots to sell in the sweet spot of lot sales: $150–$1,500 (source: eBay Live!).

- List in the Wholesale subcategory (available under many categories, using Search), as shown in Figure 2-3.

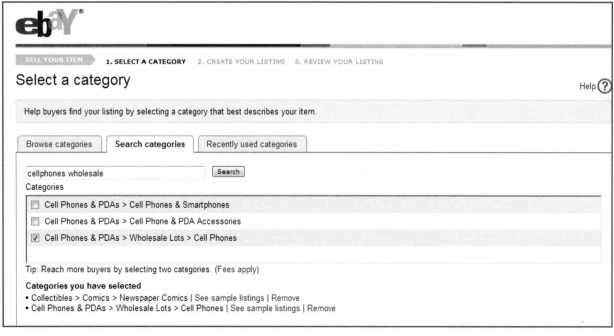

Figure 2-3: *List your bulk lots in the Wholesale subcategory.*

Target Selling with Your Sales Data

To assist you in analyzing your sales data so you can make listing decisions, such as which sales format to use (bidding or fixed-price), what listing durations and ending times seem most effective, which categories are doing best, and several other sales metrics, you can receive Sales Reports from eBay. The basic (although limited) Sales Report is free (your seller's account must be in good standing, must have sold at least one item in the last four months, and must have a feedback rating of at least 10). The more robust Sales Report Plus incurs a $4.99 monthly fee but doesn't have minimum requirements to subscribe.

Selling Tools
- Accounting Assistant
- Blackthorne Basic
- Blackthorne Pro
- eBay Certified Providers
- eBay Solutions Directory
- File Exchange
- Picture Manager
- Sales Reports
- Selling Manager

1. Click **Site Map** on the eBay header.

2. Under Selling Tools, click **Sales Reports**.

3. On the Sales Reports Overview page, view the side-by-side comparison of the products:
   - To sign up for the basic Sales Report, click the Sales Report **Sign Up Now** button, click **Sales Reports (Free)**, and click **I Agree To These Terms**. If you don't meet the requirements for a free subscription, you will be offered only the Sales Reports Plus option.
   - To sign up for Sales Reports Plus, click the Sales Reports Plus (Free) **Sign Up Now** button, and click the **I Agree To These Terms** button. After accepting the terms and conditions, you'll receive a congratulatory page and an e-mail with welcome information.

4. View your report from My eBay (your initial report might take up to three days to generate). Under My Subscriptions on the sidebar, click **Sales Reports**. Your Sales Summary will look similar to Figure 2-4.

My Subscriptions
Sales Reports

	Sales Reports Sign Up Now!	Sales Reports Plus Sign Up Now!
Description	See a high-level view of your most recent activity, including a summary of your: • Sales • Ended Listings • Successful Listings % • Average Sale Price • eBay and Paypal fees	See in-depth views of your most recent activity. Sales Reports Plus offers everything in the basic product PLUS: • Metrics by Category • Metrics by Format (e.g. Fixed Price) • Metrics by Category & Format • Metrics by Ending Day or Time for all formats • Buyer counts • Detailed eBay fees • Unpaid Item Credits Requested • Ability to show or hide sections • Download capabilities
Subscription Fee	FREE !	FREE !
Requirements	Sales Reports	Sales Reports Plus

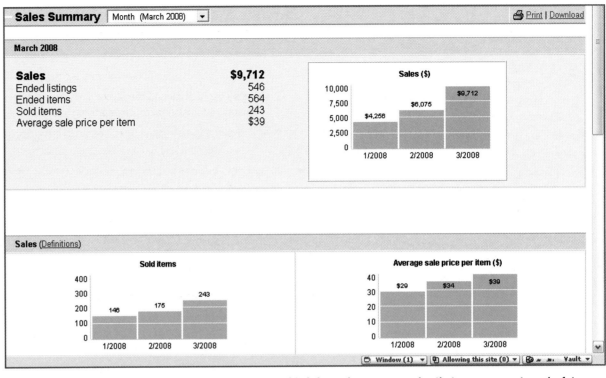

Figure 2-4: *Sales reports are available from eBay and provide information on your sales that you can use to make future selling decisions.*

Gain a Competitive Awareness

eBay is a highly open market—there aren't many secrets associated with a transaction. This can be a proverbial double-edged sword at times. If you find an item that sells extremely well, it won't be long before others pick up on your good fortune. It may be simply the product you are selling that increases your sales, the category where it's listed, the appearance of your listing, or a combination of these and other factors. Conversely, there's nothing stopping you from mining competitor information on eBay (and beyond) and picking the best-of-breed data to emulate. To this end, eBay goes out of its way to share best practices, lessons learned, and success stories. (eBay makes money, regardless

QUICKSTEPS

MAKING IT EASY FOR YOUR BUYERS

A timeless sales strategy and competitive advantage is to make the buying experience easy and straightforward to entice buyers to return to your sales outlet. eBay offers several features you should consider that relieve the buyer of anxiety and make the purchasing process simpler.

USE COMBINED PAYMENTS

To make it more convenient for repeat buyers to make payments, you can combine the payments on multiple purchases so the buyer only has to make one payment. Besides the ease of making just one payment, the buyer might then qualify for discounts you offer based on the final purchase amount (and you can save in PayPal fees). To offer combined payment, follow these steps:

1. In My eBay, under My Account, click **Site Preferences**.

2. Under Selling Preferences, click **Show** for Shipping Preferences. The Site Preferences window expands to show shipping preferences.

3. Click **Edit** to open the My eBay: Combined Payments And Shipping Discounts page.

4. On the Combined Payments rule, click **Edit**:

   • On the Edit Combined Payments dialog box, verify that a check mark is next to Allow Buyers To Send One Combined Payment For All Items Purchased.

Continued . . .

if you or your competitor succeeds, but they would rather see you both do well and pass along those listing and final value fees!) Consider integrating these practices into your eBay business:

- Research Completed Items listings in the categories where you sell:
  - View other listings and see if your listing looks as professional as theirs (see Chapter 4 for information on improving your listings).
  - See what type of listing format seems to be getting top dollar. Are top sellers using fixed-price listings or letting the bidding process do the heavy lifting for them?
  - Check the return and shipping policies of your competitors. Especially in lower-priced, competitive sales, shipping costs can quickly sway a buyer from one listing to another.

- Stay tuned to the pulse of eBay by visiting the Community Hub and browsing discussion boards, workshops, and the latest announcements.

- Determine current trends:
  - Check out the eBay Merchandising Calendar to see what categories eBay will be highlighting on the home page in the next few months. Click **Site Map** on the eBay header, click **Seller Central** (under Selling Resources), and click **What's Hot** on the sidebar.

Shipping preferences		
		Hide
Offer combined payments and shipping	Yes	Edit
Offer flat shipping and insurance discounts	No	
Offer calculated shipping and insurance discounts	No	
Offer promotional shipping discounts	No	
Specify insurance on combined packages	No	
Offer this UPS shipping rate	Daily	Edit

- See what buyers are searching for by category. From Seller Central, click **Category Tips**. Scroll to the category you're interested in, and click the **In Demand** link. Top searches are listed according to subcategories.

- Read trade periodicals (for example, *Antique Trader*, *Sports Collectors Digest*, *Hemmings Motor News*, and *Comics Buyers Guide*) for insight into sales from storefront businesses.

- Peruse retail catalogs (*Williams-Sonoma*) to see what Madison Avenue is telling everyone will be the latest must-have items.

Category Tips

Knowledge is power, they say, and it couldn't be truer than when it comes to selling on eBay. Selling success is about being in the right place, at the right time, with the right product. Below, you'll find category-specific strategies and resources to help you become a savvy seller.

Antiques
Seller's Edge
Seller Profiles
In Demand
Discussion Board
Seller Guide

Health & Beauty
Seller's Edge
Seller Profiles
In Demand
Seller Guide
Discussion boards

MAKING IT EASY FOR YOUR BUYERS *(Continued)*

- Set the Time Period For Combined Purchases to the time period you want.

5. Click **Save**.

USE SHIPPING DISCOUNTS

You can combine shipping discounts by specifying rules for flat shipping (when your items are combined into one package using the flat-rate shipping costs) or for calculated shipping (where your buyer's shipping cost is based on his or her ZIP code, promotional shipping discounts (where you may offer special discounts to promote your listings), and insurance offerings.

To enable the shipping discounts features for existing listings:

1. In My eBay, under My Account, click **Site Preferences**.

2. Under Selling Preferences, click **Show** for Shipping Preferences. The Site Preferences window expands to show shipping preferences. Click **Edit**.

3. Under the Combined Shipping Discounts area, click **Create** to open a specific shipping rule pane.

4. On the specific shipping rule pane, either open the drop-down menu and click the option you want, or click the option buttons. Follow the tips to set your shipping rules.

5. When you have selected the option you want, click **Next** and a message will be displayed with the options you have set.

6. Click **Save**.

Edit Combined Payments
To offer combined shipping on your listings, you need to offer combined payments. After the time period expires, buyers will have to check out for each item one at a time.

☑ Allow buyers to send one combined payment for all items purchased.
Time period for combined purchases : 7 days ▼

TIP

You can also offer or change your combined shipping discounts from an item listing. In My eBay, click your item listing link to display your listing. At the top of your listing, click **Create Shipping Discounts**. On the specific rule you want to set or change, click **Edit**. Using the Tip in the shipping combined payment window, select your options, click **Next**, and then click **Save**.

Add Skype Chat and Call buttons to your item
Revise your item
Sell a similar item
Create shipping discounts

Establish an eBay Brand

Ask anyone in Outer Mongolia if they'd like a Coke, and they'll probably smile and say, "Yes, thank you." They may never have drunk one, but chances are they know what it is. Ask these same people if they'd prefer an "Acme Cola," and they will probably give you a blank look. The difference is that Coca-Cola (and its variants) is one of the world's most recognized brands, while Acme Cola isn't well known beyond the bathtub it's made in. The classic definition of a *brand* is a name, design, term, or symbol that identifies a product. As an eBay business, chances are you didn't make the product you're selling (although there are many craftspeople who sell their wares on eBay), but you still can work on establishing an identity on eBay that buyers will remember and trust. Brand loyalty can be a powerful prime mover for repeat sales. Four areas exist where you can personalize your eBay business's presence and create a branding aura for you and/or your product.

Browser Earl says: "Find companies that design and create branding material at http://solutions.ebay.com."

DESIGN A KILLER LISTING TEMPLATE

Just as many books are judged by their covers, the fortunes of many eBay sellers are made or lost based on their listing templates. A template that has too few pictures, doesn't show enough detail, lacks depth in its description, or whose layout conveys amateurism can quickly turn off a prospective buyer. Develop the skills to work with Hypertext Markup Language (HTML), the language used to create Web pages, or get someone to create a listing template for you. eBay provides many templates you can use for free, but much like clip art, it tends to lose its effectiveness when viewers notice it used elsewhere. See Chapter 4 for an in-depth dissection of eBay listings.

CREATE A LOGO

The easiest way to personalize your business or product is with a logo. Consistency is the key element in establishing a brand. That is, consistency in how your design complements your business, product, or organization (nonprofit charitable organizations are discussed in Chapter 9). The design should be simple and small enough to see clearly on eBay promotional venues, such as About Me pages and eBay Stores.

EMPLOY AN ABOUT ME PAGE

An About Me ⓜⓔ page lets you showcase your brand. You can add information about your business, display listings you have for bid, show feedback you've received, and provide links to off-eBay Web sites, including your own (see Figure 2-5). Chapter 10 describes how to create an About Me page.

CROSS-PROMOTE

The adage "the whole is greater than the sum of its parts" aptly applies to the use of cross-promotion in eBay to build a branding sense among your bidders and buyers. A free eBay feature lets you advertise other items you have for bid or sale when a buyer bids on or views a purchased listing (or, for eBay Stores, when a buyer views your item), as shown in Figure 2-6. Also, if you have an eBay Store, items you have in the general listings are integrated with your store items, and you'll have a unique Internet address (URL—Uniform Resource Locator) for your store's home page that you can use off-eBay to drive

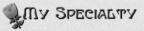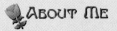

Figure 2-5: *About Me pages are easy to set up and let you tell buyers about yourself and your items.*

Save on shipping This seller offers shipping discounts on combined purchases.

Beadworx Red & Blue Parrot on Perch
Wire Glass Bead NWT

Buy It Now or Best Offer   US $35.99

Time left: 3d 17h 44m

Rawcliffe Pewter West Highland White
Terrier Keychain

20% OFF *Buy It Now* price: US $4.79

Original price: ~~US $5.99~~

Country Artists Working Cowboy & Horse
Sculpture NIB

20% OFF *Buy It Now* price: US $79.19

Original price: ~~US $98.99~~

Ganz Leather Horse Figure Brown

Buy It Now or Best Offer   US $10.99

Time left: 5d 1h 11m

📓 Visit seller's Store

Figure 2-6: Leverage your listings and eBay Store items through cross-promotion.

ENLISTING eBAY TO HELP YOU CROSS-PROMOTE

You can have eBay provide bidders and buyers links to other items you have for sale when they show interest in a particular item.

1. On the My eBay Views sidebar, click **Marketing Tools**.

2. Under Item Promotion, click **Cross-Promotion Settings**.

   Item Promotion
   ■ Cross-Promotion
     Defaults
     Settings
   ■ Favor🖑 Seller Top

3. You can see whether you are set up to automatically participate in the eBay cross-promotion. If the options are checked, you are all set—cross-promotions will automatically appear to buyers.

4. Click the options you want, and click **Apply,** as shown in Figure 2-7.

customers to your items. See Chapter 6 for more information on eBay Stores and Chapter 10 for more information on using cross-promoting, in and outside of eBay Stores.

You can tailor your cross-promotions to match your items. For example, if you are selling gold rings, you can display other gold rings when a buyer bids on or views a purchased item, or views a gold ring listing in an eBay Store. To customize your cross-promotion:

1. Click **My eBay** on the eBay header.

2. Click **Marketing Tools** in the sidebar.

3. On the Marketing Tools page, click **Edit** next to Cross Promotion Defaults.

4. On the Cross Promotion: Defaults page, click **Create New Rule**.

5. Click **Select An eBay Category** under either of the two selling situations, and then follow the prompts to tailor your categories.

When someone bids on or wins an item matching these criteria:
Select an eBay category

Promote items matching these criteria:
Select an eBay category

[Continue >] Cancel

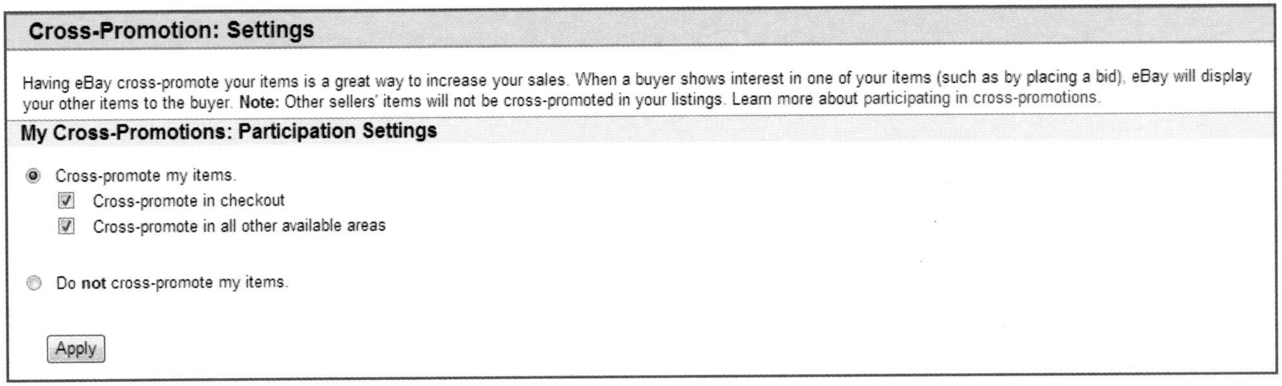

Cross-Promotion: Settings

Having eBay cross-promote your items is a great way to increase your sales. When a buyer shows interest in one of your items (such as by placing a bid), eBay will display your other items to the buyer. **Note:** Other sellers' items will not be cross-promoted in your listings. Learn more about participating in cross-promotions.

My Cross-Promotions: Participation Settings

⦿ Cross-promote my items.
- ☑ Cross-promote in checkout
- ☑ Cross-promote in all other available areas

⦾ Do **not** cross-promote my items.

[Apply]

*Figure 2-7: **Let eBay help in your cross-promotional campaign.***

Acquire Inventory

To keep your eBay business engine fueled, you need merchandise, which can come from a myriad of sources. Inventory can be procured from traditional eBay sources, such as garage sales, but to ramp up your business to higher sales, you'll want to explore sources used by retail businesses, including buying from wholesalers, using drop-shipping outlets, and buying from abroad.

Find Items the Old-Fashioned Way

Not all eBay businesses tap into manufacturers' sales representatives, import from China, or otherwise buy from traditional wholesale markets. Many eBay businesses just improve on obtaining items from the traditional sources they used when they started out, except now they do it more efficiently:

- **Basements, attics, and closets** provide the most readily available and lowest-cost items (you already own them). Include items of friends and relatives that can be had for nothing or next to it.

- **Thrift stores** contain hidden treasures that can be ferreted out with a sharp, experienced pricing eye and persistent scouring. Go (early) on promotion days to obtain even deeper discounts.

TIP

Don't overlook the sales potential in countries other than the United States. eBay has Web sites in 27 other countries (as of spring 2008), with billions of potential buyers. Some top PowerSellers have reported as much as 40 percent of their sales are for items shipped outside the United States. People around the globe want American merchandise. See "Import from Abroad" later in the chapter for information on buying and selling globally.

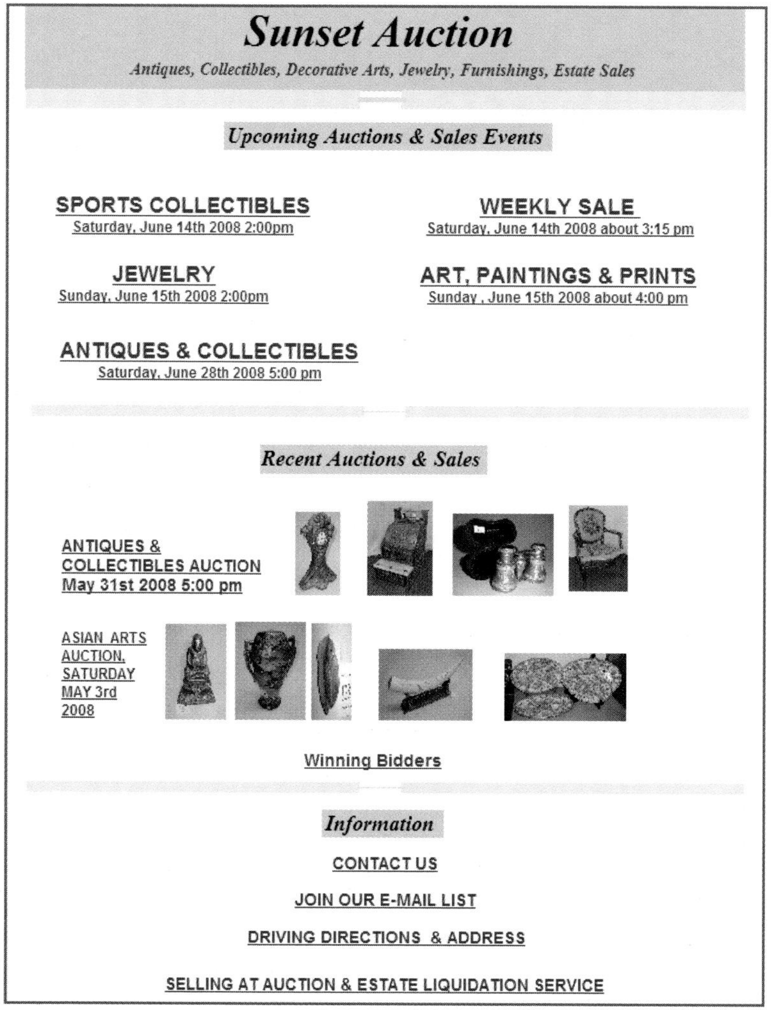

Sunset Auction

Antiques, Collectibles, Decorative Arts, Jewelry, Furnishings, Estate Sales

Upcoming Auctions & Sales Events

SPORTS COLLECTIBLES
Saturday, June 14th 2008 2:00pm

WEEKLY SALE
Saturday, June 14th 2008 about 3:15 pm

JEWELRY
Sunday, June 15th 2008 2:00pm

ART, PAINTINGS & PRINTS
Sunday , June 15th 2008 about 4:00 pm

ANTIQUES & COLLECTIBLES
Saturday, June 28th 2008 5:00 pm

Recent Auctions & Sales

**ANTIQUES &
COLLECTIBLES AUCTION**
May 31st 2008 5:00 pm

**ASIAN ARTS
AUCTION,
SATURDAY
MAY 3rd
2008**

Winning Bidders

Information

CONTACT US

JOIN OUR E-MAIL LIST

DRIVING DIRECTIONS & ADDRESS

SELLING AT AUCTION & ESTATE LIQUIDATION SERVICE

Figure 2-8: Attend live auctions to network with others in your merchandise lines and learn about auctioning.

> **CAUTION**
>
> Buying the contents of mini-storage units whose owners failed to continue payments is a classic example of caveat emptor (buyer beware). Typically, the storage unit management periodically hires an auctioneer to sell off their inventory of unpaid units. By law, in many states, management cannot open the unit until the auction, at which time the lock is cut. The bidders, in real time, then get a chance to view the contents from the door and place a bid on all the contents. So what really is in that box labeled "Guns" or "Jewelry?" There are stories of people who, in cahoots with the storage management and auctioneer, seed a unit with junk, hazardous materials, and other hard-to-get-rid-of items, and then apply deceptive arrangement and eye-candy labeling to sell these items to unsuspecting bidders.

- **Garage sales** are typically announced in your local paper and on your nearest telephone pole. Get out early, map out your route, and be done before brunch. Seek out sales that start on Friday—you'll avoid many amateur buyers (they have day jobs) and get first look at the freshest merchandise.

- **Estate sales** liquidate the contents of a household. The quality of merchandise can range from the trappings of the rich and famous to items more commonly found in Dumpsters. Depending on how the contents are sold, you can purchase individual items, as in a garage sale; or you can make a bid to purchase the entire lot. Check the auctions section in the classified section of your newspaper for upcoming sales. To find leads on buying an entire estate, network with estate-planning lawyers and other professionals who often assist survivors with liquidating family assets.

- **Live auctions** provide great experience in the world of bidding and overall auction psychology (see Figure 2-8). Check out your Sunday paper for upcoming events. Most cost very little, if anything, to attend and provide invaluable pricing data, networking, and usually entertaining auctioneers.

QUICK**FACTS**

UNDERSTANDING THE JARGON OF WHOLESALING

People use business terms every day, often without truly understanding their meanings. There's no law against that, but when dealing with goods and services worth more than a few dollars, it's vital you know what you're talking about (your supplier, wholesaler, competitor, and customer probably do):

- **Brand** is a name, design, term, or symbol that identifies a product.

- **Distribution (or sales) channel** is comprised of a hierarchy of persons or businesses that move and/or sell products from the manufacturer to the consumer.

- **Manufacturer's agent** is a middleman who sells goods from a manufacturer for a commission on what is sold.

- **Middleman** is a euphemism for any person or organization that buys from wholesalers and sells to retailers. Legitimate middlemen, such as distributors or *manufacturer's agents,* add value to the sales channel through packaging, transportation, or consolidation, but many are an unnecessary layer in the hierarchy and simply increase the cost of goods to the retailer.

Continued . . .

TIP

Before you approach a wholesaler to open an account, ensure you have a state business license and/or resale certificate. See Chapter 1 for more information on choosing and establishing a business entity.

Acquire Wholesale Sources

A classic way to run an eBay business is to buy at wholesale and sell at retail (or at what the highest bidder is willing to pay). Unfortunately, until you've established yourself as a high-volume seller, many wholesalers do not want to bother with smaller accounts. That's not to say they won't sell to you—they just don't seek you out. Consider these issues when trying to line up a wholesaler:

- Research the manufacturer for the product you want to sell. Many companies simply place their brand name on a product made by another company. The classic example is the Sears Kenmore brand—Kenmore washers are actually made by Whirlpool. You may have to do some sleuthing to locate the manufacturer, as most branded products don't generally advertise their true roots. Check manuals, nameplates, and service centers to find the OEM (original equipment manufacturer).

- Contact the manufacturer's sales department and ask for a list of their wholesale suppliers.

- Contact the wholesale suppliers and request to set up an account. Prepare for questions about your business and sales potential. Give honest answers and, if rejected, move on to the next supplier on your list.

- If you don't have the success, time, or desire to do the leg work, consider purchasing a list of suppliers that have been screened and are willing to work with online sellers. Be aware that a Google search will turn up legitimate as well as questionable providers. The eBay Solutions Directory lists several providers of wholesale items whose reputations have been verified; however, you won't be the only eBay business trying to sell their products.

PowerSeller Sally says: "Buy merchandise from other dealers. A seller may be overstocked on an item or may not have enough manpower to get it all listed. Other sellers can be a fantastic supply source for saleable merchandise."

PowerSeller Sally says: "If it were easy to set up a wholesale account, every seller on eBay would have one!"

1

3

4

5

6

7

8

9

10

Buy Wholesale on eBay

You've got to love the marketing folks at eBay. Not only do they provide the mechanisms for you to sell your items in an efficient and inexpensive manner to a worldwide market, but they also provide you a channel to buy your items wholesale on eBay "in an efficient and inexpensive manner *from* a worldwide market." To find items to buy in quantity and at a hopefully lower *wholesale* price each:

1. On the eBay header, click **Categories**, and the All Categories window will open.

2. Look through the Category items. At the end of many of them will be "Wholesale Lots." If you click this line, you will see a listing of all the wholesale lots for that category.

> Art (188226)
> Direct from the Artist (25352)
> Art from Dealers & Resellers (160567)
> Wholesale Lots (2307)
> *See all Art categories...*

3. You will need to narrow your search considerably, as many eBayers use wholesale lots to sell their single items.

Import from Abroad

Buying from outside your borders opens your buying opportunities to markets where other eBay businesspersons don't often venture. Many businesses avoid global transactions for a good reason, but if you're willing to learn the ropes, there are untapped buying opportunities. You can import through traditional channels on your own or use eBay to help you in the process.

Show only
- ☐ Items listed with PayPal
- ☐ Buying Options
  - Auctions ▼
- ☐ Free Shipping
- ☐ Completed listings
- ☐ 🎁 Gift items
- ☑ Items listed as lots
- ☐ Listings
  - Ending within ▼
  - 1 hour ▼
- ☐ Number of bids
  - ☐ to ☐
- ☐ Items priced
  - ☐ to ☐
- [Show Items]

TIP

To find wholesale items for sale or bid on eBay, include keywords such as "lot," "bulk," "resale," and "wholesale" in your search. Under the Search Options sidebar in listings pages, click **Items Listed As Lots**, and click **Show Items** to see bulk items for sale in a given category. Scan eBay for wholesale items that are incorrectly listed or that are not placed in the proper category. You can often obtain saleable merchandise at bargain prices because a seller did not know the proper way to list his or her items.

NOTE

If you are a PowerSeller, you can find more options in the Reseller Marketplace, only available to PowerSellers. Here, manufacturers, eBayers with excess inventory, liquidators, and others offer their inventory for sale.

TIP

Stay one step ahead of other eBay businesses by keeping in touch with international economic factors. A few years ago, Mexico was the place to go to purchase wholesale, cheap, metal garden sculptures and outdoor architectural structures, such as archways and trellises. Now, China's massive steel industry has spawned a plethora of metal fabricators for the export market, and "Mexican Iron" is quickly being usurped in quality and price.

Professor Polly says: "The best way to discover the duty on a specific item is to contact your local U.S. Customs office, since they are the agency that will be assigning the duty amount."

NOTE

Not too many years ago, the rage in importing antique furniture was the arrival of a shipping container from England or France at your local antique dealer's parking lot. One dealer we know used to make five or six European buying trips a year (and enjoyed a nice vacation while amassing enough items to fill a container). Times have changed. Due to post- 9/11 tightened security and related measures associated with bringing containers to the United States, this dealer has stopped importing containers altogether.

UNDERSTAND IMPORT FACTORS

Many headaches and costs are associated with an import business, and for most eBay business with relatively low sales volumes, it may not be worthwhile. The main limitations to buying abroad are determined by:

- What you buy:

    - Many items do not adhere to U.S. safety, Environmental Protection Agency (EPA), and other standards. For example, several news accounts have highlighted the toxic lead that was contained in toys made in China.

    - Items of cultural importance may not be allowed outside the borders of a country. For example, in Turkey, items more than 100 years old are not generally allowed to leave the country.

    - Some items just have higher duty rates than others (as a twist on the previous bullet, antiques more than 100 years old can enter the United States duty-free).

    - Heavy items may incur prohibitive per-item shipping costs, unless you buy in very large quantities.

- Where you buy it:

    - Duty rates are broadly assigned by country. Duty rates for goods entering the United States are extracted from the Harmonized Tariff Schedule Annotated (HTSA) of the United States, published by the United States International Trade Commission (www.usitc.gov/tata/hts). Most countries enjoy "Column 1 of the Duty Rates," or favored nation, rates. Items from unfavored "Column 2" countries pay a higher rate, as shown in Figure 2-9.

- How you bring it into the country:

    - Bringing them with you is the easiest way to bring items back to the United States. You can simply produce the items for inspection, and informal verbal declarations when driving across a border or simple Customs forms used when arriving by plane or boat are painless.

    - Shipping by mail is an acceptable entry method because you don't need to be personally present at the point of entry. When the United States Postal Service (USPS) receives an overseas package that contains dutiful items, it's passed to a Customs agent, who reviews Customs forms on the package and determines any duty fees. The package is given back to the USPS, where, upon delivery to the recipient, the duty and Customs handling fees are collected.

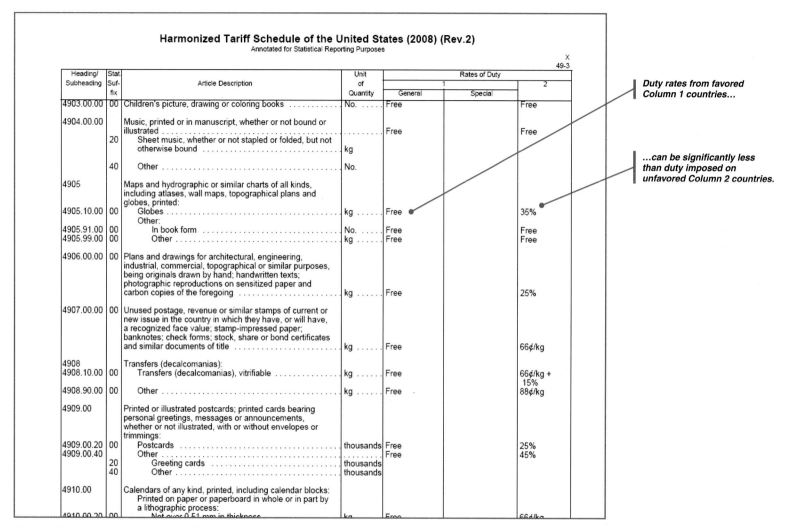

Harmonized Tariff Schedule of the United States (2008) (Rev.2)
Annotated for Statistical Reporting Purposes

X
49-3

Heading/ Subheading	Stat. Suffix	Article Description	Unit of Quantity	Rates of Duty 1 General	Rates of Duty 1 Special	Rates of Duty 2
4903.00.00	00	Children's picture, drawing or coloring books	No.	Free		Free
4904.00.00		Music, printed or in manuscript, whether or not bound or illustrated	....	Free		Free
	20	Sheet music, whether or not stapled or folded, but not otherwise bound	kg			
	40	Other	No.			
4905		Maps and hydrographic or similar charts of all kinds, including atlases, wall maps, topographical plans and globes, printed:				
4905.10.00	00	Globes	kg	Free		35%
		Other:				
4905.91.00	00	In book form	No.	Free		Free
4905.99.00	00	Other	kg	Free		Free
4906.00.00	00	Plans and drawings for architectural, engineering, industrial, commercial, topographical or similar purposes, being originals drawn by hand; handwritten texts; photographic reproductions on sensitized paper and carbon copies of the foregoing	kg	Free		25%
4907.00.00	00	Unused postage, revenue or similar stamps of current or new issue in the country in which they have, or will have, a recognized face value; stamp-impressed paper; banknotes; check forms; stock, share or bond certificates and similar documents of title	kg	Free		66¢/kg
4908		Transfers (decalcomanias):				
4908.10.00	00	Transfers (decalcomanias), vitrifiable	kg	Free		66¢/kg + 15%
4908.90.00	00	Other	kg	Free		88¢/kg
4909.00		Printed or illustrated postcards; printed cards bearing personal greetings, messages or announcements, whether or not illustrated, with or without envelopes or trimmings:				
4909.00.20	00	Postcards	thousands	Free		25%
4909.00.40		Other	....	Free		45%
	20	Greeting cards	thousands			
	40	Other	thousands			
4910.00		Calendars of any kind, printed, including calendar blocks: Printed on paper or paperboard in whole or in part by a lithographic process:				
4910.00.20	00	Not over 0.51 mm in thickness	kg	Free		66¢/kg

Duty rates from favored Column 1 countries…

…can be significantly less than duty imposed on unfavored Column 2 countries.

Figure 2-9: Duty rates start in the HTSA based on a country's trading status and are then applied based on a U.S. Customs officer's assessment of the item.

Global Sites

Choose Site ▾ | Go |

- Freight shipments are how most international trade is conducted and is not generally recommended for businesses new to global shipping. You or your agent (to whom you will need to pay fees) will need to quickly arrange movement of the merchandise from the shipper's warehouse to Customs to avoid *demurrage* (warehousing costs) and then produce invoices, bills of lading, and Customs forms to determine the duty owed. In the post-9/11 world, shipments are being visually inspected more and more, and you will be responsible for associated costs to open containers and remove shipping and packing materials.

BUY GLOBALLY ON EBAY

Many eBay users avoid global transactions because of the extra work and potential pitfalls involved with conducting business outside the borders (see "Understand Import Factors"). Their reluctance can be your opportunity to acquire unique items that every other eBay business isn't fighting over. The "At a Glance" statistics on eBay's Global Trade page show you the monetary incentive to consider eBay's global potential. eBay provides searching to its worldwide sites and offers a lot of useful information to help you navigate the labyrinth of currency fluctuations, shipping costs, language problems, and other issues.

At a Glance

- Users: 147,000,000
- Listings: 431,000,000
- Trade Volume:10,602,000,000

- eBay Marketplace Research
- Seller Education
- Sell Internationally
- Shipping Center

1. On the eBay header, click **Site Map**.

2. Under Selling Resources, click **Sell Internationally**.

Browser Earl

Browser Earl says: "Get items from around the world at http://pages .ebay.com/globaltrade."

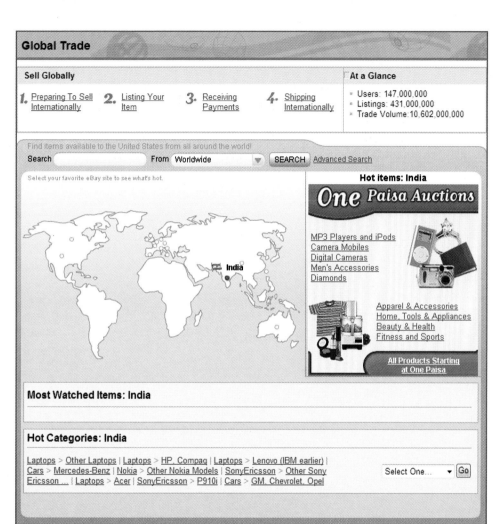

Figure 2-10: eBay provides a portal to global buying and selling.

3. On the Global Trade page, shown in Figure 2-10:

- Type keywords to search global sites for items (see "Buy Wholesale on eBay" earlier in the chapter for keyword hints for wholesale listings).

- Click an eBay worldwide site's flag or link to display that country's "Hot Items" and "Hot Categories."

- Scroll down and click one of the many resource links to learn more about the aspects of buying and selling internationally.

Use Drop-Shipping

So you want to become an eBay business, but you live in a studio apartment without a square foot of space to store inventory? Not to worry—you can conduct a successful eBay business without ever buying, seeing, or touching your items. Using *drop-shipping,* you establish a relationship with a wholesaler, who will package and ship items you sell directly to buyers (even with a mailing label using your company name). As far as the buyer is concerned, the billiard table he or she received came from your studio apartment. You pay the drop-shipper the wholesale cost of the item and shipping and handling costs. Of course, the trick to making this work is finding a reputable and reliable company with which to partner. Doing a search on Google will produce pages of potential drop-shipping sources, but as with most things on the Internet, it's best to get a second opinion before you do business. To find companies vetted by eBay that drop-ship or that provide lists of companies that do:

1. Click **Site Map** on the eBay header.

2. Under Selling Tools, click **eBay Solutions Directory**.

3. In the Solutions Directory, under Selling Solutions, click **Sourcing**.

■ Sourcing
Find new products to sell on eBay.

4. Click the links of the solution providers that indicate they offer drop-shipping services, as shown in Figure 2-11.

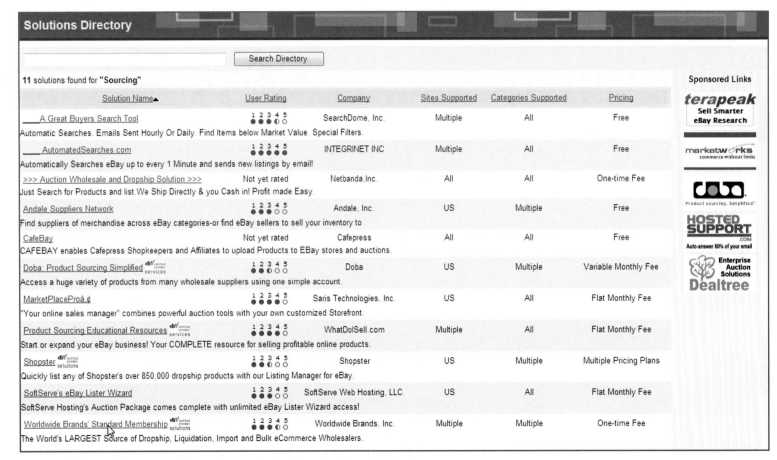

Figure 2-11: Drop-shippers provide a way to conduct an inventory-free eBay business.

Chapter 3
Creating eBay Business Processing Centers

From garage sale seller to PowerSeller, you have to accomplish a sequence of operations and processes to sell on eBay. It doesn't matter if you work off a legal pad or if you use commercial auction-management software. All merchandise on its way to eBay buyers requires a certain level of attention from you during its tenure under your ownership or control. The better organized and more efficient you become, the more time you will have to pursue other eBay selling opportunities and, ultimately, you will become a more profitable business.

In this chapter you will learn that no matter what level of selling you are at, you can benefit your eBay business by utilizing the concept of *processing centers* to handle the various tasks necessary to acquire, list, sell, ship, and finalize a sale.

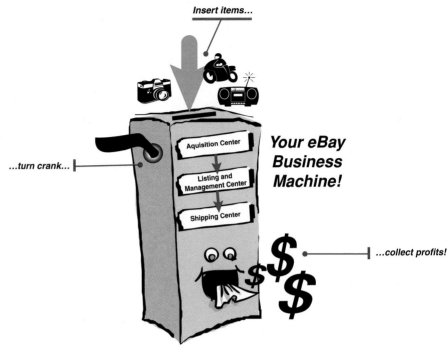

Figure 3-1: *Items need to travel, virtually if not physically, through a prescribed path in your eBay business.*

QUICK**FACTS**

PROCESSING ON THE FAST TRACK

An item's journey through your eBay business follows a typical flow, as shown in Figure 3-1. The main processing centers include:

- The **Acquisition Center** logs a new item into your inventory database (this can be a simple notebook; a dedicated database/spreadsheet program, such as Microsoft Excel; or auction management software, such as Selling Manager Pro) and includes sales cost, date of acquisition, and source, and assigns an inventory number, if applicable. The information gathered during the acquisition phase can be integrated into your inventory accounting system.

- The **Listing and Management Center** photographs and describes the item, researches similar items for pricing and category selection, and creates and submits the contents of your listing form to eBay or to your auction-management system. Listings are monitored for bidding activity, and responses are provided to bidder/buyer inquiries. The management portion of this center works with your accounting system to process incoming payments and releases items to the Shipping Center when funds have cleared.

- The **Shipping Center** provides materials and equipment for easy and professional packaging. Liaisons and accounts with shippers are established to maximize convenience (daily pickups) and minimize costs.

Process Incoming Items

Chapter 2 describes several strategies you can use to acquire items. But once you've purchased the merchandise, what do you do with it? Quite a bit, actually, although the norm is closer to just placing the item in the nearest available space on a shelf or on the floor. The more time and energy you devote to get merchandise properly introduced into your system, the greater the efficiency dividends you will receive during the time the product spends with your business. The upfront time to establish inventory controls and attend to accounting details will quickly become the "gift that keeps on giving."

Capture Purchase Data

In the zeal to acquire and purchase merchandise, it's easy (and tempting) to throw all of the receipts and other documentation into a file folder or shoebox and deal with it when the need arises (usually April 14). Though this method might serve casual eBay sellers, as your eBay business volume increases, you will need a more systematic approach to documenting your purchases. The best time to do that is close to the time of purchase, when your memory is fresh and any paper trails are still close at hand. Whether your system is a notebook with lined columns, an Excel spreadsheet, or accounting or auction-management software, you have to dedicate the time to log the captured data.

SET UP A SIMPLE SYSTEM

With a program such as Excel, you can create a basic spreadsheet that lists the key information you need when purchasing an item. Create columns to record data on each item you purchase for resale. Table 3-1 describes the columns, and Figure 3-2 shows an example of a sample spreadsheet. (See *Microsoft Office Excel 2007 QuickSteps*, published by McGraw-Hill, for information on creating and using spreadsheets).

USE AN ACCOUNTING PROGRAM

Keeping accurate records of inventory costs, selling prices, shipping and handling, overhead, and other associated costs is the foundation to satisfying government reporting requirements, as well as keeping on top of the financial health of your business. Some accounting programs (such as Intuit's QuickBooks Simple Start/Basic/Pro/Premium series) do extremely well at the business of accounting, but aren't typically geared toward the business of listing items for sale on eBay. Although you may find you can "force" one to do this, it's best to look at these programs as part of an overall suite of tools you might employ and not the sole solution.

SPREADSHEET COLUMN	DESCRIPTION
Purchase Date	The date the item was purchased.
Category and Subcategory	Places items into the eBay categories you will probably list them under. Once categorized, you can sort your items by category or subcategory.
Item Name	A short name identifying the item.
Number	An internal inventory number you can use to track the item.
Description	A narrative area where you can add any amplifying information about the item, especially information you will want to use when listing the item.
Total Purchase Price	The total amount paid for the item or lot, including tax.
Item Price	The price you paid for each item or lot (include any commissions or fees).
Tax	The cost of any sales tax on the item or lot (if you have a resale number from your state, you should not have to pay sales tax when purchasing items you are selling).
Quantity Purchased	The number of identical items you purchased or the number of lots (for multiple items, determine if you will sell them individually or by lot).
Onhand	An inventory metric designed to let you know how many items are left from a multiple-item purchase. Initially, the Quantity Purchased and Onhand columns for such items will be identical.

Table 3-1: Information Recorded for Resale Items

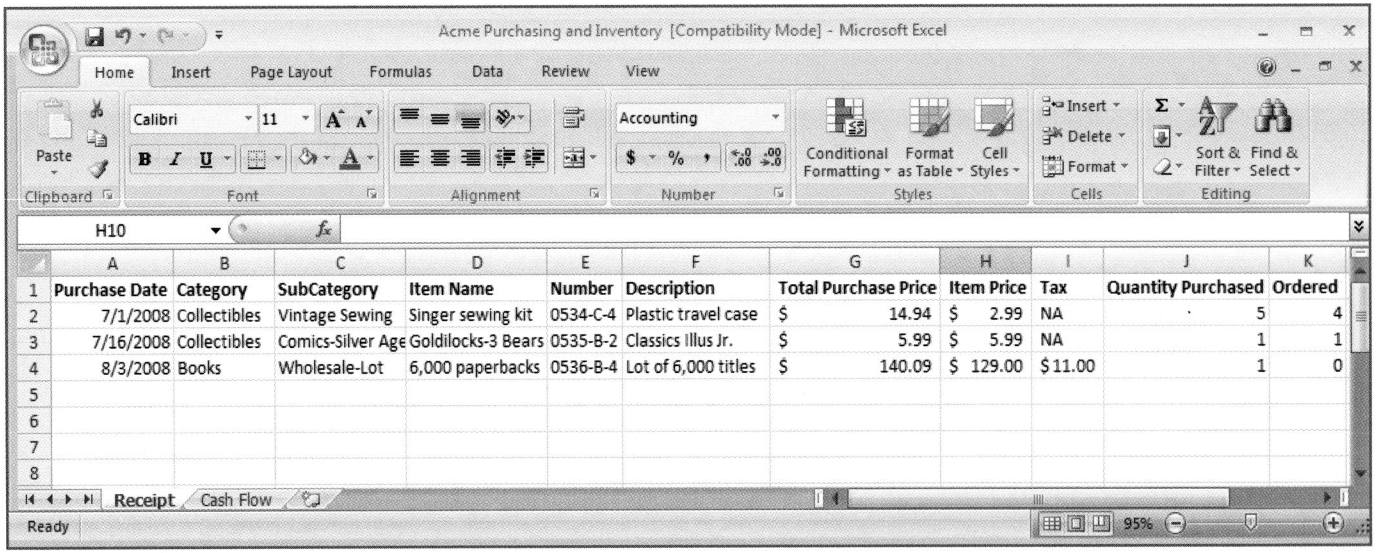

Figure 3-2: Spreadsheet programs, such as Excel, are great for creating your own first purchasing and inventory-tracking systems.

The key to capturing your business data is to get it entered into a digital, portable format. Your needs and experience with various financial and inventory systems will change as your business grows and matures, but as long as the data is on your computer, you will be able to convert, copy, export, import, and otherwise recycle the data without losing or having to re-enter it. Ensure that whatever system you use can convert data to common formats, such as text (.txt) and comma-separated value (.csv) files, Excel (.xls), and Intuit's QuickBooks (.qbw).

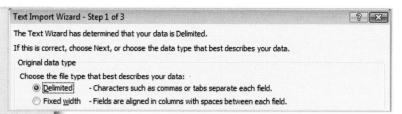

USE AN EBAY TOOL OR SERVICE

eBay provides several auction-management tools and services you can use to organize and manage your sales, from the views in My eBay (with or without the added functionality of online services, such as Selling Manager Pro)

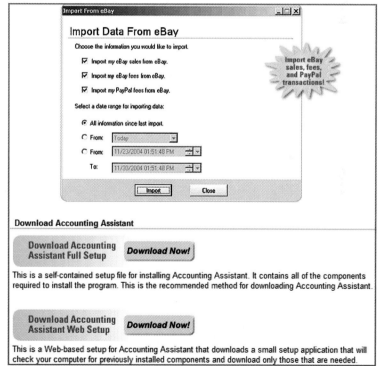

Figure 3-3: Choose a download method to start importing eBay data into a QuickBooks account.

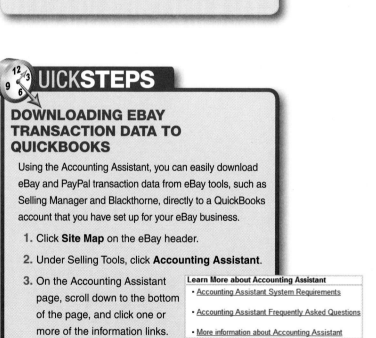

QUICKSTEPS

DOWNLOADING EBAY TRANSACTION DATA TO QUICKBOOKS

Using the Accounting Assistant, you can easily download eBay and PayPal transaction data from eBay tools, such as Selling Manager and Blackthorne, directly to a QuickBooks account that you have set up for your eBay business.

1. Click **Site Map** on the eBay header.

2. Under Selling Tools, click **Accounting Assistant**.

3. On the Accounting Assistant page, scroll down to the bottom of the page, and click one or more of the information links.

   Learn More about Accounting Assistant
   - Accounting Assistant System Requirements
   - Accounting Assistant Frequently Asked Questions
   - More information about Accounting Assistant

4. When ready, click the method you want to use to download the Accounting Assistant, as shown in Figure 3-3.

to desktop tools, such as the comprehensive Blackthorne Pro. Though these services and tools do a credible job of helping you manage listings and interact with buyers, they are not intended to replace specialized accounting and inventory control systems your business might require. If your needs aren't too demanding, you can "game" these tools and services to approximate the services provided by more robust offerings. For example, eBay's free Turbo Lister program provides an optional field you can use for inventory information, as shown in Figure 3-4. See Chapters 4 and 5 for more information on using specific auction management tools and services.

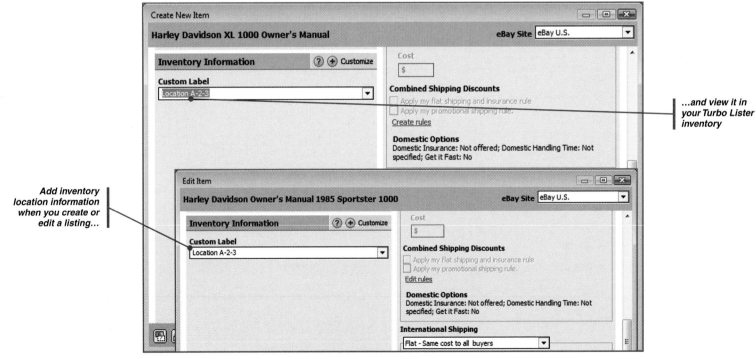

Figure 3-4: You can add inventory data to your listing in Turbo Lister by using the optional Inventory Information sub-window in the Create New Item form.

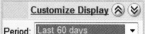

Control Your Inventory

Even if you sell just a few items a week, you need an inventory-management system that stores and organizes your merchandise and that reflects the number of items available if you deal in lots, bulk, and other multiple-item sales.

CREATE THE STOCKROOM

Storage solutions can be as simple as arranging a typical college-dorm shelving system consisting of 1ft. x 12 ft. planking and cement blocks in a spare bedroom, or you can lease commercial warehousing space lined with steel racks to handle larger inventory needs similar to what you see in the "big box" stores. The goal is to develop an infrastructure that satisfies several criteria:

- Match the storage system to the type of items you sell. Don't store Ford E-350 transmissions using a dorm shelving system or use expensive racks with weight limits in the hundreds of pounds to hold jewelry.

- Dedicate a safe, secure space. Even if you need to share a room, garage, or building between your eBay business and other uses, segregate your eBay inventory by distinct lines of demarcation. Not only are you trying to prevent theft, but you don't want to commingle your inventory with personal or other business items. There's nothing more embarrassing than having to inform a buyer his or her item cannot be shipped because the item has seemingly grown legs.

- Think ergonomics. Design the storage system so that heavy items are accessible without any undue bending, there is enough room to provide easy ingress and egress, and safety measures are installed to prevent items falling from above.

ORGANIZE THE INVENTORY

An organization system needs to be applied to your inventory so items can be easily and quickly stored, located, and retrieved.

1. Assign a locator system to your storage infrastructure. For example, "A-2-3" could be used to identity the "A" rack, number "2" shelf, and third ("3") position on the shelf. Label your storage system in a clear but nonpermanent manner (you'll probably tweak the system a few times before you're satisfied with it).

2. Identify the item with the locator number. Annotate the item's record in your software with the locator code. For example, in Turbo Lister, you have an optional Custom Label

field you can use to add inventory text, or you can add the locator code to the Excel spreadsheet you've created. Also, print out a copy of the item's record and keep it with the item.

	D	E Inventory	F
1	Item Name	Number	Description
2	Singer sewing kit	0534-C-4	Plastic travel case
3	Goldilocks-3 Bears	0535-B-2	Classics Illus Jr.
4	6,000 paperbacks	0536-B-4	Lot of 6,000 titles

3. Be disciplined. Ensure that all the people involved in your operation understand the system you've set up and that they use it all the time. All it takes is for one item to show up on a table without identifying documentation to lose the efficiencies you've worked hard to create.

KNOW HOW MUCH YOU HAVE

If you only sell distinct items (by definition, you should only have one of each), you probably don't need to worry about tracking quantities, but if you sell multiple items, you need to have an accurate picture of your inventory. If you use eBay and third-party inventory or listing-management software, the software will deduct your total quantity on hand by the number of items

in your sales. If your system is less sophisticated, you'll need to make the changes manually and then be attentive in your bookkeeping.

Create and Manage Your Listings

The Listing Center, the middle link in the overall eBay business cycle, (see Figure 3-1), is where you perform the actions and functions that are unique to selling on eBay. This center is comprised of sub-centers, including:

- **Listing Central** is where you research items, develop descriptions, select categories, determine selling prices, and enter the item into the Sell Your Item form or into a listing program, such as Turbo Lister. This area can be as simple as a stand-alone computer, or its function can be parsed out to several stations that feed into a common listing form.

NOTE

The functions performed in the Listing Management and Customer Service sub-center typically can be combined with those in the Listing Center; that is, it does not require additional equipment or space from that in the Listing Center where you create listings. Unless your goal is feedback scores that qualify you for the eBay "shooting stars," you should find enough downtime on your listing computer(s) to use them for managing your listings. If you are "shooting" for shooting stars, you'll probably need additional hardware and software to support your growing business.

Yellow shooting star (⭐) = 10,000 to 24,999 points
Turquoise shooting star (⭐) = 25,000 to 49,999 points
Purple shooting star (⭐) = 50,000 to 99,999 points
Red shooting star (⭐) = 100,000 points or more

TIP

The standard eBay Sell Your Item form (and its more simplified brother, the Create Your Listing form for auction-only listings) provides the basic framework for the workflow needed to list an item, but you can design policies and a physical layout that support greater time and flow efficiencies. For example, photograph items upon receipt, and use the pictures to write the listing instead of the physical item. This way, the item is placed into inventory once and kept there until retrieved for shipping. Also, some items are bulky and don't lend themselves well to handling while you are working on your computer.

QUICKFACTS

OUTFITTING A LISTING CENTRAL AREA

Your workspace and equipment can be as simple or as complex as you desire.

SET UP A SINGLE USER/SMALL BUSINESS DESKTOP

- **Computer and software.** You don't really need the latest and greatest—probably any functioning computer you've bought in the last few years will work just fine. Your biggest expense probably will be for third-party software to enhance or replace the free tools and services provided by eBay. For example, photo editing software to supplement the meager offering in the eBay Enhanced Picture Services and auction management software to replace or upgrade My eBay.

Continued . . .

- **Photography Studio** provides a suitable environment to digitally photograph or scan the item to accentuate its features, identify any points of contention, and basically sell the item from a visual perspective.

- **Listing Management/Customer Service** is where you track the completed listing from the start of the sale to final payment, respond to buyer and bidder inquiries, and work with others in the business to answer questions about the item during the sale. This is also where you handle disputes, payment and shipping issues, and other post-sale problems.

Work with Listings

After an item has been entered into your purchasing and inventory systems by your Acquisition Center (see "Process Incoming Items" earlier in the chapter), it's time to pass the baton (and item) to Listing Central, the area where the item is entered into the eBay system and monitored by you. As a low-volume, occasional seller, you can get away with the inefficiencies of having to share equipment, space, and time between eBay selling and other activities. When ramping up your sales, however, you need to borrow from industry practices and strive toward an assembly-line process that allows you to quickly move items through the elements of the listing-creation process. Of course, if you sell similar or multiple items, much of the work can be minimized.

QUICK**FACTS**

OUTFITTING A LISTING CENTRAL AREA *(Continued)*

- **Monitor.** A large, higher-resolution screen will allow you to view more space in a single view and will let you see the details in your pictures that many of your buyers will be seeing.

- **Internet connection.** A broadband connection should be considered mandatory. The time you will spend creating or uploading listings, checking e-mail, and doing research will warrant the expense.

- **Digital camera and scanner.** Unless you have special needs, any newer, medium-quality equipment should work just fine. You don't need the most expensive, highest-megapixel camera to capture images for display on a monitor (see Chapter 4 for more information on taking pictures).

- **Scale or device for measuring the weight of the item.** When creating the item listing, you'll need the shipping specifications, which require the weight and sometimes the dimensions of the item. Although this equipment is needed for creating the listing, it is also needed in the Shipping Center.

SET UP A HIGH-VOLUME LINE

In addition to the essential equipment described for a single user/small business, other considerations need to be taken into account for higher-volume sellers:

- **Networked computers, printers, and other peripherals.** Larger operations will need several workstations to concurrently access business records, listings, and other related data. A typical wired networking scheme is a peer-to-peer local

Continued . . .

TIP

For information on developing management skills, consider *The QuickSteps Guide to Skills for New Managers* by Marty Matthews and Sherryl Christie Bierschenk (McGraw-Hill, 2008).

RESEARCH YOUR ITEMS

To create accurate listing titles and descriptions, determine the best selling format (auction or Buy It Now), and price your items where they will sell for the best price-to-volume ratio, you need to know your items:

- Search for the item on eBay to determine an item's value by checking the Completed Listings for identical or similar items. View Completed Listings by opening a category's listings, clicking the **Completed Listings** check box on the left sidebar, and clicking **Show Items.**

- Search for the item using search engines, such as Google, to cast a wider net and see what you can find in other auctions, brick-and-mortar stores, classified ads, and wherever else the search engine mines information. Or use specialized Web sites that feature your type of item.

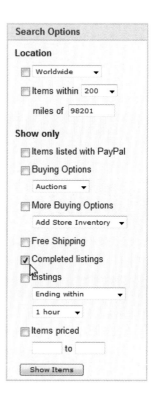

- Visit libraries, antique malls, and shows to purchase or borrow reference books on antiques and collectibles, and to network with other dealers. Collectors' shows are one of the best places to gather information (and inventory) in any of the collectible fields. You will be able to network with both dealers and collectors. This will allow you up-to-the-minute information on trends, buying and selling patterns, and additional data that might enable you to enhance your eBay listings. Your eBay sales will be greatly enhanced when buyers can tell from your listings that you have knowledge of your field.

OUTFITTING A LISTING CENTRAL AREA *(Continued)*

area network (LAN), as shown in Figure 3-5. Wireless networks today are inexpensive alternatives, especially if your physical layout makes running cables difficult. The biggest operations will need to consider dedicated servers with the inherent increased expense of more robust equipment and software.

- **Employees.** As your business grows, so will the need for more personnel to keep up with your listings volume. Hire personnel with specific tasks in mind, for example, people with photography experience to take item pictures and people who are familiar with the items you're selling. Contact your state business offices to properly set up accounts to collect unemployment and worker's compensation-related taxes (see Figure 3-6), as well as setting up a payroll system to collect federal and state income, Social Security, and Medicare taxes (see the "Downloading eBay Transaction Data to QuickBooks" QuickSteps for information on using QuickBooks). If you are not familiar with hiring and managing employees, get assistance from local business groups and consider taking classes offered by many community colleges.

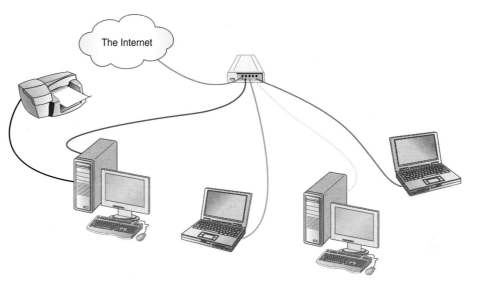

Figure 3-5: You know your eBay business is growing when you start having to invest in networked computers and peripheral equipment.

If you are a collector, you might find it productive to start your eBay business with sales in your area of expertise.

- Contact others who sell, collect, manufacture, or use the item you're trying to sell. You will be surprised at how much information you can get from other eBay sellers.
- Use grading and authentication services to bolster your customers' confidence in the condition (grading) and authenticity of an item by having an independent, experienced professional examine it (see the "Finding a Grading or Authentication Service" QuickSteps.)

Figure 3-6: Along with the productivity increases associated with hiring employees, you will also increase your administrative workload and filing requirements.

FINDING A GRADING OR AUTHENTICATION SERVICE

eBay offers sellers (and buyers) a list of independent companies that help determine if an item is in good condition and that will attest to an item's authenticity:

1. Grading services comment on an item's condition—what grade is a specific coin, for instance? Is it mint condition? Good? Poor? The grading system depends on what item is being graded, so coins would differ from antique furniture, for example. A grading service can also tell you if the item has had restoration procedures performed on it or if it is in its original state. Often, restoration on a painting, comic book, or paper document is hard for the untrained eye to detect. Some collectibles can be devalued by as much as 50 percent if signs of restoration are present.

2. Authentication services verify that an item is genuine. For example, Professional Sports Authenticator (www.psacard.com) offers an authentication service, PSA/DNA, which uses a synthesized DNA technology to look at an autograph that is available on eBay and renders an opinion as to whether it is genuine.

3. Click **Site Map** on the eBay header.

4. Under Selling Resources, click **Opinions, Authentication & Grading**. Scroll down to view the categories of graders and authenticators, as shown in Figure 3-7.

5. Click the link for the service you're interested in using.

TIP

Find the most inquisitive and creative person or employee in your business and put him or her in charge of researching items and preparing listings.

PREPARE AND SUBMIT THE LISTING

After researching and collecting the raw information for an item, the data needs to be incorporated into a selling form that will ultimately become the listing Web page. The technical knowledge required of the person preparing the selling form will depend on the method you use to create your listing and how much customization you add to it. For example, listing items with the simplified Create Your Listing form (auction listings only) and the standard Sell Your Item form that allows you to customize your listing, using eBay Picture Services to host images, and using prebuilt templates requires little but fundamental computer skills. However, if you create your listings from scratch using Hypertext Markup Language (HTML), host your own photographs, and use custom listing or management software, the new computer user would be challenged. Chapter 4 describes how to create listings to maximize sales using tools such as Turbo Lister, shown in Figure 3-8.

TIP

To a receive a quick and inexpensive appraisal of an item you're selling, click the **What's It Worth To You** link at the bottom of the Opinions, Authentication & Grading page (see the "Finding a Grading or Authentication Service" QuickSteps). After creating an account and providing basic information, such as category, description, and pictures, and any amplifying information required by their appraiser, you will be able to download an appraisal certificate.

General

Contact What's It Worth To You for an online appraisal.

Contact the International Society of Appraisers to find an appraiser in your local area.

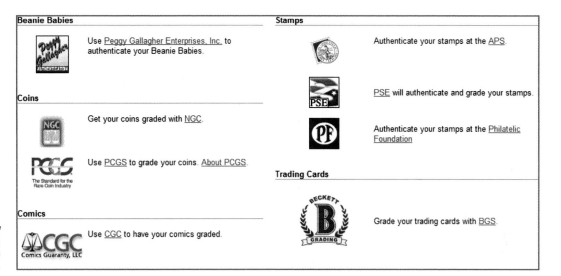

Beanie Babies

Use Peggy Gallagher Enterprises, Inc. to authenticate your Beanie Babies.

Coins

Get your coins graded with NGC.

Use PCGS to grade your coins. About PCGS.

Comics

Use CGC to have your comics graded.

Stamps

Authenticate your stamps at the APS.

PSE will authenticate and grade your stamps.

Authenticate your stamps at the Philatelic Foundation

Trading Cards

Grade your trading cards with BGS.

Figure 3-7: eBay provides a list of grading and authentication services that will help ensure buyers of the validity or quality of an item.

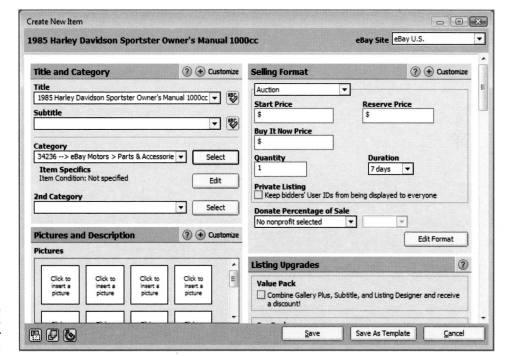

Figure 3-8: Turbo Lister provides a concise listing format and tools to create listings on your local computer that you can upload to eBay.

TIP

You can purchase ready-made "boxes" that provide the proper environment for taking pictures of smaller items, such as jewelry. For example, Cloud Dome (www. clouddome.com) offers a translucent dome that evenly diffuses ambient light, includes a universal camera mount, and can even accommodate larger items with an extension.

CAUTION

Third-party auction- and listing-management software often includes features to send automatic e-mail responses to buyers' inquiries. These have their place if you receive the inquiry after hours or if you're temporarily unavailable. However, while it's better to send anything in lieu of providing no response, make sure to follow up with a personal response to retain customer goodwill.

SET UP THE PICTURE ZONE

As a casual seller, you probably spent an inordinate amount of time preparing the background to take pictures of your items, putting the equipment away when you were finished, and then repeating the process every time you listed a new item. A necessity when you are limited by space and equipment constraints, but not a process you want to continue as your listing volume increases. To streamline the picture-taking process, dedicate the space you need—commensurate with the type and size of items you're selling—and leave the "studio" intact so you can quickly introduce subsequent items. When setting up the picture area, consider:

- **Lighting.** Use natural lighting, light bars, and other light sources you can install and leave in place once you've found the illumination satisfactory, as shown in Figure 3-9. Avoid using a flash if you can. Pictures taken with a flash tend to produce undesired results, such as creating reflections off glass or other shiny surfaces. Some items lend themselves well to outdoor/natural light photography. Consider this option with smaller and more portable items, if it's convenient—you probably don't want to climb up and down five flights of stairs to shoot photos outside.

- **Camera mounts.** Set up a tripod on the floor or a table, and adjust it for optimal picture taking. Remove the camera for safekeeping at the end of the day, but leave the tripod in place for a quick setup for the next photo opportunity.

- **Scanners.** A good place to set up a scanning station is with your photo studio. Set up a computer in your studio with your scanner and digital camera software and memory card readers, and connect it to other networked equipment in your business.

- **Backgrounds and backdrops.** Whether your items are small or large, you will want to place your items on top of or in front of appropriate backgrounds to accentuate them. For example, for large items, you could install rods similar to curtain or shower rods on a wall so you could easily slide on a different background from your stock.

Assign Customer Service and Listing-Management Functions

As soon as a listing is submitted, you begin a new phase in the life cycle of an eBay sale. Initially, you will begin to receive e-mails from prospective buyers and bidders inquiring about the item. Concurrently, you will need to handle

Figure 3-9: ***Set up an area where you can leave lighting, backgrounds, and other equipment in place for repeated use.***

several potential issues with current or past listings, such as canceling a bid, whether to limit buyers and bidders for a listing, feedback concerns, canceling or ending a listing early, and dealing with unpaid items. Each situation can involve several hours and many e-mails, but to protect your eBay reputation, you need to invest the effort to try and reach equitable resolutions (Chapter 5 describes how to handle several issues you might have with buyers and ways to protect your eBay business). Customer service-related concerns and activities include:

- Assign personnel to ensure that someone is responsible for customer service issues and that such things aren't left to be handled on an ad hoc, random basis. Preferably that person will have the patience and tact to interact with potentially irate customers. As your volume increases, so will situations like "lost in the mail" packages, customers who want refunds (for any number of reasons), and other issues that will steal time from your duties. If you can designate a person to handle these issues, you will be freeing your time to facilitate sales.

- Develop escalation procedures to ensure you have clear guidelines, preferably written, that inform employees on how to handle recurring issues (for example, when to grant return authorization to a buyer) and when to inform you or other final-decision makers when a delicate situation is brewing.

- Schedule times to review inquiries. You cannot just get up in the morning and field the current e-mails in your inbox. Check your e-mail throughout the work day and also occasionally after hours, since eBay usage doesn't stop at 5 o'clock.

RECEIVING WIRELESS EBAY E-MAIL ALERTS AND INSTANT MESSAGES

You can receive eBay alerts and instant messages (IM) on a wireless device, such as a smartphone, Blackberry device, or on a cell phone with the requisite capabilities. In other words, you never need to wonder what is happening with your eBay sales (or purchases)—perfect for price checks when you are at a distributor, auction, or collectors' show. You can receive the following types of notices, both when you're bidding on eBay to buy merchandise and when you're selling:

- When someone outbids you
- When an auction ends and you learn whether you are the high bidder
- When someone leaves you feedback
- When a buyer pays for an item of yours
- When an item of yours sells or does not sell
- A buyer completes checkout

To receive either IMs or wireless e-mails, start from My eBay:

1. From My eBay, under My Account on the My eBay Views sidebar, click **Notification Preferences.**

2. Under Notification Preferences, click **Show** to the right of Notification Delivery Format.

3. In the Delivery Options area, shown in Figure 3-10, click **Subscribe** next to the type of service you want, IM or SMS (Simple Message System) text message alerts on your cell phone-capable device. (Unlike IMs, eBay will charge you $ 0.25 per auction item for up to ten alerts per item.)

4. Follow the prompts to subscribe to the service.

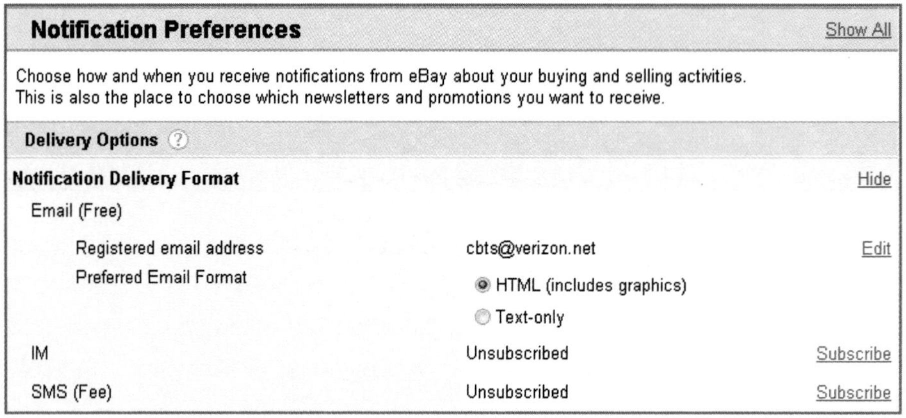

My Account
- Personal Information
- Addresses
- Notification Preferences
- Site Preferences
- Feedback
- PayPal Account
- Half.com Account
- Seller Account
- Donation Account
- Subscriptions

Figure 3-10: *Select the type of notification service to which you want to subscribe.*

- Transition items to the Shipping Center after payment has been received and cleared. PayPal payments seamlessly integrate with My eBay selling views and management software, but you will have to monitor receipt of several other forms of payments.

Develop a Shipping Center

The shipping phase begins when you receive notification that payment for the item has cleared. The next step is to retrieve the item from its place in inventory, package the item, and hand it off to a delivery service.

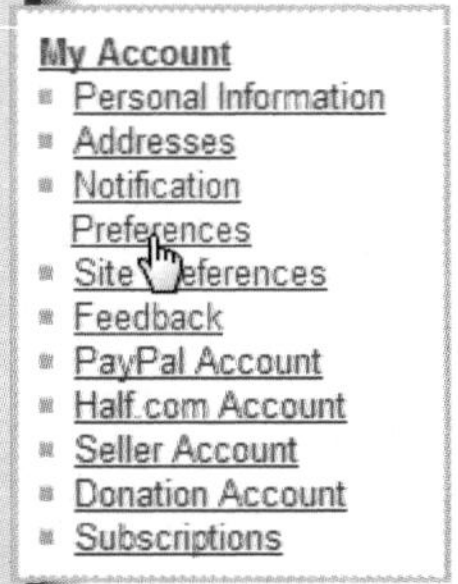

There are more opportunities to gain efficiencies in your operation during the shipping phase than in any other aspect of the eBay sale. On the other hand, this is the one area that can quickly negate everything good you've done to secure a sale and solidify your eBay reputation. You have control over several aspects of the process, and you can incorporate safeguards into your Shipping Center, but once the item is turned over to a shipping/delivery service, you are pretty much out of the picture. Although you cannot ride shotgun with your packages to ensure their safe and timely delivery, you can take reasonable steps to minimize shipping problems.

Create an Efficient Packaging Area

Similar to your photography studio (see "Set Up the Picture Zone" earlier in the chapter), the area where you package items should be a semi-permanent location where you have room to work and easy access to materials you need to package items you sell.

Envision a clear, horizontal, elevated workspace where you can place the packaging container and have the elbow room to add cushioning material and secure the package with tape. Do what it takes to make sure the space remains cleared. Available horizontal workspace is always at a premium in a business and quickly becomes the target of opportunity for other people and other uses. A few packaging pointers include:

- Keep packaging material within arms' reach to minimize trips to find boxes, Styrofoam peanuts, labels, and tape. Visit some of the professional packing businesses in your area, such as The UPS Store, to see what they do to streamline the packaging process. Figure 3-12 shows a typical packaging business's setup. Also, locate your packaging area near your entrance to minimize handling for pickups or place packages on carts for ease of shuttling (or arrange for USPS/UPS pickups from your place of business).

Figure 3-11: *A recycled audio/visual cart finds new life as an "expediter" in this eBay business.*

Hopper-style Styrofoam peanut dispenser

Packaging Scales

Boxes in various sizes

Figure 3-12: Utilize the efficiencies of workflow, space, and location of materials the professional packagers use when setting up your own packaging area.

- Cut costs on packaging material by buying in bulk or receiving them for free. (See the "Getting Free Packaging" QuickFacts.) Don't reuse material unless it's not obvious you are reusing it. Nothing screams "AMATEUR" more loudly to a buyer than receiving a box that has vestiges of its past life, such as old labels, frayed tape, and dirty packaging material.

It's ecologically unfortunate and hard on the bottom line when you send a used but still sturdy cardboard box to the landfill or recycler for the simple reason that it contains markings from its previous life. You can return a box to almost new condition by using a spray mark-over product. Similar to spray paint and offered in white and tan to match the color of typical shipping boxes, the ink dries quickly and masks addressing, hazardous material warnings, and the scars left over from removing adhesive labels. Check with your local shipping and packaging businesses to purchase a spray mark-over product, such as those offered by Marsh (www.msscllc.com).

Access Shipper Services

Shipping packages through eBay gets easier all the time as better relationships are developed between eBay and its shipping partners, currently United States Postal Service (USPS), UPS, and freightquote.com (for packages over 150 pounds). These relationships develop into the tools you can use in the various selling forms that let you easily select mailing options and services from the shipping partners, relieving you of many time-consuming tasks. Depending on the tool or service you employ, you can:

- Choose the carrier and level of service you want to offer

- Show customers their costs upfront through flat-rate or calculated rates
- Print for-free shipping labels and Customs forms for international shipping
- Track packages
- Link with an inventory control system

For more information on eBay shipping in general and each of its shipping partners, eBay provides a great clearinghouse at the Shipping Center, shown in Figure 3-13.

1. Click **Site Map** on the eBay header.

2. Under Selling Resources, click **Shipping Center**. On the left sidebar, click links for information on several shipping options and features.

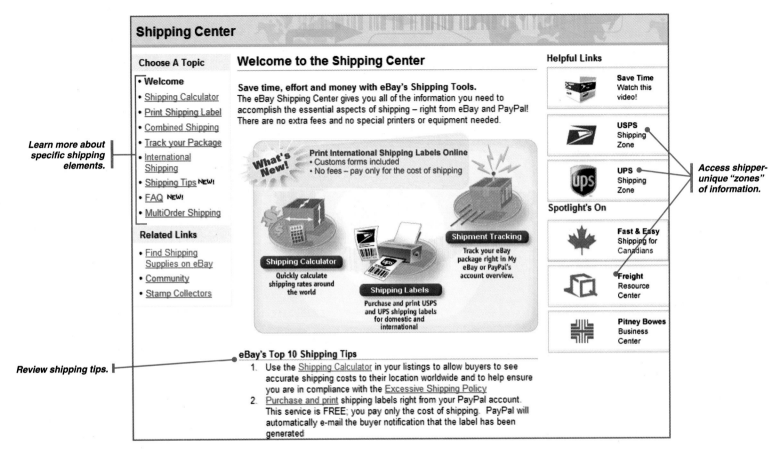

Learn more about specific shipping elements.

Access shipper-unique "zones" of information.

Review shipping tips.

Figure 3-13: eBay's Shipping Center provides a one-stop shopping place for information on shipping services and features.

–Or–

On the right sidebar, access information on how the individual shippers are set up to ship within the eBay system.

–Or–

Review the Top 10 Shipping Tips at the bottom of the page.

Cut Shipping Costs

One of the slicker features eBay has provided over the years is to offer buyers a combined shipping discount when purchasing multiple items from a single seller. The seller sets up rules that govern costs for calculated, flat-rate, or promotional shipping, and life is good (set up combined shipping in My eBay's Site Preference page). Well, it's good if you're selling commodity-type items that have a standard weight and size that you can plan for in advance of your packing needs. However, if you sell distinct items that come in all shapes, sizes, and weights, you can run into situations where the anticipated package will not conform to the combination of items purchased and added expense will be required. To avoid these potential headaches, many sellers simply work out a "worst-case" shipping cost to the most distant state and apply that flat-rate cost to each item. (If contacted by a buyer located close to the shipping point, adjustments can be made to their invoice for the reduction in shipping charges.)

One of the first questions that comes up when speaking of eBay shipping is, of course, "Which carrier is cheaper, USPS or UPS?" Well, it depends. One rule of thumb is to use USPS for lighter items, say, under three pounds and UPS for heavier items. Another plug for UPS is their Special Pricing Program for eBay sellers that provides significant savings over USPS pricing when shipping is processed through eBay and PayPal. You simply need to have both a UPS and PayPal account (go to http://pages.ebay.com/ups/home.html).

Browser Earl says: "If you use the USPS counter service at your local post office, be sure to take advantage of the merchants/business line available at many offices. You can avoid the lengthy general-mailing lines that tend to develop around peak service times, such as the noon hour and in advance of the holiday period."

QUICKFACTS

GETTING FREE PACKAGING

You can get a lot of free packaging items from the three main eBay shippers delivered to your door (packaging material is labeled for its intended level of service, for example, USPS Priority Flat Rate boxes):

- **United States Postal Service (USPS).** The USPS provides limited materials from their local post offices. On the USPS home page (www.usps .com), under Shipping Tools, click **Supplies**. On the Postal Store page, select the items you want delivered, and proceed to checkout, where you will need to establish an account (forms, labels, and Priority/Express boxes and envelopes are free; other items incur a charge).

- **UPS (United Parcel Service).** On the UPS home page (www.ups.com), click the **Shipping** tab, and then click **Get UPS Labels, Paks, And More** on the sidebar (you must log in with your UPS account information to access these free items).

Continued . . .

Order

Priority Mail Large Flat Rate Box

Pack of 10

12" x 12" x 5-1/2"
Minimum order: 1
Maximum order: 8

No Charge

QUICK**FACTS**

GETTING FREE PACKAGING (Continued)

- **FedEx (Federal Express).** On the FedEx home page (www.fedex.com), under the Package/ Envelope tab, point to **Manage**, and click **Order Supplies** (requires a FedEx account). FedEx is not one of 'Bay's preferred shipping partners, but when you need to get a package to someone yesterday morning, FedEx is there for you.

- **eBay.** Click **Site Map** on the eBay header, and under Selling Resources, click **Shipping Central.** Click **Find Shipping Supplies On eBay** on the sidebar to display "almost free" listings in the Shipping & Packing category, as shown in Figure 3-14.

For even greater cost efficiencies, if you're shipping regularly, consider getting a UPS Daily Pickup Account. If you incur at least $60 a week in shipping charges, a mere $8 per week can get you a driver to stop by daily and pick up your packages. At the current price of gas (and not to mention your time) that's quite a deal. Contact the UPS New Accounts Sales Group at 800.877.1509 to investigate other pricing options and get a daily (Monday-Friday) visit from Brown.

eBay Sellers may be eligible to Save up to 31% on UPS Shipping
LEARN MORE

Additionally, after you sign up, when you print a label through PayPal, you'll pay less for a five pound package shipped UPS Ground from New York to Chicago than you would pay for Priority Mail or Parcel Post.

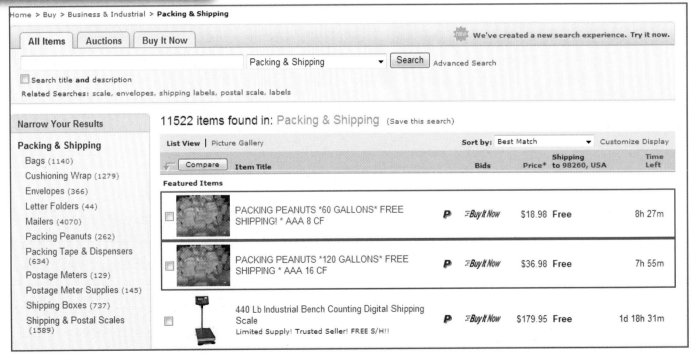

Figure 3-14: In the vein of "eating one's own dog food," eBay itself is a great resource for finding deals on packaging to ship eBay items.

Chapter 4
Creating Super Listings

eBay sellers live and die by their listings. An eBay listing is your all-encompassing sales force, combining several brick-and-mortar parameters, such as advertising, window dressing, warranty and return policies, delivery service, and pricing, into a single, concise Web page. The listing has to attract buyers and, in most cases, tell them *and* show them what they need to know to bid on or purchase an item. You also need to provide the necessary information to ensure the buyer understands shipping and related costs. Most new and low-volume sellers quickly realize the importance of adding keywords to aid in searches, writing accurate descriptions, and including quality pictures, but an eBay business also looks for ways to gain efficiencies in how listings are created, taking advantage of tools that streamline the listing process. Finally, listings can become a cornerstone of a selling strategy—holding listings in your listing program for uploading to eBay when a selling opportunity presents itself.

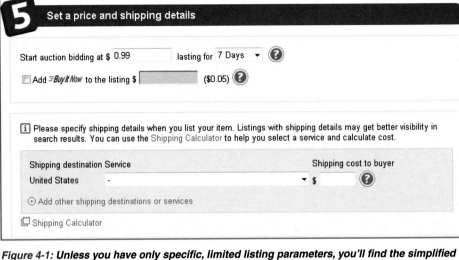

Figure 4-1: *Unless you have only specific, limited listing parameters, you'll find the simplified Create Your Listing form under-optioned for your listings needs.*

Employ Listing Strategies

When you create a listing, whether you use eBay forms or other listing software, you have several opportunities to make decisions that can greatly increase your sales potential. Though not all strategies work all the time, and some are not suitable for every item you sell, they provide a framework you can use to create successful listings.

Reduce Fees

You have two primary ways to make a profit on eBay: receive more revenue or reduce your expenses. The eBay marketplace will determine the amount you receive for items; thus, this component is largely out of your hands. However, you do have a lot of control on cutting expenses, and one key area is in listing fees. The simplified Create Your Listing selling form (see Figure 4-1) and the Sell Your Item form do a fine job for the occasional and beginning seller, but inexperience can be costly in terms of the price you pay for tasks you can do more cheaply, or for free, using other means. Table 4-1 describes several alternatives to eBay fee-based features.

PowerSeller Sally says: "The key difference between a PayPal Premier and Business account is that a Business account allows multi-user access."

eBAY FEE-BASED FEATURE	FEE	ALTERNATE METHOD USED BY eBAY BUSINESSES
Scheduled Start Time allows you to start a listing at a future date and time.	$0.10.	Use listing software to create listings, and then save them until you are ready to submit them and start the listing (eBay's Turbo Lister is free).
eBay Picture Services provides an interface to select pictures from your local system and perform common picture-editing functions, such as rotating and cropping.	$0.15 per picture (the first one is free). $0.75 for a pack of one to six extra-large pictures (up to 800 x 800 pixels). $1.00 for a pack of 7 to 12 extra-large pictures (up to 800 x 800 pixels).	Host your pictures using a free hosting server (generally provided by your Internet service provider), and edit pictures using a low-priced image editor, such as Adobe Photoshop Elements, or, if you don't mind the upload and download times, a free Web-enabled program such as Adobe Photoshop Express (www.photoshop.com/express).
Listing Designer lets you choose a theme and layout for your listing design.	$0.10 (free for Selling Manager Pro subscribers).	Create a listing template using a Web page–creation program (for example, Microsoft Expression Web), and use a listing program (for example, Turbo Lister, Selling Manager Pro, or a third party).
PayPal provides a convenient, safe payment option; you can transfer funds from a buyer's PayPal account or accept credit card payments.	Personal Accounts: Free transfers between PayPal accounts; does not accept credit card payments. Business/Premier Accounts: 2.9 percent + $0.30 for a transaction fee, up to $3,000. Other fees and qualifications for items priced above $3,000 apply.	No alternative. Recommend you obtain a Business/Premier account and offer PayPal as a payment option. You do not want to exclude the millions of buyers who prefer using their PayPal accounts. Also, PayPal provides an alternative to obtaining your own merchant credit card account for buyers who prefer using a credit card for payment.

Table 4-1: Alternatives for eBay Fee-Based Features

Nonfiction Books

Category
Pet, Animal Care (3263)
Back to all options

Sub-Category
Birds (228)
Cats (249)
Dogs (1412)
Fish (156)
Horses (380)
Reptiles, Amphibians (55)
Other (196)

Format
Hardcover (1690)
Softcover (1341)
Mixed Lot (37)
Other (108)

Special Attributes
1st Edition (250)
Signed (19)

Condition
New (835)
Used (2002)

Use Item Specifics

The more you can do to assist buyers in finding items you have for sale or bid and the more details you provide about your items, the greater your chance for increased sales. The Item Specifics feature comes in two options:

- **eBay-generated Item Specifics** are only available for certain listing categories. They allow you to tag your item from a list of detail labels that are attuned to the item and the category it's listed in. For example, when listing a book in the Nonfiction category, you have the opportunity to define it by sub-categories, format, condition, publication year, and by special attributes, such as whether it's signed. A bidder or buyer will be able to filter their search based on these definitions you provide.

- **Custom Item Specifics** are available for categories that don't support eBay-generated Item Specifics. You can create your own Item Specifics detail labels and definitions, or you can modify suggested ones eBay may offer.

SELECT FROM eBAY-GENERATED ITEM SPECIFICS

To use Item Specifics to list an item:

1. In your listing form (such as the Sell Your Item or Turbo List form), after selecting a category that supports the Item Specifics feature, the Item Specifics details will be displayed. Click the down arrow next to each detail label, and select the definition that most closely matches your item, or enter information such as dates, as shown in Figure 4-2.

2. Complete the listing. Your Item Specifics selections appear in your View Item page at the top of the item description.

Item Specifics - Nonfiction Books			
		Category:	**Pet, Animal Care**
Format:	**Softcover**		
Publication Year:	**1997**	Condition:	**Used**
Special Attributes:	--		
See Reviews			

CREATE YOUR OWN ITEM SPECIFICS

If the category you choose in the listing form does not support a static list of Item Specifics provided by eBay, you can modify eBay suggestions or create your own list of detail labels and definitions to provide pertinent information about your item to buyers/bidders, as shown in Figure 4-3.

1. In the listing form, after selecting a category, you might see some suggested detail labels and definitions provided by eBay. Some can be modified or removed, and some cannot. To modify a detail label or definition, click the down arrow next to the control you want to change, click **Enter A Custom Detail** or **Enter Your Own** (depending on the form you are using), and type the new label or definition.

Figure 4-2: Select detail definitions that most closely describe your item from the Item Specifics details provided by eBay.

Spell check your custom detail.

Remove a label/ definition set.

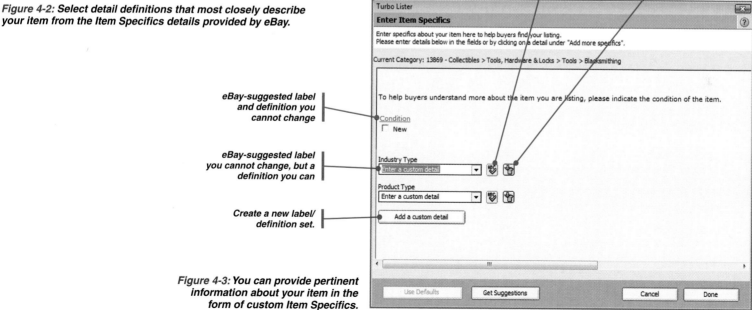

eBay-suggested label and definition you cannot change

eBay-suggested label you cannot change, but a definition you can

Create a new label/ definition set.

Figure 4-3: You can provide pertinent information about your item in the form of custom Item Specifics.

NOTE

Unfortunately, there is no master list of categories that support eBay-generated Item Specifics. eBay is continually adding their Item Specifics to more categories. Check the General Announcements in the Community Hub frequently to stay on top of eBay changes.

QUICKFACTS

SELECTING ITEMS TO SELL WITH PRE-FILLED ITEM INFORMATION

eBay only supports a limited number of items with pre-filled item information. Periodically review the General Announcements available on the Community Hub to see if eBay has added any items to the list. The categories and attributes that are currently supported include the following (not all subcategories within each of the listed categories necessarily support pre-filled item information).

SELECT ENTERTAINMENT CATEGORIES

- **Books**: ISBN (International Standard Book Number), title, author
- **Movies**: UPC (Universal Product Code), title, director
- **Music**: UPC, title, artist
- **Video Games**: UPC, title
- **Tickets**: Venue name, city, state/province, date, time, event

SELECT ELECTRONIC CATEGORIES

- **Digital Cameras**: Brand, product line, resolution, MPN (manufacturer part number)
- **PDAs**: Manufacturer, personal digital assistant (PDA) series, screen, MPN

continued . . .

TIP

Product finders that buyers use to find items can display the details you used when creating a listing either as links (see "Use Item Specifics") or as drop-down list boxes.

Women's Dresses Finder

Occasion: Formal Gown
Sleeve Style: Any
Dress Length: Full-Length
Size Type: Petites
Size: 6P
Main Color: Black
Condition: Pre-Owned
Search Keywords: dress,formal
[Show Items]

–Or–

To remove a label/definition set, click **Remove** or the Delete button next to the controls.

–Or–

To add a new detail label and options, click **Add A Custom Detail**. Customize the label and definition as described in Step 1.

2. Complete the listing. Your custom Item Specifics appear in your View Item page at the top of the item description.

List Efficiently with Pre-filled Item Information

For many listing categories, you can have eBay fill in many of a product's attributes from data maintained by eBay. The attributes are generic—you will want to add Item Specifics to provide details about your item (see "Use Item Specifics"). For example, pre-filled information on books doesn't include a Condition attribute, but you can combine Item Specifics to provide that information. Also, for items that have stock photos available, you can omit taking your own pictures. To use pre-filled item information:

1. In your listing form, select a category that supports the Pre-filled Item Information feature (see the "Selecting Items to Sell with Pre-filled Item Information" QuickFacts). Turbo Lister provides immediate feedback to let you know if a category supports pre-filled item information, as shown in Figure 4-4. Click **Continue**, **Next**, or otherwise to move to the next step in the listing process.

SELECTING ITEMS TO SELL WITH PRE-FILLED ITEM INFORMATION

(continued)

- **Cell Phones**: Brand, service provider, display, MPN

- **Camcorders**: Brand, MPN, product line, model

OTHER CATEGORIES

- **Home & Garden**: Brand, model, product type (Blenders sub-category)

- **Sporting Goods**: Club type, brand, model (Golf Clubs subcategory)

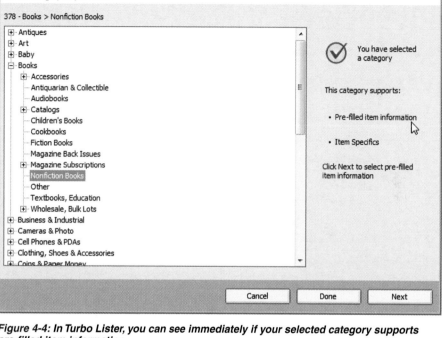

Figure 4-4: In Turbo Lister, you can see immediately if your selected category supports pre-filled item information.

Professor Polly says: "The value of using visibility upgrades decreases significantly the more unique the item you're selling. If you're offering a one-of-a-kind or rare item, a simple search by potential buyers will likely bring up only a few choices."

2. Select search criteria to find items in eBay's pre-filled database that most closely match the item(s) you are selling. Depending on the category you are selling in, you might be able to provide specific information, such as the MPN, to conduct a more direct search.

3. Confirm that you want pre-filled item information, and click **Search** or **Continue** to display items that match your search criteria.

4. Indicate the item that most closely matches the one you're selling, and continue with the next listing step. Your item's pre-filled information, stock photo, and Item Specifics options are displayed, as shown in Figure 4-5.

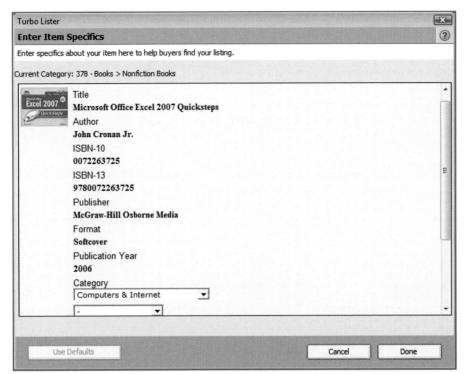

Figure 4-5: *Pre-filled item information, a stock photo, and Item Specifics save you a lot of time and effort when creating listings.*

Use Visibility Upgrades

You have several options to try and attract attention to your listing. Whether their cost justifies their advertising potential to bring more bidders to your auction is one of those great philosophical questions for the ages, although eBay is ready to help you overcome any reluctance with fee sales and upgrade packages, as shown in Figure 4-6.

In the listing upgrades area, select the upgrades you want for your item:

- **Gallery Plus** ($0.35) adds an Enlarge icon 🔍 next to the picture in your listing as it appears in search results, allowing a mouse pointer rollover to provide potential bidders/buyers an instant enlargement.

- **Gallery Featured** ($19.95) enhances the Gallery Plus feature by adding your listing to the Featured Items section in Gallery pages (as well as in the standard Gallery list).

- **Bold** ($1.00) accentuates your item title with boldface type.

- **Border** ($3.00) frames your listing with a purple border.

- **Highlight** ($5.00) surrounds your listing details with a colored background.

NOTE

Effective February 20, 2008, eBay eliminated the Gallery fee. eBay now provides for free a thumbnail picture you choose of your item next to your listing and lists your item and picture in Gallery View.

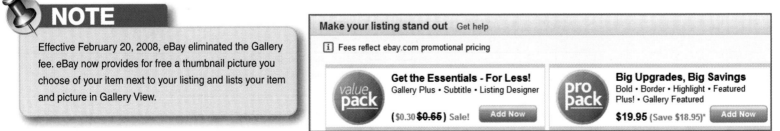

Figure 4-6: *eBay offers periodic sales on its listing upgrades and combines listings enhancements into packages for additional savings.*

TIP

Buyers expect choices when they shop at a store. An eBay business is no different—you want to satisfy that expectation by ensuring you constantly have items available for bid or for Buy It Now sale. The most cost-effective way to keep a quantity of items for sale is to open an eBay Store (see Chapter 6), where listings can have a much longer lifetime at a lower listing fee. The bottom line is that you want to make sure that when buyers search your eBay User ID in response to a listing that interests them, they are rewarded by plenty of listings advertising your other merchandise, as shown in Figure 4-7.

- **Featured Plus!** ($19.95) adds your listing to the Featured Items area of its category list (usually at the beginning) and in the list generated by a search (as well as in the standard auction and search listings).

- **Home Page Featured** ($39.95 single listing/$79.95 two or more listings) provides a randomly selected exposure to your listing under the Featured Items list on the eBay home page (listings are rotated—it's likely your listing will appear, but is not guaranteed), as well as on the Featured Items list on the Buy Hub page and on the item's category page.

From our Sellers

- Brand New Maxam 71pc Pneumatic...
- MAKE MONEY ONLINE BE THE BOSS...
- INSTAL KITS TO MAKE AUTOS RUN ...
- Acai Berry Juice Antioxidant. ...
- BRAND NEW NEXTEL ic602 602 HYB...
- BUNN B10 Classic 10-Cup Home C...

See all featured items

- **Gift Services** ($0.25) adds a Gifts And Services icon next to your item title, lists your item in Gifts View, and attracts bidders and buyers to your gift services, such as gift wrapping and direct shipping to the gift's recipient.

Figure 4-7: Use techniques such as offering sales (from your eBay Store) to get your listings in front of as many buyers and bidders as you can.

Professor Polly says: "You have the freedom to add your own pictures, shipping instructions and terms, return policy, and links to the item description (see Figure 4-8). Your only limitations are eBay's selling policies and some restrictions on using HTML and JavaScript functions to perform unauthorized actions."

Create a Listing Template

A listing template records and saves an item's selling form with all of its detail so that you can reuse it to create a listing for another similar item.

Templates provide several benefits, including:

- **Consistency** across all your listings is assured. You can create a layout, add a theme, and apply consistent links and guidelines for your buyers.

Auction Terms and Shipping & Handling
*** READ CAREFULLY BEFORE BIDDING ***

AUCTION TERMS AND WINNING BIDDERS
By bidding you agree to ALL the terms of sale stated below. All winning bids are final! You will receive emails about your win, and package shipping information – PLEASE provide your email address for this purpose. Questions about bids, buy it now, best offer or other general questions contact David at davidt@cultureandthrills.com or call (813) 968-1805. **Feedback will automatically be left for the winning bidder after feedback is left for us.** Good Luck!

PAYMENT: Payment is expected **within 10 days of notification!** Please pay for winning bids on time. We accept checks, money orders, credit cards and PayPal (unless otherwise noted in item description). Those paying with a BEST OFFER must pay for insurance on the item(s). Contact us (813) 968-1805 if you have any questions. **PAYMENT IN U.S. FUNDS ONLY. Make check or money order to: David T Alexander.**

SHIPPING AND HANDLING TERMS: The shipping and handling fee covers processing your item(s) both in and out of our warehouse, packing materials, consignment costs, and costs of transporting your item(s) to the post office, in addition to the postal fees. Since many items come from outside sources and incur consignment fees, we must impose this fee to continue to offer items at the lowest possible minimum bid. This allows us to offer the widest possible variety of material from many sources, while giving each bidder a chance to get the best available deal. Insurance and other special services are optional costs. We can combine shipping for multiple orders. Large/heavy items cost more than the standard rate to combine. **Contact Debbie at debbiea@cultureandthrills.com for any shipping questions.**

- **Shipment inside the USA:** Buyer pays standard fo Express or other services are extra – please let optional for most items – yet recommended. Larger

- **Shipment outside the US:** Buyer must pay exact fo on the invoice. Standard 1st Class International do will require Global Priority shipment for tracking - Express or other services are extra – please let special services or insurance available. If necessar

INSURANCE: Insurance is optional (but recommended). damaged in transit, we will not be held responsible. In t ONLY those who have PAID for insurance will either re items (if available) or and equal value credit on anothe fees).

You can use a template to create your own listing persona...

...and redirect buyers from the staid eBay boilerplate to your custom text.

Shipping and handling

Ships to
Worldwide

Country: United States ▼

Shipping and Handling	To	Service	Insurance
US $1.75	United States	Standard Flat Rate Shipping Service	None

Return policy

Return policy not specified.
Read item description for any reference to return policy.

Figure 4-8: You can use the listing template to add more information about your policies than you can using the default tools in selling forms.

LEARNING ABOUT HTML

To learn more about HTML, the language of the Web, you can check out eBay's listings of commonly used tags and use other readily available resources. eBay provides a "starter kit" of tags you can reference to get started typing your own descriptions, terms, and conditions.

1. Click **Help** on the eBay header.

2. On the eBay Help page, type <u>html</u> in the Search The Help Pages text box, and click **Search Help Pages**.

3. Click the **HTML Tips** help topic link. Tags are listed according to usage categories.

Many HTML tags are combined with one or more *attributes* that modify what the tag does—for example, in the Use Color section of the HTML Tips page, the <FONT> tag is modified by the color attribute to add color to text.

Tag	How to use it	What it looks like
<font color=*color*> </font>	Bid <font color=green> now</font> and you may win!	Bid now and you may win!
<font color=*color*> </font>	Bid <font color=blue> now</font> and you may win!	Bid now and you may win!

- **Speed** is of the essence when posting listings. You can create a template for each product category in which you sell that is tuned to the category specifics. For example, if you sell books, you could create a picture gallery layout that includes a larger picture for the cover and several smaller picture placeholders for the back cover, title page, and copyright pages.

- **Test** several ways to sell a product so that you can easily re-create the listing that is most successful.

In order to achieve the results you want from a listing template, you should be comfortable working with HTML, the language of Web pages; or use WYSIWYG (What You See Is What You Get) tools to create Web pages in much the same way you use a word processor. Most listing forms provide tools for common editing functions, such as changing fonts, text size, and creating lists, as shown in Figure 4-9, but lack the flexibility and breadth of features you can employ using HTML or a full-fledged HTML editor, such as Microsoft Expression Web.

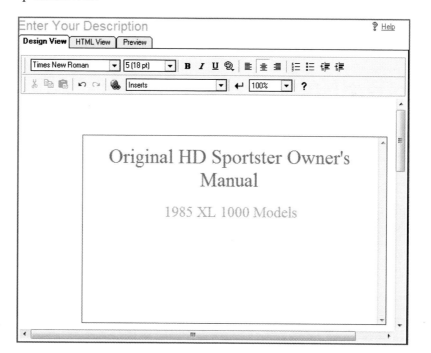

Figure 4-9: Use listing tools, much like you would a word-processing program, to add formatted text.

TIP

The easiest way to lay out a listing template is to use one or more *tables*. Tables provide a grid of rows and columns that make alignment easy, make creating borders and separator lines a snap, and let you place pictures within the confines of individual cells (see Figure 4-10). Depending on the HTML editor you use, you can even design tables by simply drawing the rows, columns, and cells you want.

Add Your Own Pictures

Pictures that your buyers and bidders see in your item's View Item page (and in Web pages in general) are not actually an integral part of the page; they are hosted, or linked, to the Web page from the Web server where they are located. Pictures you upload using eBay Picture Services are hosted on an eBay server and are displayed using eBay formatting. If you want to add pictures for free and display them where you want, you will need to store them on a Web server that allows anonymous access; that is, it does not require a user name and password. All you have to do is add some HTML to your item description that points to the stored location.

You can link to as many pictures of your item as you want.

1. Review your pictures in an image-editing program, such as Adobe Photoshop Elements. Crop, size, and add any effects to present the item as you want (see "Take Quality Pictures" later in this chapter).

2. In the selling form's HTML tab or text box, or in a text editor, use the **IMG** tag and **SRC** attribute (see the "Learning About HTML" QuickFacts for descriptions of HTML terms, such as tag and attribute), and type <IMG SRC="*URL to picture*">. For example, if your picture, FrontCover.jpg, is hosted on acmehosting.com in a folder named Jones, you would type <IMG SRC="http://acmehosting.com/Jones/FrontCover.jpg"> on the page where you wanted the picture to appear.

   –Or–

   If using a WYSIWYG HTML editor, place your insertion point where you want the picture in your listing template Web page, and type the picture's URL in an Insert Picture dialog box or a similar interface.

3. Preview your description and make any desired changes.

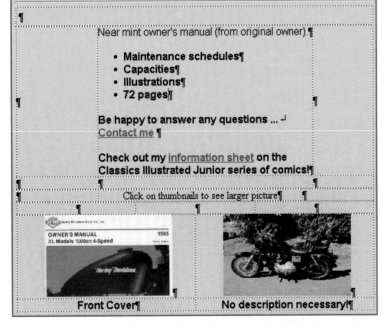

Figure 4-10: Tables provide a grid so you can easily align and lay out content on a Web page.

TIP

If you want the bidder to see text when he or she moves the mouse pointer over the picture, add the ALT attribute to the IMG tag. For example, typing <IMG SRC="http://acmehosting.com/Jones/FrontCover.jpg" ALT="1985 HD Sportster Owner's Manual"> will cause the words "1985 HD Sportster Owner's Manual" to appear when the mouse pointer is moved over the picture.

Take Quality Pictures

The fastest, cheapest, safest, and easiest way to obtain pictures for use on a selling form is to use a digital camera (unless the items are flat and can be placed on a flatbed scanner). For images that are designed to be displayed online, even a low-cost digital camera will be adequate (and thousands are for sale on eBay!).

You don't need to be a professional photographer or own a studio to produce quality pictures that capture a bidder's interest. There are several basic photographic pointers, however, that you can use to separate your listings from the pack.

THINK COMPOSITION

Photographic composition defines the detail, orientation, and symmetry of the picture. In eBay parlance, this boils down to taking pictures that focus on the item you are selling. If you are selling a tabletop item, concentrate on the item itself, not on how well you can set a table. Close-up pictures show details a buyer will be interested in; save the panoramas for your next trip to the Grand Canyon!

THINK SIZE

That new gazillion-megapixel camera takes great pictures, as evidenced by the striking print that comes off your inkjet printer. Most bidders and buyers, however, don't want to wait the two and a half hours it would take to download that picture. Use a *resolution* that is suitable for viewing online (anything over 100 pixels is unnecessary). Also, *size* relates to composition—a small picture makes it hard to see detail. eBay recommends a 1024×768 (pixels) size.

UTILIZE GOOD LIGHTING

Dark, backlit, and shadowed pictures show you are either an amateur photographer or haven't taken the time to create a quality picture—neither of which adds to your selling potential. Use a flash, unless you have added auxiliary lighting or have good natural lighting. There is no additional cost to take several shots with a digital camera until you have one that provides your item in its "best light."

CREATE A MINI-STUDIO

Even if you are a casual seller, it is worth your time to set up an area that provides a pleasing environment for your pictures. For example, if selling furniture, you might have a kit of backdrop sheets, clamps, floodlighting, and a dolly available. When selling small items, such as glassware, you might line an open box with fabric to create an instant setting or purchase a commercial light box, such as the Cloud Dome (www.clouddome.com).

Create Listings Using Turbo Lister

To your buyers and bidders, an item listing on eBay is all they care about. It's what tells them what an item is, how it looks, how much it costs, and how it will arrive. To you, efficiently creating and posting listings on eBay is just as important. According to an informal survey taken from the Community Hub's Auction Listing discussion board, the tool used by an overwhelming number of eBay sellers in the small-to-medium range to create and post listings is Turbo Lister, eBay's free listing tool.

Turbo Lister provides a more concise listing form than the Sell Your Item form, and you can use it to create thousands of listings offline that you can upload to eBay at any time. You can duplicate listings; set defaults for auction, fixed-price, real estate ad, and eBay Store listings; import your listings from eBay; and easily modify listings.

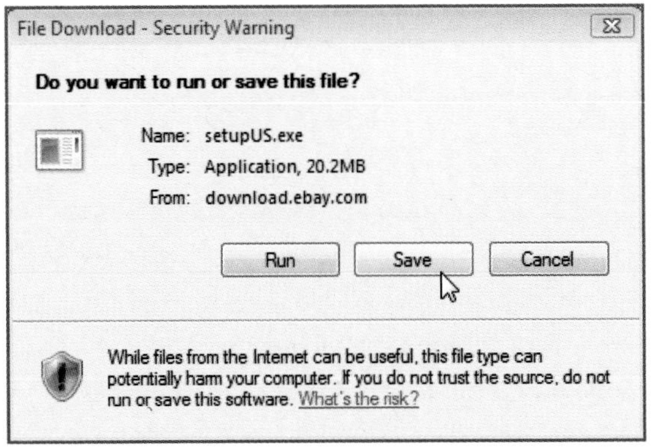

Install Turbo Lister

Turbo Lister is available from eBay for download and installation.

1. Click **Site Map** on the eBay header.

2. Under Selling Tools, click **Turbo Lister**.

3. On the Turbo Lister page, click **Download Now**.

Download Now!

4. In the File Download - Security Warning dialog box (see Figure 4-11), click **Save**, and in the Save As dialog box that appears next, select where on your local system you want to save the 20-megabyte (MB) file. Click **Save**. The file setupUS.exe will start downloading to your computer.

5. Open the file to start its installation program. Installation files are uncompressed, and then the installation wizard begins. If you want to install Turbo Lister on multiple computers, you can reuse this file and avoid having to download the file more than once.

6. Follow the installation wizard prompts to complete the installation.

Figure 4-11: Save a copy of the Turbo Lister installation file to your computer so you'll have it for any future needs and avoid having to download it again.

NOTE

The first time through while installing Turbo Lister, you will have to build a link on eBay that connects to the new Turbo Lister files. You will be led through setting up this link, reentering your eBay User ID and password, and agreeing to the linking of eBay to Turbo Lister. Then you will verify that your contact information is correct and select either to create a new item or to synchronize data with eBay. If you are creating a listing for the first time, you will be led through filling in the Create New Item form. This first-time procedure differs from that which you'll use after you have some listings.

Create a New Listing

You create new listings using a single interface into which you enter the details of your item.

1. After you have installed Turbo Lister and have created some initial listings, you can start Turbo Lister by double-clicking the shortcut icon added to your desktop by the installation program.

–Or–

Click **Start**, click **All Programs**, click **eBay**, and click **eBay Turbo Lister 2**.

In either case, the Turbo Lister window opens, as shown in Figure 4-12.

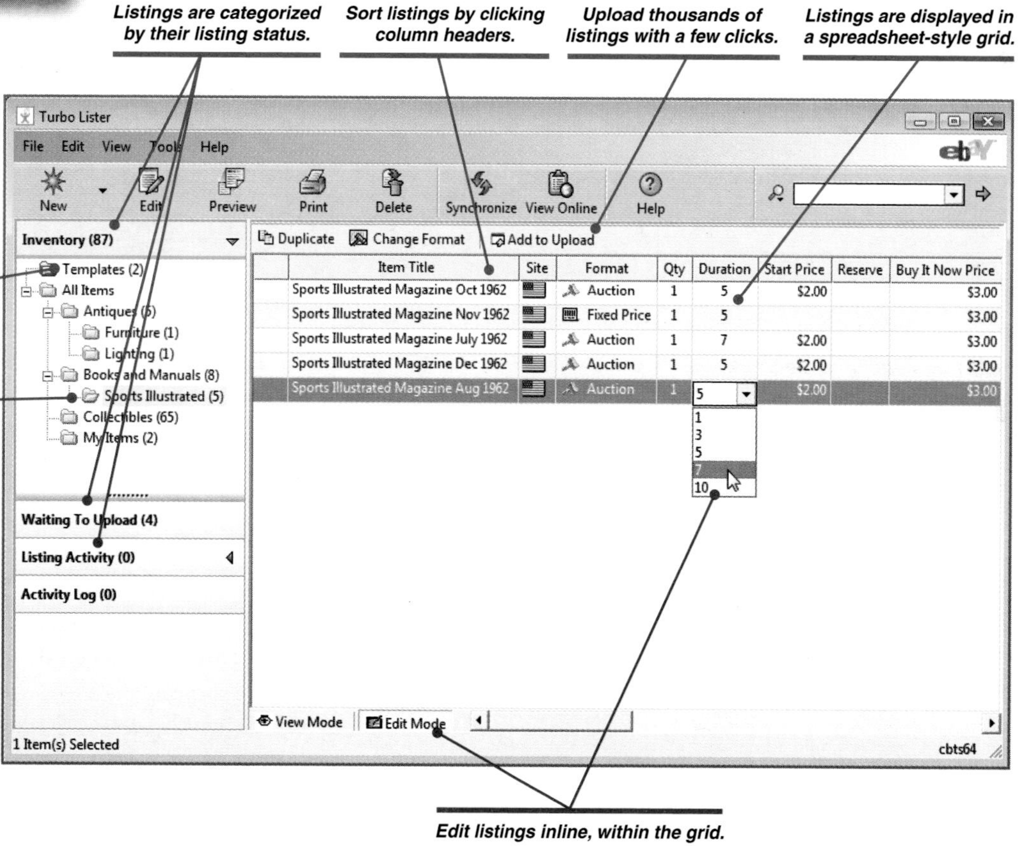

Listings are categorized by their listing status.　　*Sort listings by clicking column headers.*　　*Upload thousands of listings with a few clicks.*　　*Listings are displayed in a spreadsheet-style grid.*

Store templates for future use.

Create folders to organize listings in inventory.

Figure 4-12: The Turbo Lister window shows listings in various stages, as well as the tools to support them.

Edit listings inline, within the grid.

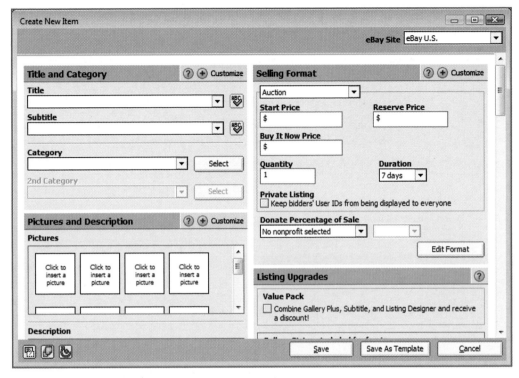

Figure 4-13: *Turbo Lister mimics the listing areas on the Sell Your Item form, making the transition a snap.*

2. Click the **New** button on the Turbo Lister toolbar, and click **Create New Item**. The Create New Item window opens, as shown in Figure 4-13, divided into sections that correspond to the similar sections on the familiar Sell Your Item form.

- **Title And Category** provides text boxes for the listing title and optional subtitle (both with spell checker support), and lets you select the listing category and an optional second category.

- **Pictures And Description** provides areas to upload pictures using eBay Picture Services or add Uniform Resource Locators (URLs) for self-hosted pictures (click the **Customize** button, and click **Self-hosted Pictures** to add a new tab to the Pictures area), as well as access to a description builder, where you can type or paste in your item description and use the optional Listing Designer to add a professional layout to your text.

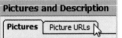

- **Inventory Information** provides you the opportunity to add custom inventory information to help organize your items, such as a label or number (see Chapter 3).

- **Selling Format** provides controls that allow you to choose between selling formats (i.e., auction vs. fixed price), determine pricing and quantity you are offering for sale, set the duration of the sale, and establish charitable donations through eBay Giving Works (see Chapter 9).

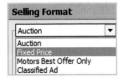

NOTE

This book assumes you have a basic understanding of eBay and does not delve deeply into areas that you already know from listing or buying at least a few items. To a large degree, the listing process in Turbo Lister is the same as that used in the Sell Your Item form, and similar procedures and concepts are not repeated. If you need a refresher on eBay basics, read *eBay QuickSteps*, 2nd Edition by Carole Matthews and John Cronan (McGraw-Hill, 2007).

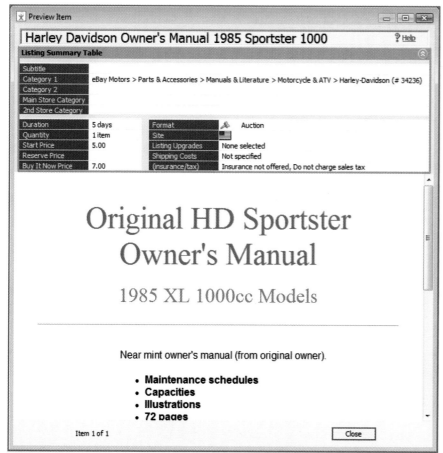

TIP

To see a summary of your listing choices and options, and to view your item description as you build it, as shown in Figure 4-14, click the **Preview** button 🖭 on the bottom of the Create New Item window.

- **Listing Upgrades** lets you select for-fee upgrades to make your listings stand out from the pack (see "Use Visibility Upgrades" earlier in the chapter).

- **Shipping Options** allows you to set shipping pricing, choose carriers and levels of service, advertise your handling time, and apply combined shipping rules.

- **Payment Methods** lets you identify the forms of payment you will accept.

- **Buyer Communication** lets you choose whether to offer Skype, the Internet-based chat and voice service, as a way for buyers/bidders to contact you.

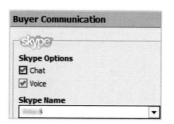

- **Instructions And Policies** lets you add text to specify your return policy (eBay requires that you specify what your return policy is, even if it's only to state that you don't accept returns), set any buyer requirements (such as blocking those buyers below a certain feedback score), and add any miscellaneous instructions. (If you create your own listing template/item description, you are probably better off including your instructions and policies there instead of force-feeding them into the Create New Item controls.)

3. When finished, click **Save** to add the listing to the item folder you selected when first starting to create the item, from where you can then select it for upload to eBay.

–Or–

Click **Save As Template** to add the listing to your Templates folder, where you can then open it and save it to one of your item folders, as-is or with minor changes, once or as many times as you want.

Figure 4-14: Preview your listing as you build it and review listing selections in one concise view.

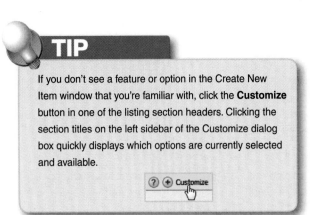
Add Additional eBay Sites to Turbo Lister

If you are planning on selling on eBay sites other than eBay U.S., you will need to identify them and add any updates Turbo Lister requires. (Chapter 2 describes the benefits of the global marketplace.)

1. On the Create New Item/Edit Item window, click the **eBay Site** down arrow in the title bar, and click **Add Additional Sites**.

2. Select the site(s) where you want to list items, as shown in Figure 4-15, and click **OK**.

3. In the Updates Found dialog box, click **Download** to add updates to your Turbo Lister installation that will allow listing on the site(s) you selected.

4. Click **Backup** if you are presented with an opportunity to back up your database of listing data. (If you choose not to back up, skip to Step 6).

Please select all the eBay sites where you list items.

☑ eBay U.S.	☑ eBay Canada
☑ eBay United Kingdom	☐ eBay Australia
☐ eBay Austria	☐ eBay Belgium (French)
☐ eBay France	☐ eBay Germany
☐ eBay Italy	☐ eBay Belgium (Dutch)
☐ eBay Netherlands	☐ eBay Spain
☐ eBay Switzerland	☐ eBay Hong Kong
☐ eBay India	☐ eBay Ireland
☐ eBay Malaysia	☑ eBay Canada (French)
☐ eBay Philippines	☐ eBay Poland
☐ eBay Singapore	

OK   Cancel

Figure 4-15: Choose the eBay global sites where you want to list your items.

5. In the Backup Database dialog box, click **Backup Reminder** to change the default number of days (seven) Turbo Lister provides between backup reminders. Accept the default location for your backup file (in Windows Vista, it is *Username*\Documents\ Turbo Lister Backup), or click **Browse** and select a new folder. Click **OK** in the Backup Database dialog box when you are ready to start the backup.

6. After the database is compacted and backed up (if you chose to do so), updates are downloaded and installed (it might take several minutes).

USING INSERTS

You can use inserts to create and save text segments for use in future item descriptions. You can have up to five inserts of up to 1,000 characters each. For example, you could make an insert out of shipping and handling instructions, a logo, or text formatted with HTML tags, as shown in Figure 4-16.

1. In the Description section of the Create New Item or Edit Item window, click **Description Builder**.

    Description Builder

2. On the Design View or HTML View tab in the Enter Your Description pane, click the **Inserts** down arrow on the toolbar:

3. Click **Create An Insert** to name and type (or paste) the text for the insert.

    –Or–

    Click **Edit Your Inserts** to remove or change existing inserts.

    –Or–

    Click in the item description area where you want the insert placed, and click the name of the saved insert you want. eBay also provides pre-built inserts for links to your other items for sale, a link that adds you to the buyer's Favorite list, and a link to PayPal promotions.

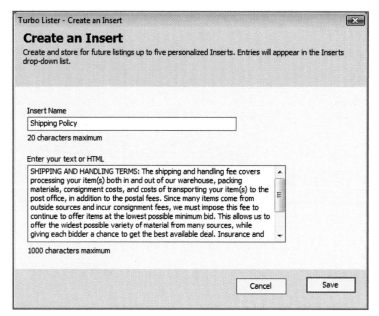

Figure 4-16: Create inserts to save snippets of texts for repeated use.

Create Listings Quickly

Turbo Lister was created to make efficient use of your time. It offers a few tricks for quickly creating listings. You can easily duplicate existing listings for use with similar items (see "Modify Listings" for information on changing an existing listing) or save listings to be used as a template for future listings. A template acts as a more "permanent" copy from which you can easily find (in the Templates folder) and reuse listing information, whereas making a duplicate of an item is fine as long as you still have the original listing in your inventory.

CREATE DUPLICATE LISTINGS WITHIN THE CREATE NEW ITEM OR EDIT ITEM WINDOW

Click the **Create Another** button at the bottom of the respective window (in the Create New Item or Edit Item window, you must have entered a minimum level of information, such as the item category). The current listing is saved and added to your Turbo Lister inventory.

CREATE DUPLICATE LISTINGS WITHIN THE TURBO LISTER WINDOW

1. In the Turbo Lister window, select the listing(s) you want to duplicate from the grid in the right pane. To select noncontiguous items in the list, hold down **CTRL** and click the items you want selected. To select a contiguous listing of items, click the first item in the list, hold down **SHIFT**, and click the last item in the list.

2. Right-click the selection and click **Duplicate Item(s)** from the context menu.

   –Or–

   Click **Duplicate** in the right pane above the listings grid.

   –Or–

   Press **CTRL+D**.

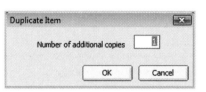

3. In the Duplicate Item dialog box, type the number of additional copies you want, and click **OK**.

CREATE A LISTING FROM A TEMPLATE

1. Click the **New** down arrow on the toolbar, click **Create Item From Template**, and click the template you want to use.

   –Or–

   Open the **Templates** folder in the Folder List, select a template from the grid, and then click **Item From Template**.

   Select the Templates folder in the Folder List...   ...select the template you want to use...   ...click Item From Template

2. In the Select Folder To Save Item dialog box, click the folder where you want to save the listing. (You can create new folders in the Folder List, displayed in the left pane of the Turbo Lister window. Right-click the folder where you want to create a subfolder, and click **New Folder** on the context menu. Type a name for the folder, and click **OK**.) Click **Save**.

3. Make any changes to the listing in the Edit Item window (see "Modify Listings" next), and click **Save**.

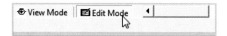
TIP

To change the format of a listing in the right pane grid, in either View or Edit Mode, select the listing and click **Change Format** Change Format above the grid. In the Change Format dialog box, select the format you want, and click **OK**. (You can also modify Item Specifics and Listing Designer features for a selected listing in the grid by selecting their respective commands from the Edit menu.)

Change Format

What format would you like to change your item(s) to?

○ Auction
⊙ Fixed Price
○ Motors Best Offer Only
○ Classified Ad

TIP

Double-click a listing in the grid to open it in the Edit Item window.

Modify Listings

You can modify listings in several ways, including changing fields as the listings appear in the right pane, opening up the Edit Item window (an individual listing similar to the Create New Item window), or applying changes to multiple listings simultaneously.

CHANGE LISTINGS IN THE RIGHT PANE

Probably the most profound change incorporated in the upgrade to Turbo Lister 2 was the ability to make changes directly to select fields in the right pane, eliminating the need to open a separate editing window.

1. At the bottom of the Turbo Lister window, enable inline editing by clicking the **Edit Mode** button to change from the default View Mode (which only displays listing information).

⊕ View Mode | ☑ Edit Mode ◀

2. Click the field in a listing that you want to change (sometimes you have to click a second time). If the field is editable, you will be able to edit the entry (similar to editing an entry in a spreadsheet such as Microsoft Excel) or select from a drop-down list. If a field does not respond to your actions, you will need to edit its information within the listing's individual Edit Item window (described next).

3. Repeat for other fields and listings.

CHANGE LISTINGS INDIVIDUALLY

You can make changes to individual listings and sequence through them in different ways.

1. Select a listing in the grid, click **Edit** on the toolbar, and make changes to the item attributes in the Edit Item window, shown in Figure 4-17.

2. To save the item and return to the Turbo Lister window, click **Save**. Repeat the process for any other listings you want to change.

–Or–

Use the Next and Previous buttons to cycle through other listings you want to edit.

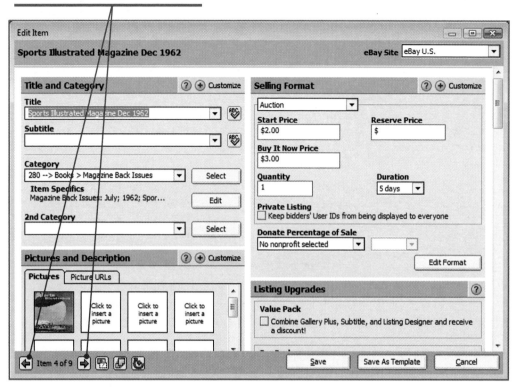

Figure 4-17: The Edit Item window displays the same listing areas as the Create New Item window, with the addition of buttons to cycle through listings for continued editing.

To change items in sequence, prior to clicking the Save button, click **Next Item** or **Previous Item** at the bottom of the Edit Item window (see Figure 4-17) to display the attributes of the adjoining listing in the current folder without returning to the right pane grid. (If you selected items in the grid, the sequencing will only include the items you selected.) Continue clicking Next Item or Previous Item to move to the next listing. Click Save when you've reached the last item you want to change. All items that have been edited will be saved, and you'll return to the grid.

MAKE CHANGES TO MULTIPLE ITEMS AT ONCE

1. In the right pane grid, select the listing(s) you want to modify. To select noncontiguous listings in the grid, hold down **CTRL** and click the items you want. To select contiguous listings, click the first listing in the list, hold down **SHIFT**, and click the last listing in the list.

2. Right-click the selection and click **Edit Multiple Items**.

   –Or–

   Click the **Edit** menu, and click **Edit Multiple Items**.

3. In the Multiple Values window (similar to the Edit Item/Create New Item windows), make changes to any available attributes (some attributes, such as Category, may not be changed if the selected items do not have identical choices). Changes will apply to all selected items. Click **Save** when finished. Changes are made, and the new listing format is reflected in the right pane grid for all selected listings.

Upload Items to eBay

When you create listings in Turbo Lister, you are creating them in a separate program from eBay. To use them in eBay, you first must identify the listings you want to sell on eBay and place them in a "waiting" area, where you can check on their fees and desired sales schedule. Then, you complete the process and upload your listings to eBay to start selling within their respective selling formats, such as auction or fixed-price.

1. Open the folder in the Folder List that contains the listings you want to upload to eBay. Folders and sub-folders help you organize your inventory by product line, supplier, or other means to help you quickly find the listings you want to send to eBay.

2. Select one or more items in the listing inventory, and click **Add To Upload** above the grid. In the Add To Upload dialog box, click **Go Upload**.

   –Or–

   Drag selected listings from the grid to the Waiting To Upload section in the Folder List, and then click the **Waiting To Upload** header to display the listings in the grid.

3. To schedule a listing to start other than immediately after upload (a scheduling fee of $.10 applies for each listing), select the listing and click **Schedule** above the grid. In the Schedule Listing To Start dialog box, shown in Figure 4-18, select the date and time to start the listing. You can schedule item listings to start up to three weeks in the future. For multiple selected items, you can have them start at intervals from one minute to one hour. Your scheduling choices will appear in the grid in the Start Date & Time column.

4. To check on listing fees, click **Calculate Fees** above the grid to get a calculation for all listings in the Waiting To Upload grid.

   –Or–

   Select the item(s) you want to calculate, click the **Calculate Fees** down arrow, and click **Calculate Fees For Selected Items**.

   Fees are tabulated in the Fees column at the right end of the listing row.

Figure 4-18: Time your listings' start to take advantage of listing sales on eBay and other scheduling advantages.

Item Title	Site	Pre-Filled Information	Start Date & Time
Sports Illustrated Magazine July 1962		Not available	4/10/2008 7:30 PM
Harley Davidson Owner's Manual 1985 Sportster 1000		Not available	ASAP
Sports Illustrated Magazine Dec 1962		Not available	ASAP
Classics Illustrated Junior- Sleeping Beauty		Not available	4/6/2008 7:00 PM

5. When finished scheduling and editing listings (you can edit listings here as you did listings in inventory, though fewer fields are displayed), click **Upload All** above the grid to send all listings to eBay for sale.

   –Or–

   Click the **Upload All** down arrow, and click **Upload Selected** to send only selected listings to eBay.

   –Or–

   Click the **Upload All** down arrow, and click **Upload To Selling Manager** to include the listings in this eBay auction-management tool (see Chapter 5 for information on Selling Manager Pro and third-party offerings).

Professor Polly says: "It's generally best to list your items so that the listing ends in the evening, around 8 to 11 P.M. Eastern Time. Most people in all U.S. time zones are home from work at this time and are able to check eBay. Your listings will be visible to the most potential buyers on the day they close."

Chapter 5
Managing Your eBay Business

Managing an eBay business includes the activities that surround your listings after they are created. You will have a listings inventory to track and have to decide the most advantageous timing to submit items; you will need to consider selling restrictions to limit your sales to certain buyers; you will need assistance to keep track of a listing's life cycle (e-mails, payment, shipping, feedback, relisting, and unpaid items); and you will need to utilize auction-management software to help integrate all these aspects of the eBay business so they operate more automatically and in higher volumes than the beginning eBay seller.

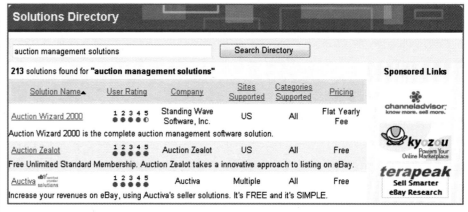

QUICKFACTS

UNDERSTANDING AUCTION-MANAGEMENT SOFTWARE

Hundreds of auction-management programs are available that can make dealing with listings in volume more convenient. At some point, these programs become a necessary investment of time and money. The breadth of features, cost, and flexibility range from the free views provided in My eBay to third-party programs exemplified by the Complete Solutions listed in eBay's Solutions Directory, as shown in Figure 5-1. No matter which program you decide to use, you should consider several options when choosing an auction-management system.

Subscription-based or purchase-pricing models determine whether you pay an upfront fee for software you install on your computer, whether you pay a periodic subscription fee to have services available to you online, or whether you pay both. The subscription-based model allows users to test the program without a large up-front investment, and makes it easier to change to other programs if the need arises. Also, changes to the software are typically done at no additional cost. An auction-management system you purchase outright limits your investment to a one-time amount, but you will generally be charged for major changes and upgrades.

A complete auction-management program should provide a number of functions, including

- Track listing inventory
- View scheduled and active listings
- Relist unsold items
- Automate e-mail, feedback, and invoicing
- Track payment and shipping
- Produce reports and accounting information
- Provide image hosting

Figure 5-1: *There is no shortage of auction-management programs for eBay that advertise themselves as your "complete solution."*

In this chapter, you will see how to achieve a more efficient selling model by using eBay and third-party software. While we cannot explore every feature and nook and cranny of these programs, you will have a good idea of their potential. You will also learn how to handle unpaid items and unscrupulous buyers, and discover other ways to protect your business.

Browser Earl says: "Access the eBay Solutions Directory by clicking Site Map on the eBay header and, under Selling Tools, clicking eBay Solutions Directory."

PowerSeller Sally says: "Auctiva is a free auction-management program used by many PowerSellers on eBay. Auctiva has enough functions to do the work of one extra person in your business. One less weekly salary can make a difference in your bottom line!"

The use in this chapter of Selling Manager Pro and Auctiva (www.auctiva.com), an eBay-Certified Solutions Provider, to illustrate some auction-management software features is not an endorsement for eBay businesses to quit using their current systems and jump on either of these programs. Selling Manager Pro, whose marketing spiel is shown in Figure 5-2, provides a small-to-medium eBay business a set of features to conduct day-to-day operations within the familiar My eBay interface. While you get Selling Manager (Pro's little brother) free when opening a Basic Store, you might (assuming you have a Store) want to at least try the free 30-day trial period and see if the added features in Selling Manager Pro are worth the $15.99 a month to you (when your business grows and you upgrade to a Premium eBay Store, Pro is then provided free). Auctiva is a free, full-featured, Web-based program that may be all you need. A popular choice used by large-volume PowerSellers is the ChannelAdvisor Complete suite of selling, searching, price comparison research, and Web site integration (www.channeladvisor.com/products).

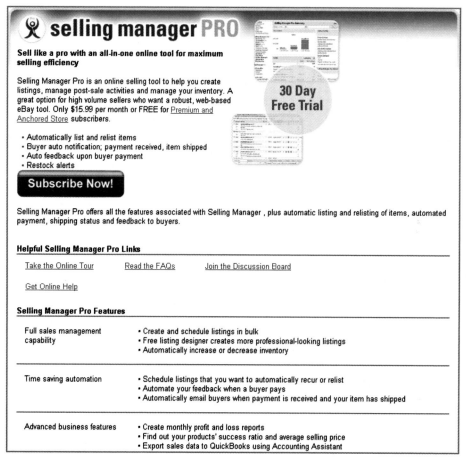

*Figure 5-2: **Selling Manager Pro adds auction-management and listing enhancements to the selling area of My eBay.***

Manage Listings

As your eBay business grows, you will need to have listings available to keep a constant flow of items for sale. It's much more efficient to have the listings already created and waiting to be submitted to eBay than scramble to create the listing as your ideal posting time approaches (Chapter 4 describes how to use Turbo Lister to create and hold listings). Auction-management software can

Active Listings (8 listings)   🖨 **Print** **Customize Display**
Once a listing ends, it will move into Sold or Unsold listings depending on whether you have a buyer.

Item title ▾

Store Category	Status	Format	
All ▾	All (8) ▾	All (8) ▾	**Search** | Hide Search Options | Clear Search

☐ Title	Product	Custom Label	Format	Current Price	# of Watchers	Bids	# of Questions	Time Left ▽	Action
☐ Culinary Arts Institute The Scandinavian Cookbook	Culinary Arts Institute Cookbooks	[Add]	📋	*Buy It Now* $4.00	0	--	0	29d 22h 31m	Send to Online Auction ▾
☐ Culinary Arts Institute The Hungarian Cookbook	Culinary Arts Institute Cookbooks	[Add]	📋	*Buy It Now* $4.00	0	--	0	29d 22h 09m	Send to Online Auction ▾
☐ Culinary Arts Institute The French Cookbook									
☐ Sports Illustrated June 1962									
☐ New York Times Apollo 11 Splash Down Announcement									
☐ Devil in the Church and His Snares Laid to Destroy...									
☐ 1985 Harley Davidson Sportster 1000cc Owner's Manual									
☐ Olympia Challenge Bowl One Program, PAC 8 vs BIG 10									

auctiva
Powerful Solutions for eBay Sellers

Welcome, cbts64   Help \| Community \| Refer a Friend \| Add a Link \| Sign Out

Classes & Tutorials click here   Events: **4 - 0 - 0**

HOME   LISTINGS   IMAGES   PROFILES   INVENTORY   STORE   SALES   EDUCATION   MY ACCOUNT

New Listing \| Saved Listings \| Scheduled \| Active \| Closed \| Folders

Auctiva Active Listings

Filter Listings

Listing Type: All Listings ▾   Title ▾ **Search**
Folder: All Folders ▾
Go

Move selected item(s) to: No Folder ▾ **Move**   Items/Page 25 ▾

Active Listings

Revise **Add Images** **Stop Auto-Relist**

1

☐	🔺	Title	Folder	Quantity	Bids	Watches	Hits	Current Bid	High Bidder	End Date
		Olympia Challenge Bowl One Program, PAC 8 vs BIG 10								
☐		(270242359230) 30 day	Imported Listings	1	0	0	N/A	--		6/30/2008 1:23:49 PM PST
		1985 Harley Davidson Sportster 1000cc Owner's Manual								
☐			Imported							6/30/2008

Figure 5-3: Most auction-management programs provide similar information for your current listings.

help track your listings inventory, let you know when you need to reorder items, use templates to sell identical items, and provide other listing shortcuts. Auction-management software also needs to keep you informed of the status of listings you've already submitted, as well as provide the tools to view and manage the listings:

- **Active listings** are currently for sale or bid (see Figure 5-3).
- **Scheduled** (or *pending*) listings have been assigned a time and date to become active.
- **Sold** listings are your selling successes.
- **Unsold** listings are not your selling failures; they are your inventory of items to be relisted.

Quickly Sell Bulk or Similar Items

If you buy in bulk, you can use auction-management software to quickly create a listing from a previously created listing (or *template* as it's called in

A *template* is simply a term used to describe the framework and contents of a listing that is saved and available for repeated use. For example, when buying in bulk and selling the items individually, a template can be duplicated without any modification except for the auction's start time. Templates also can be duplicated to retain layout and other options you want to keep across all your listings and then modified to provide a different description, unique pictures, and other criteria, such as different shipping considerations.

Selling Manager Pro). With a few clicks, the software can create a new listing, document the number of items you have on hand, and let you know when to reorder based on a threshold you determine. Each auction-management program performs the process in different ways, but they follow a general set of steps similar to the following:

1. Create the listing template using the auction-management program, provided it supports listing creation (see "Create a Listing Template in the Auction-Management Program").

   –Or–

   Create the listing template in another program, and export it to the auction-management program. For example, Selling Manager Pro accepts data in a template created in listing programs such as Turbo Lister (see Figure 5-4). Chapter 4 describes how to create a listing template in Turbo Lister.

   –Or–

   Convert your listings to a spreadsheet format that your auction-management software can accept.

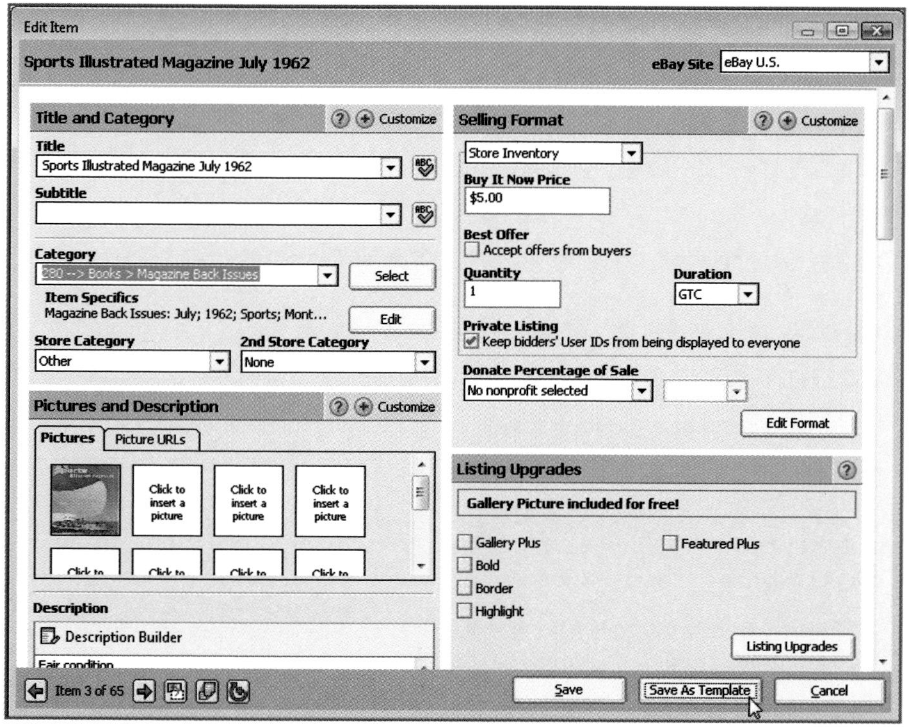

Figure 5-4: *You can save a template by simply saving a listing you've created in a program such as Turbo Lister.*

To upload a Turbo Lister listing to be used in Selling Manager Pro (as a *template*), in Turbo Lister, move the listing from the **Inventory** folder in the Folder List to the **Waiting To Upload** folder. Click the **Tools** menu, and click **Send All Listings To Sales Manager Pro**. Type a product name in the small dialog box that appears, and click **OK**. The listing (template) is uploaded into the Product Inventory view, as shown in Figure 5-5.

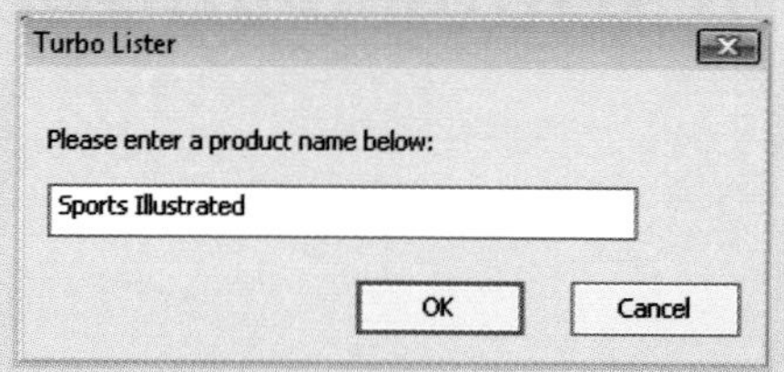

Product name created
by you in Turbo Lister

Listings from Turbo Lister automatically
go into a Selling Manager Pro folder of
the same name as a template.

	Product Inventory ▾	Custom Label	Folder Name	Available to List	Scheduled	Active	Sold	Unsold	Success Ratio	Avg Selling Price	Last Submitted	Action
☐	**Sports Illustrated Magazine**	[Add]	Sport Illustrated	6	0	1	0	0	0%	$0.00	Jun-08-08	
	Sports Illustrated June 1962: Sports Illustrated June 1962											Assign Automation Rules ▾
☐	**QuickSteps** Excel		Turbo Lister	0	0	0	0	0	0%	--	--	
	Template 1: Microsoft Excel 2007 QuickSteps											Assign Automation Rules ▾

Figure 5-5: *Listings created in Turbo Lister can be uploaded to Selling Manager Pro as templates and are displayed in the Product Inventory view.*

2. Organize the listing by creating folders according to the variances of your inventory. For example, if you sell books, you could create folders for fiction, nonfiction, and others that mimic the selling categories in eBay or your eBay Store categories.

Manage Folders: All

Folder: **All** (1 product)

☐ Name	Comments	Last Modified
☐ 📁 Cookbooks (0)		Jun-08-08 13:32:26 PDT
☐ 📁 Manuals (0)	Vehicle, m/c, and misc	Jun-08-08 13:33:27 PDT
☐ 📁 Newspapers (0)	Noteworthy articles	Jun-08-08 13:32:50 PDT
☐ 📁 Sport Illustrated (0)	Back issuees	Jun-08-08 13:32:15 PDT
☐ 📁 Turbo Lister (1)		Jun-08-08 12:28:43 PDT

[Add Folder] [Edit] [Move] [Copy] [Delete]   Total Inventory Folders: 5

3. Update the total number of items you have available to list (see "Adjust Your On-Hand Quantity").

4. Submit the listing to eBay.

5. Repeat Step 4 to add an identical listing.

   –Or–

   Edit the template to use for similar items, and submit the listing.

Create a Listing Template in the Auction-Management Program

Many listing-management programs simply do just that—manage listings. They offer few, if any, tools to create a listing. For example, Selling Manager Pro allows you to create a template (actually, it's the same as a listing) using a form similar to the Sell Your Item form—not considered the most efficient way to create a listing by higher-volume sellers, though it works.

1. Create your item description using your favorite means (for example, by using a Web design/editing program, such as Microsoft Expression).

2. In My eBay, under Selling Manager Pro, click **Inventory**.

Selling Manager Pro
▪ Inventory (11)
▪ Scheduled

TIP

Once you amass several templates under a given product, it can become tedious to edit each one individually, especially when you are making the same change in each. To speed up the process, Selling Manager Pro (and other management programs) offers a means to do bulk editing—that is, applying the same change to all selected templates. To start the process in Selling Manager Pro, in Product Inventory view, select the product whose templates you want to change, and click **Edit Templates**. Choose the templates you want to change, select **Edit Templates In Bulk**, select the field(s) you want to change, and then edit them. The change will propagate to each template.

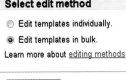

Select edit method

○ Edit templates individually.
● Edit templates in bulk.
Learn more about editing methods.

[Continue >] | Cancel

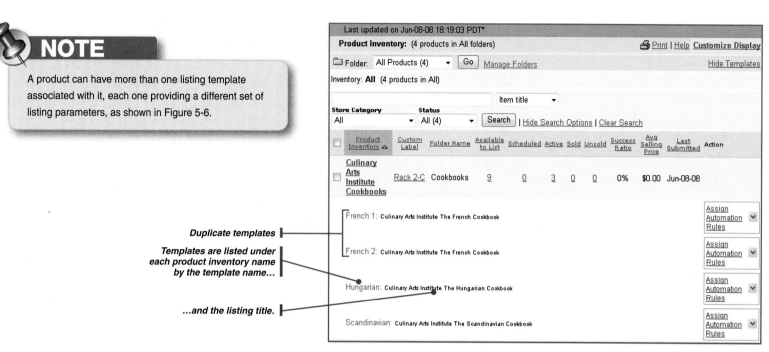

Duplicate templates

Templates are listed under each product inventory name by the template name...

...and the listing title.

Figure 5-6: *Listing templates for a product can be duplicates or can contain minor changes that let you experiment with listing options.*

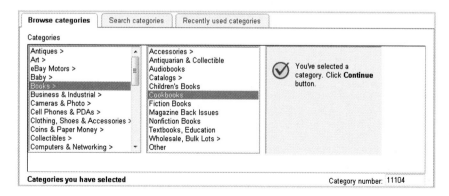

3. In the Product Inventory view, click **Create Product**.

4. In the Create New Product page, shown in Figure 5-7, provide a name, folder, quantity, and average cost for the item. Optionally, click the **Alert Me If Quantity Available To List Is Less Than** check box, and type a minimum threshold quantity. Add any vendor information, and click **Save & Create Listing**.

5. In the Create A Template: Select A Category page, use the category picker to choose an eBay category by browsing, searching for keywords, or selecting from categories you've used recently. Click **Continue**.

*Figure 5-7: **Listing-management programs provide tools that you can use to set up product-specific criteria to track quantity and speed reordering.***

6. Continue setting up the template using the Create Your Listing form, shown in Figure 5-8, used in eBay to list individual items. Add your own item description; add a link to self-hosted pictures or use eBay Picture Services; add listing upgrades; and determine pricing, duration, shipping, and payment options.

7. When finished, click **Save Only**. The template is added to the list of templates available for a product.

–Or–

If you want to make the listing/template active on eBay, as well as adding to the list of templates available for a product, click **Submit & Save Listing**.

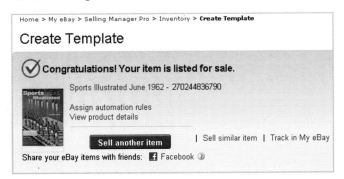

Adjust Your On-Hand Quantity

The inventory function in an auction-management program typically offers a way to help you keep track of the number of multiple items you have for sale. As you list items for sale, the number is automatically reduced to provide a real-time picture of your current inventory. Usually, you enter your on-hand quantity when you first create the item or product category and the software will keep track of things from there as you sell them. Both Selling Manager Pro and Auctiva (see Figure 5-10) offer features that provide inventory details and generate notifications when the quantity drops to a certain level (which means you are selling!). The following sections show how Selling Manager Pro handles

QUICKSTEPS

ADDING AN ACTIVE LISTING TO YOUR TEMPLATE COLLECTION

If you have an active, older listing that didn't originate from a template, for example, a Good 'Til Sold Store Inventory item that's been in your Store for awhile, and you acquire additional similar items or otherwise want to add it your template collection, there is typically a way for you to save the listing as a template without having to find the original (which is probably long gone). This is how it's done in Selling Manager Pro:

1. On the My eBay sidebar, under Selling Manager Pro, click **Active**.

2. Select the listing by clicking the check box to the left of its title.

   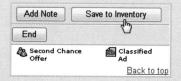

3. At the bottom of the view, click **Save To Inventory**.

4. On the Save To Inventory page, save the template to a new or existing product, template, and folder. Optionally, provide a custom label (can be an inventory location, SKU, or some other identifying information), quantity you have, and average cost, as shown in Figure 5-9.

5. Click **Save To Inventory** to add the listing as a template to the Product Inventory view (see Figure 5-6).

Almost analogous to the standard eBay Sell Your Item form | Added section distinguishes the two forms

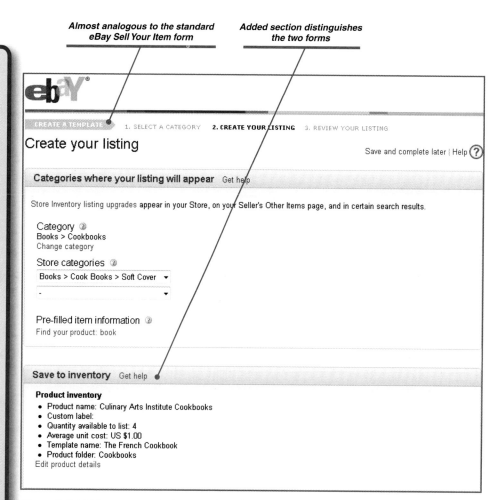

Figure 5-8: *Listings are created as templates in Selling Manager Pro using a form similar to eBay's standard Create A Listing form.*

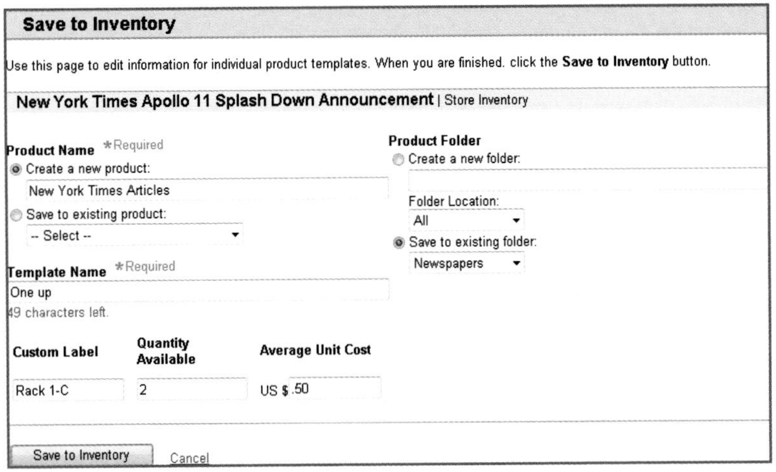

Save to Inventory

Use this page to edit information for individual product templates. When you are finished, click the **Save to Inventory** button.

New York Times Apollo 11 Splash Down Announcement | Store Inventory

Product Name *Required
○ Create a new product:
New York Times Articles
○ Save to existing product:
-- Select --

Template Name *Required
One up
49 characters left.

Product Folder
○ Create a new folder:

Folder Location:
All

● Save to existing folder:
Newspapers

Custom Label	Quantity Available	Average Unit Cost
Rack 1-C	2	US $ .50

Save to Inventory   Cancel

Figure 5-9: You can add existing listings to your product inventory in Sales Manager Pro.

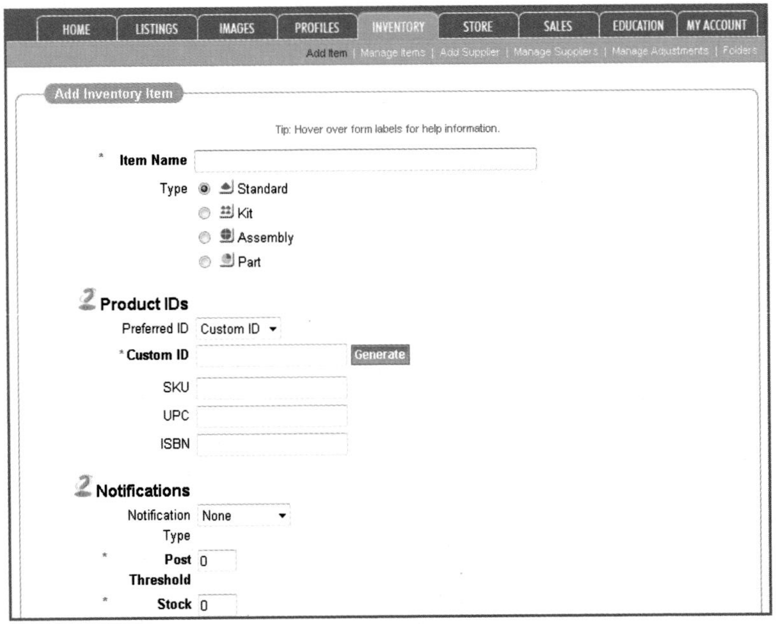

Figure 5-10: The inventory system in Auctiva provides a straightforward means for adding and managing your stock and suppliers (see Figure 5-7 to compare with the interface used by Selling Manager Pro).

basic inventory control. (See "Create a Listing Template in the Auction-Management Program" earlier in the chapter to see how Selling Manager Pro sets up an initial item/product.)

ADD QUANTITY WHEN CREATING A PRODUCT IN AUCTIVA

1. From the Auctiva home page, click the **Inventory** tab.

2. On the Inventory page, click **Add Item** on the links bar below the Inventory tab.

3. On the Add Inventory page (see Figure 5-10), add the identifying information for the items. In the Initial Adjustment area, type the date of the day you received the item and the quantity.

4. Add any optional details you want regarding the item, including a picture and description (they will come in handy when you list the item), place the item in a folder to help organize your inventory, and click **Save & Create New**, as shown in Figure 5-11.

Figure 5-11: Auctiva provides more robust fields to identify your new product than Selling Manager Pro.

Update Quantity

Enter the quantity for your product.

Product Name	Available to List	Action	Quantity
Culinary Arts Institute Cookbooks	9	Add ▾	5

[Update Qty] [Cancel]

Figure 5-12: **You can update your on-hand quantity of products in Selling Manager Pro at any time.**

QUICKFACTS

USING THE SELLER DASHBOARD

Another aspect of managing your eBay business is to constantly gauge your success as an eBay seller in the eyes of eBay. Your Detailed Seller Ratings (DSRs) from buyer feedback (see the "Reviewing Your Feedback Profile" QuickFacts later in the chapter) and quantity of sales have direct bearing on whether your listings will rise toward the top in Best Match searches by prospective buyers (the eBay default search), as well as determining PowerSeller discounts. Assuming you have at least ten DSRs in the last year, the Seller Dashboard will give you a snapshot of several metrics that will help you see where you stand, as shown in Figure 5-13 (if you're not a PowerSeller, you'll see how close you are to becoming one).

To view the Seller Dashboard, you can click links in your My eBay My Account sidebar or on your Selling Manager/Selling Manager Pro Summary pages.

CHANGE QUANTITY AFTER A PRODUCT IS CREATED

If you acquire more items, break some, lose them in your inventory count (which means your inventory system needs a second look or someone is stealing from you), or otherwise need to adjust your quantity, it's simply a matter of choosing the product and changing the number. (Unlike many accounting programs, where there are typically auditing safeguards to prevent adjustments after the fact.). Here's how it's done in Selling Manager Pro:

1. In Product Inventory view, select the check box to the left of the product whose quantity you want to change, and click **Update Quantity**.

2. In the Update Quantity page, shown in Figure 5-12, click the **Action** down arrow. Click **Add** to increase the current count.

   –Or–

   Click Remove to decrease the current count.

3. In the **Quantity** text box, type the amount the product has increased or decreased.

4. Click **Update Qty** to make the change.

View Listings by Current Status

An auction-management system needs to keep you informed of the status of a listing, from the time it's created to its submission to eBay. After the sale is made, it needs to ensure the item is paid for and shipped, and that data is fed back into accounting and inventory systems. That's a tall order, and unless you're at the top tier of eBay sellers, the cost to accomplish all that seamlessly will be more than you probably want to spend. The best solution is to accomplish as much as you can—at the lowest possible cost—using an auction-management program and then supplement the pieces of the system that are not handled automatically with manual processes. The interface provided by My eBay, and optionally supplemented by Selling Manager/Selling Manager Pro, provides a lot of information inexpensively (the monthly subscription to

View your current PowerSeller discount.

See how your trailing 12-month DSR ratings compare with the eBay average.

Access the Seller Dashboard from My eBay

Gauge how high your listings will appear in Best Match searches...

...and understand why

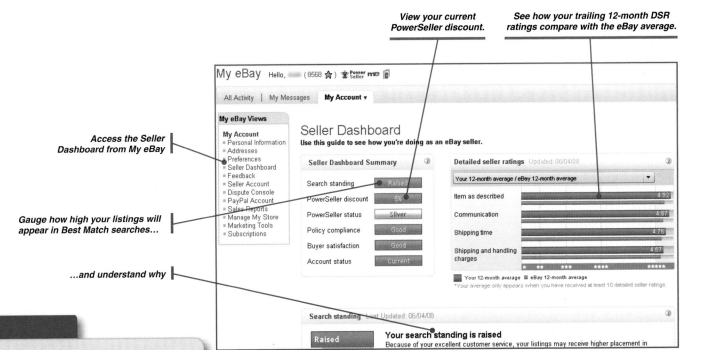

Figure 5-13: The Seller Dashboard provides a summary and specifics on several metrics of your eBay account that directly affect your bottom line.

TIP

eBay offers several auction-management functions for free in its All Selling view of My eBay. The All Selling view is especially good at tracking a listing's status once a sale or auction has started. If your business is new or you don't have more than 50 active listings, you probably can rely on My eBay to keep you on track.

NOTE

You can automatically have Selling Manager Pro (and other auction-management programs) relist unsold items (see "Relist Items Automatically" later in the chapter) and make changes to the listing that might increase your selling success (see the "Changing a Listing for Success" QuickFacts). This is in contrast to selecting items in the My eBay Unsold view and relisting them individually.

Selling Manager Pro is $15.99 as of this writing, and Selling Manager is free for a Basic Store owner).

1. Click **My eBay** on the eBay header.

2. On the sidebar, under All Selling (if you're using My eBay without Selling Manager) or under Selling Manager/Selling Manager Pro (if a subscriber), click the relevant link to view items submitted to eBay in the following status categories:

All Selling
- Scheduled
- Selling
- Sold
- Unsold

Selling Manager Pro
- Inventory (4)
- Scheduled
- Active (8)
- Unsold
- Sold (84)

- **Inventory** (Selling Manager Pro) displays templates of your inventory organized by product.

- **Scheduled** lists items that are scheduled to start at a future time (up to three weeks from the time you submit each listing). You can reschedule items to start at a new time and date.

CHANGING A LISTING FOR SUCCESS

Consider changing your listing to resolve the following potential problems after attempting to sell an item one or more times:

- **Item is too expensive.** Start the bidding at a lower starting price, remove the reserve price, or lower the Buy It Now price. Consider offering the Best Offer option for Buy It Now items, in which buyers suggest a price.

- **Item payment options are too restrictive.** Accept additional methods of payment.

Confirm Your Purchase

Important: ▓▓▓▓ requires immediate payment for this item with PayPal. Learn more.

- **Item cannot be easily found in searches.** Change the category, add a second category, or change the title to contain better keywords.

- **Item doesn't attract buyers.** Take new pictures to give a better presentation or to show more detail; rewrite the item description to describe its selling points; or add upgrades, such as a bordering or highlighting.

- **Item shipping and handling charges are excessive.** Eliminate any handling fees, charge exact shipping, and write off your time and incidental expenses for this particular item. For more costly items, consider offering free shipping (Chapter 10 describes sales and shipping promotions you can offer for eBay Store items).

MY eBAY SELLING ICON	DESCRIPTION
	A buyer completed checkout
	A buyer has not completed checkout
	Item paid for by buyer
	Item not paid for by buyer
	You've refunded payment to buyer
	You've shipped the item
	You have not shipped the item

Table 5-1: Selling Icons Used in My eBay Views

- **Selling** (or **Active**) lists items currently for sale or bid. You can quickly see how many bids have been placed, how many users are tracking your item in their Watching view, and the time remaining for the sale. You also can access links to sell similar items, change the listing, end the listing early, and change cross-promotion settings.

- **Sold** displays listings for completed sales and provides a visual record of the actions you should perform to complete a sale with a winning buyer or bidder. Table 5-1 lists some examples.

- **Unsold** displays items available to be relisted for sale. eBay provides a refund for the initial listing fee if you sell the item the second time you list it. You need to satisfy several criteria to relist the item, such as pricing it less than or equal to the original price.

Automate Your eBay Business

The key feature of any auction-management program is its ability to relieve you from repetitive tasks by automating actions that are the same for listing after listing. For example, how many different ways can you phrase positive feedback for someone buying an item from you? If it was a normal sale—that is, the buyer paid on time and didn't beleaguer you with e-mails or otherwise cause problems—he or she is a "Great Buyer!" So why not just set up a few responses and automatically send positive feedback? The most popular, and

PowerSeller Sally says: "Lower shipping charges will attract more buyers, as well as keep the Shipping And Handling Charges portion of your Detailed Seller Rates above the threshold to maintain your PowerSeller discount!"

recommended, automatic listing feature is Checkout, offered by eBay (and used by many other listing programs). At its simplest, the winning bidder or buyer is presented with a Pay Now option that confirms shipping and final pricing, and encourages them to pay right away. If you offer PayPal, the Pay Now button ⟨Pay Now⟩ is always displayed when the listing closes.

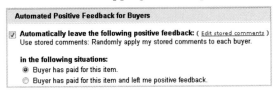

TIP

Customize the Checkout page that your buyers and winning bidders see with a logo and custom message. In My eBay, click **Marketing Tools** on the sidebar. On the Marketing Tools sidebar, under Logos And Branding, click **Customize End Of Auction Emails**. On the Customize page, click **Change** to the right of End of Auction Email. As shown in Figure 5-14, you can upload a .jpg file of your logo, sized to 310 x 90 pixels, and click the **Include My Logo Located At The Following Web Address (URL)** check box. Preview the image by clicking **Test Your Logo** (if you have an eBay Store, your option will be to include your Store logo). Type in plain text your message, using the AutoText to insert specific information about you, your buyer, and the item. Click **Save** when finished.

Logos and Branding
- Customize End of Auction Emails
- Customize Invoice

NOTE

If you use a third-party auction-management program, it probably offers a similar feature to eBay's Checkout but refers to it by a different name, such as ClickOut, to automate the checkout process for buyers and winning bidders.

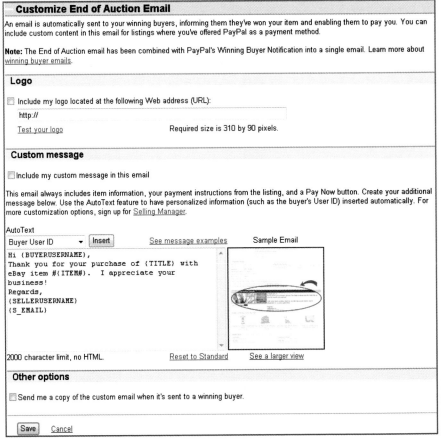

Figure 5-14: *Customize your automated Checkout pages and e-mails with your own logo.*

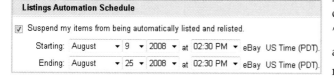

Payment from buyers	
Use checkout	Yes
Offer PayPal on my listings	Yes

To verify Checkout is used in your listings and to turn it on if it isn't:

1. In My eBay, under My Account on the sidebar, click **Site Preferences**.

2. Under Selling Preferences, click **Show** next to Payment From Buyers. If there's a Yes to the right of Use Checkout, you're good to go. If not, click **Edit** on the right side of the table.

3. On the Payment Preferences page, click the **Use Checkout (Recommended)** check box, and click **Submit**.

Checkout Preference

When you use Checkout, a Pay Now button appears in your listing after it ends. This button helps you get paid faster by encouraging buyers to pay. Learn more about your Checkout preference.

☑ Use Checkout (recommended)
   Note: Checkout is always on in closed listings where PayPal is offered.

RELIST ITEMS AUTOMATICALLY

Your auction-management program should provide options for you to automatically relist items that don't sell on their previous attempts and allow you to wait for buyers to eventually seek out your items. (In eBay Stores, you can maintain a constant stock of merchandise for sale by choosing the Good 'Til Sold listing duration). Figure 5-15 shows rule settings you can set up when automatically relisting using Selling Manager Pro. You can also easily suspend relisting for specific periods of time, such as during times you will be away.

Listings Automation Schedule

☑ Suspend my items from being automatically listed and relisted.

Starting: August ▾ 9 ▾ 2008 ▾ at 02:30 PM ▾ eBay US Time (PDT).
Ending: August ▾ 25 ▾ 2008 ▾ at 02:30 PM ▾ eBay US Time (PDT).

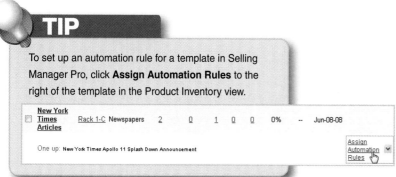

TIP

To set up an automation rule for a template in Selling Manager Pro, click **Assign Automation Rules** to the right of the template in the Product Inventory view.

| New York Times Articles | Rack 1-C | Newspapers | 2 | 0 | 1 | 0 | 0 | 0% | -- | Jun-08-08 |

One up: New York Times Apollo 11 Splash Down Announcement

Assign Automation Rules

*Figure 5-15: **Maintain a stock of merchandise for sale by setting up automatic relisting rules.***

Assign Automation Rules

Use this page to assign automation rules to the listing templates that you selected. Select a rule, specify its settings, then click the **Assign** button.

Rule: Relist continuously until an item sells ▾

This rule enables you to relist your items continuously until they sell.

Rule Settings

◉ Relist after items do not sell

○ Relist ___ days ___ hours after items do not sell *

○ Relist at 1 ▾ 00 ▾ AM ▾ US Time (PDT) *

☐ Add Best Offer

*Listings scheduled to begin in the future are an additional US $0.10. This fee may vary for items listed on international sites.
Note: You may receive an Insertion Fee Credit if your listings are eligible.

NOTE

Although you can relist an item as many times as you want, you are only eligible for an insertion fee credit for your initial sale if the first relisting results in a sale and satisfies a few other criteria. The sale must be a single-quantity, auction, or fixed-priced format; and the new starting price must be equal to or less than the initial price. Also, you can only relist with a reserve price if you initially listed with one, and the reserve price must be equal to or less than the first reserve price.

SEND SECOND CHANCE OFFERS

Second Chance offers are a way for you to notify bidders that they can buy your item(s) even if they didn't win the auction. Nonwinning bidders (or *back bidders*) can be offered a chance to buy an item under a few conditions:

- The winning bidder didn't pay you.
- The reserve price was not met.
- You have duplicate items for sale but did not list them as a multiple-item (Dutch) auction.

Some auction-management programs will automatically send Second Chance offers based on criteria you set, such as pricing strategies.

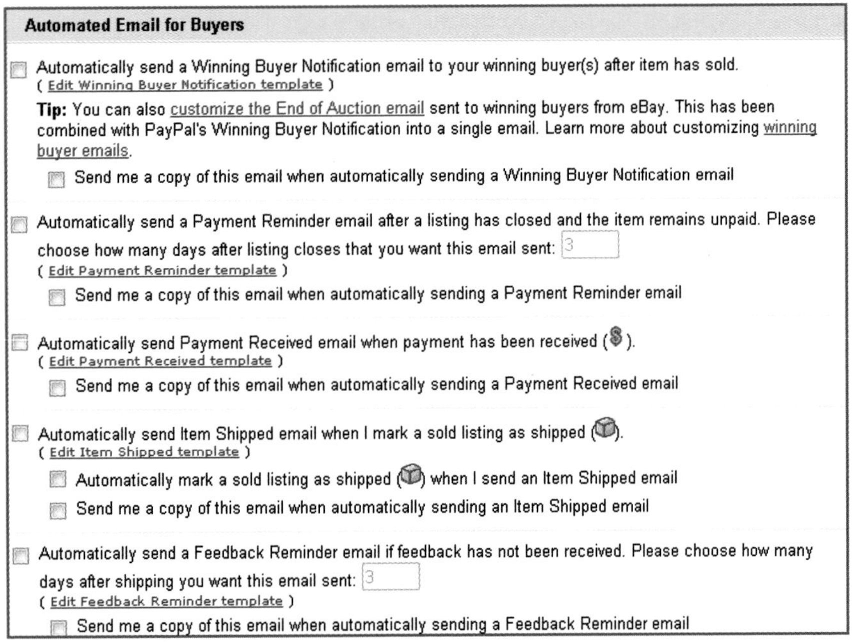
Automated Email for Buyers
Automatically send a Winning Buyer Notification email to your winning buyer(s) after item has sold.
(Edit Winning Buyer Notification template)
Tip: You can also customize the End of Auction email sent to winning buyers from eBay. This has been combined with PayPal's Winning Buyer Notification into a single email. Learn more about customizing winning buyer emails.
Send me a copy of this email when automatically sending a Winning Buyer Notification email
Automatically send a Payment Reminder email after a listing has closed and the item remains unpaid. Please choose how many days after listing closes that you want this email sent: 3
(Edit Payment Reminder template)
Send me a copy of this email when automatically sending a Payment Reminder email
Automatically send Payment Received email when payment has been received ( ).
(Edit Payment Received template)
Send me a copy of this email when automatically sending a Payment Received email
Automatically send Item Shipped email when I mark a sold listing as shipped ( ).
(Edit Item Shipped template)
Automatically mark a sold listing as shipped ( ) when I send an Item Shipped email
Send me a copy of this email when automatically sending an Item Shipped email
Automatically send a Feedback Reminder email if feedback has not been received. Please choose how many days after shipping you want this email sent: 3
(Edit Feedback Reminder template)
Send me a copy of this email when automatically sending a Feedback Reminder email

***Figure 5-16:* Your auction-management program can provide several automated e-mails, which you can customize before sending to your buyers.**

SET UP AUTOMATED E-MAILS

E-mail can be looked at as being the Eighth Wonder of the World or as the largest albatross ever hung on the neck of modern society. eBay, being an online medium, is married to e-mail to provide efficient and inexpensive contact between buyers and sellers, although much of the communication is simply notification of actions performed that can be set up for automatic release. eBay provides many automated e-mail messages for free, but you can customize the messages to a large degree using most auction-management programs, as shown in Figure 5-16.

LEAVE FEEDBACK AUTOMATICALLY

One of the more tedious eBay tasks is also one of the most important actions to ensure the overall solvency of eBay as a global marketplace. Feedback is the mechanism that provides a reputation and trust for the millions of buyers who make daily purchases on eBay sites. You need to support the effort by rewarding your buyers with positive feedback (even though you cannot chastise them with negative feedback), but the chore can sometimes stand in the way of completing the action (see the "Reviewing

CAUTION

Ensure you download data from online auction-management programs to your local system for archiving before the information is removed from the service and you can no longer access it. Most programs allow you to download the data in a format that can be read by spreadsheet programs, such as Microsoft Excel and Intuit QuickBooks accounting programs.

REVIEWING YOUR FEEDBACK PROFILE

Your eBay Feedback Profile is an important way that potential buyers can get a sense of your honesty, reliability, and overall business worthiness. It records how satisfied a buyer is with the transaction. An example can be seen in Figure 5-17. Every eBay seller knows about the value of positive feedback and the downside of its negative twin, but it's especially important to those of you who plan on using eBay to produce an income or to support a lifestyle that you treat feedback with the respect it's due. A Feedback Profile is made up of two parts: the Feedback Rating and the Detailed Seller Ratings (DSRs).

CALCULATE THE FEEDBACK RATING

The **Feedback Rating** is a general overall rating of how satisfied a buyer is with the transaction. They can measure you by selecting one of three ratings:

- A *positive rating* adds one point to your Feedback Rating.
- A *neutral rating* adds no points to the Feedback Rating.
- A *negative rating* subtracts one point from the Feedback Rating.

Continued ...

Your Feedback Profile" QuickFacts). Auction-management programs relieve you of this burden by allowing you to:

- Craft canned responses for positive feedback comments

- Automate the sending of feedback based on options you choose

Generate Reports

You need sales, shipping, and transaction fees data to enter into your accounting system and determine the financial status of your business. This will assist you in submitting periodic government filings. The reporting tools of auction-management programs can save you hours of number crunching and hundreds of dollars in bookkeeping or accounting costs (see Chapter 1 for more information on the financial and governmental issues in running an eBay business). Figure 5-18 shows a typical set of metrics your auction-management program can track, organize, and sum for you.

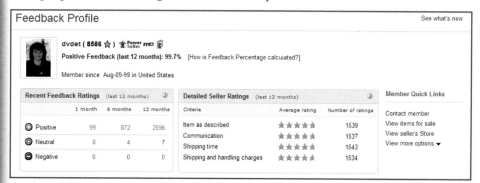

Figure 5-17: **Your Feedback Profile is what buyers will use to evaluate your honesty and responsiveness to their needs.**

QUICKFACTS

REVIEWING YOUR FEEDBACK PROFILE *(Continued)*

As of February 2008, if a buyer buys multiple times from you, the repeat submissions will count in your rating if the purchases are not made in the same week (Monday through Sunday).

CALCULATE THE DETAILED SELLER RATINGS

Detailed Seller Ratings offer a way for the buyer to judge the seller in four specific areas by clicking on a rating of one to five (poor to very good) for each criteria:

- The item received is as described
- Communication was clear and responsive
- Shipping time was as expected
- Shipping and handling charges were not excessive

The seller can only see the overall rating, not the ratings of a particular buyer.

BUILD A REPUTATION

Other buyers or sellers will know you by how you have performed in the past. Feedback ratings are like money in the bank. They are a real currency in this cyber-economy where you can't shake hands with a business partner face to face. Protect your feedback rating and DSR by going out of your way to be fair and accountable.

PROVIDE FEEDBACK

Part of being a responsible seller is to give feedback comments to your buyers. As a seller, you can only give positive ratings plus a comment. Make your comments fair and timely.

Continued . . .

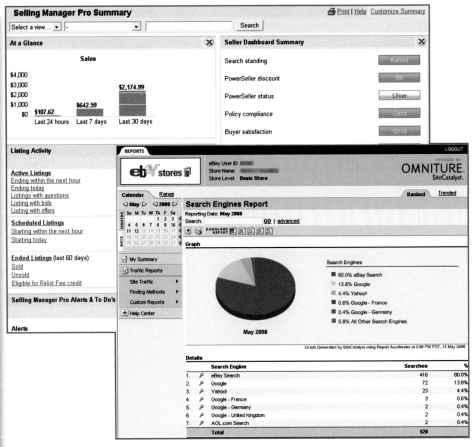

Figure 5-18: Reports are a vital part of any auction-management program.

Manage Risk

eBay is founded on the principles that people are basically good and honest, but that's not to say you can leave yourself open to unscrupulous buyers, miscommunication, and potential legal action. Managing your business risk is an unfortunate part of the eBay selling experience. However, eBay provides several features, programs, and best practices that can help you minimize the risk.

QUICKFACTS

REVIEWING YOUR FEEDBACK PROFILE *(Continued)*

HANDLE NEGATIVE FEEDBACK

If you receive negative feedback, your options are limited. Your buyer is urged to contact you to resolve any problems before leaving feedback. They must wait for seven days after a listing ends before leaving negative ratings. (If the buyer does not pay, you can file an Unpaid Item Dispute to alert eBay about the problem. See "Understanding the Unpaid Item Process" QuickSteps later in the chapter for more information.)

You can request that a buyer change his or her feedback rating, comment and Detailed Seller Ratings (DSRs). While you initiate the feedback revision process, your buyer can accept or decline your request. You should only request a feedback revision from a buyer if he or she accidently sent you negative information or if you and your buyer have now resolved the issue that initiated the negative rating, comment, or DSR. You're limited to one request per sale and your buyer must respond within 10 days (a non-response results in no changes to the feedback).

CAUTION

Setting up impediments to keep buyers from your items can limit your sales. Use buyer restrictions carefully to avoid shielding any buyers from purchasing your items except those that you feel are not worth the risk or effort.

Set Buyer Requirements

You don't have to sell your items to a buyer just because he or she has an eBay account. You have several options available to restrict the buyers with whom you want to conduct business. The most general restrictions are applicable to all bidders, based on criteria you set. More specific restrictions are available to block individual buyers (see "Restrict Bidders and Buyers" later in the chapter).

You can set up the restrictions you want from links in the selling forms, such as the Sell Your Item form, or the forms used in Turbo Lister or from Site Preferences in My eBay.

Browser Earl says: "For a reputable escrow service, use www.escrow.com, which is recommended by eBay."

To access the buyer restrictions in My eBay:

1. Under My Account on the My eBay sidebar, click **Site Preferences**.

2. Under the Selling Preferences section, click **Show**, located to the right of Buyer Requirements.

Buyer requirements	Show
Block certain eBay buyers from bidding on or purchasing your items.	

3. The Buyer Requirements window will open and the current default settings will be displayed. Click **Edit** to change it. The Buyer Requirements page will be displayed, shown in Figure 5-19.

Buyer requirements		Hide
Block buyers who:	Have received 2 Unpaid Item strike(s) within 1 Month(s).	Edit
	Are registered in countries to which I don't ship	
	Have 4 Policy Violation report(s) within 1 Month(s).	
	Have a feedback score of -1 or lower	
	Are currently winning or have bought 10 of my items in the last 10 days and have a feedback score of 5 or lower	

4. Click the restrictions you want to impose, and set any criteria available.

5. Click **Submit** when finished. The restrictions you chose are now listed in your Selling Preferences section where you click Show.

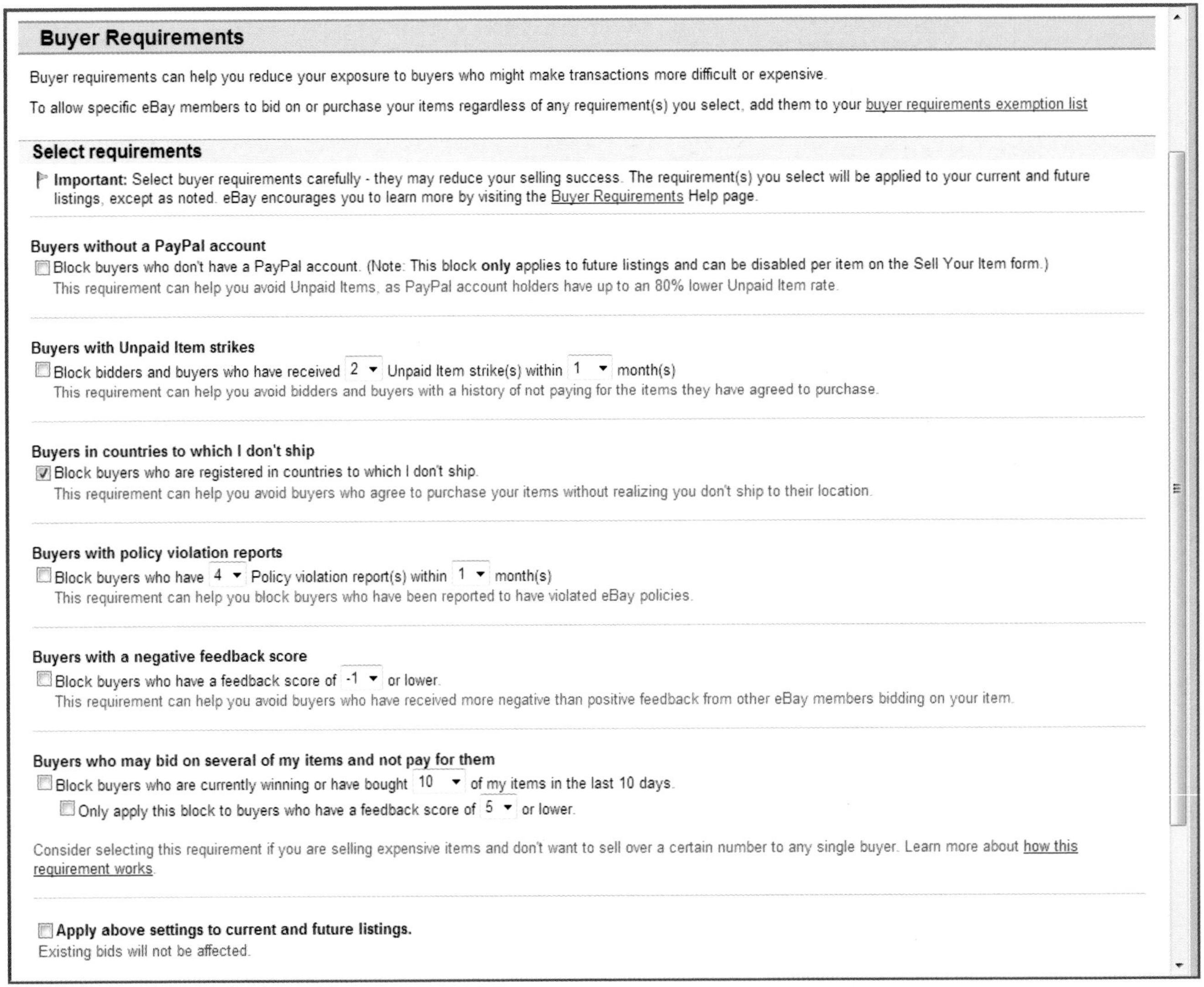

Buyer Requirements

Buyer requirements can help you reduce your exposure to buyers who might make transactions more difficult or expensive.

To allow specific eBay members to bid on or purchase your items regardless of any requirement(s) you select, add them to your buyer requirements exemption list

Select requirements

⚑ **Important:** Select buyer requirements carefully - they may reduce your selling success. The requirement(s) you select will be applied to your current and future listings, except as noted. eBay encourages you to learn more by visiting the Buyer Requirements Help page.

Buyers without a PayPal account

☐ Block buyers who don't have a PayPal account. (Note: This block **only** applies to future listings and can be disabled per item on the Sell Your Item form.)
   This requirement can help you avoid Unpaid Items, as PayPal account holders have up to an 80% lower Unpaid Item rate.

Buyers with Unpaid Item strikes

☐ Block bidders and buyers who have received 2 ▾ Unpaid Item strike(s) within 1 ▾ month(s)
   This requirement can help you avoid bidders and buyers with a history of not paying for the items they have agreed to purchase.

Buyers in countries to which I don't ship

☑ Block buyers who are registered in countries to which I don't ship.
   This requirement can help you avoid buyers who agree to purchase your items without realizing you don't ship to their location.

Buyers with policy violation reports

☐ Block buyers who have 4 ▾ Policy violation report(s) within 1 ▾ month(s)
   This requirement can help you block buyers who have been reported to have violated eBay policies.

Buyers with a negative feedback score

☐ Block buyers who have a feedback score of -1 ▾ or lower.
   This requirement can help you avoid buyers who have received more negative than positive feedback from other eBay members bidding on your item.

Buyers who may bid on several of my items and not pay for them

☐ Block buyers who are currently winning or have bought 10 ▾ of my items in the last 10 days.
   ☐ Only apply this block to buyers who have a feedback score of 5 ▾ or lower.

Consider selecting this requirement if you are selling expensive items and don't want to sell over a certain number to any single buyer. Learn more about how this requirement works.

☐ **Apply above settings to current and future listings.**
Existing bids will not be affected.

*Figure 5-19: **You can set your selling bar higher to minimize potential issues with buyers who do not meet your requirements.***

QUICKFACTS

PROTECTING THE TRANSACTION

In addition to your communications with the buyer, your attention to feedback, and the item itself, there are other practical ways in which you can protect the transaction:

- Protect your accounts by changing your passwords periodically. Keep your passwords and personal information private. Use different passwords for eBay, PayPal, and other accounts.
- Insure valuable or unique items to protect you and your buyer in case the item is damaged, broken, or lost while shipping.
- Use PayPal to pay for items or to refund money.
- Use ID Verify to give others confidence in you. Look for the ID Verify icon in your buyers and bidders.
- Become bonded through buySAFE.

I am a Bonded Seller
The buySAFE Seal on my listing indicates that:
I have passed the comprehensive buySAFE Business Inspection
Your transaction is protected by a 10-Point Guarantee
buySAFE or not at all
buysafe
Make sure it's real. Always click on the seal.

- Use credit cards to make your transactions easy and simple for buyers. Most credit card companies issue insurance for fraudulent transactions for additional protection.
- Use an escrow service for items of high value to provide assurance to buyers. The service will make sure that the item is received and approved before releasing the money to you. If there is any question regarding the item's condition, or if the buyer is dissatisfied with the item, the escrow service continues to hold the money until the item is returned to you. Be aware, however, that there are fraudulent escrow services out there.

Restrict Bidders and Buyers

You can block bidders or buyers from buying from you or bidding in an auction. You might do this in case of nonpaying bidders or buyers, or if you have had a bad experience with a buyer. You can build a list of up to 5,000 blocked buyers. Conversely, you can set up a preapproved list to sell to only buyers or bidders you select.

Browser Earl says: "To view the Buyer/Bidder Management page, go to http://pages.ebay.com/services/buyandsell/biddermanagement.html."

Browser Earl

To access buyer and bidder restrictions:

1. Click **Site Map** on the eBay header.
2. Under Selling Activities, click **Blocked Bidder/Buyer List** to open the Buyer/Bidder Management page.
3. Under Blocked Bidder/Buyer List, click **Add An eBay User To My Blocked Bidder/Buyer List**. The page shown in Figure 5-20 is displayed.
4. Type the User ID of the buyer you want to block from your auctions and fixed-price sales, and click **Submit**.

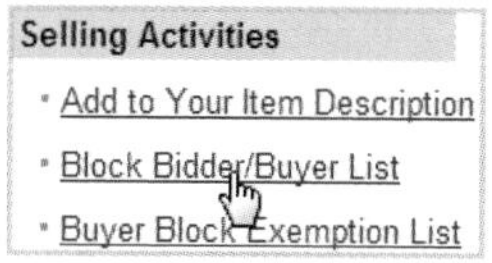
Selling Activities
Add to Your Item Description
Block Bidder/Buyer List
Buyer Block Exemption List

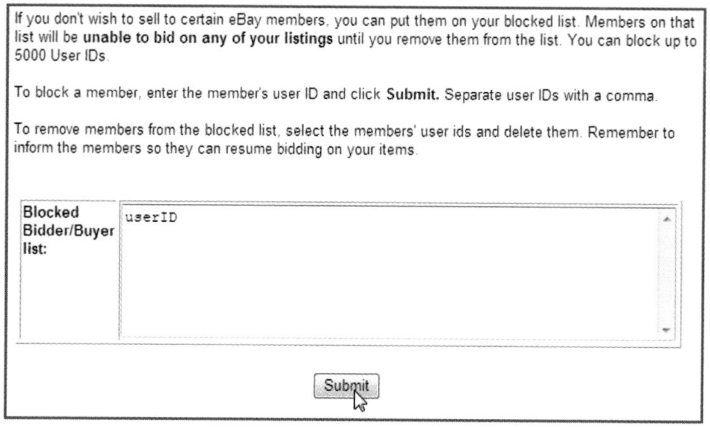
If you don't wish to sell to certain eBay members, you can put them on your blocked list. Members on that list will be unable to bid on any of your listings until you remove them from the list. You can block up to 5000 User IDs.
To block a member, enter the member's user ID and click Submit. Separate user IDs with a comma.
To remove members from the blocked list, select the members' user ids and delete them. Remember to inform the members so they can resume bidding on your items.
Blocked Bidder/Buyer list:
userID
Submit

Figure 5-20: ***You can restrict buyers and bidders from all items you list using the Blocked Bidder/Buyer List form.***

Exempt Buyers and Bidders from Blocks

You can exempt some users from the Blocked List. In other words, you can identify specific buyers to be allowed to bid in your auctions or purchase your items even though they may not pass the blocked-list criteria. You do this by including them in the Buyer Block Exempt List. Ineligible members can contact you by e-mail and request to be placed on this list.

1. Click **Site Map** from the eBay header.
2. Under Selling Activities, click **Buyer Block Exemption List**.
3. On the Buyer/Bidder Management page, click **Add A Buyer To My Buyer Block Exemption List**.
4. Click in the **eBay Members Exempted From Your Buyer Requirements** text box, shown in Figure 5-21, and type the User ID or e-mail address of the buyer/bidder you want to allow to participate in your auctions and Buy It Now listings. Separate the User IDs with commas, semicolons, or a blank space.
5. Click **Submit**.

Selling Activities
- Add to Your Item Description
- Block Bidder/Buyer List
- Buyer Block Exemption List
- Cancel Bids on Your Listing

TIP

You can remove a bidder/buyer from the blocked list or the exemption list by deleting the name from the respective list and clicking **Submit**.

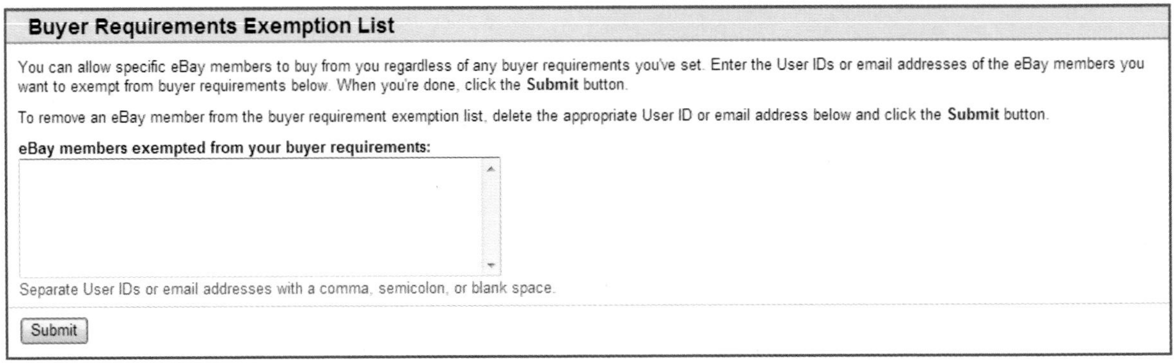

Buyer Requirements Exemption List

You can allow specific eBay members to buy from you regardless of any buyer requirements you've set. Enter the User IDs or email addresses of the eBay members you want to exempt from buyer requirements below. When you're done, click the **Submit** button.

To remove an eBay member from the buyer requirement exemption list, delete the appropriate User ID or email address below and click the **Submit** button.

eBay members exempted from your buyer requirements:

Separate User IDs or email addresses with a comma, semicolon, or blank space.

[Submit]

*Figure 5-21: **Enter a list of User IDs to exempt buyers from your Block Bidder/Buyer List.***

UNDERSTANDING THE UNPAID ITEM DISPUTE PROCESS

The Unpaid Item Dispute process utilizes eBay as a communication vehicle for you and your buyers to come to a resolution when payment is not made for an item. Although there can be many permutations to a particular situation and a variety of outcomes, if you aren't paid and don't mutually come to an agreement, you can ultimately file for a Final Value credit and become eligible for a relisting credit. The buyer can wind up receiving an Unpaid Item *strike,* which can generate a warning from eBay or, ultimately, lead to a suspension of eBay privileges. A typical situation involves these steps.

1. You file an Unpaid Item Dispute (see "Submit and Review Unpaid Item Disputes"). Typically, from 7 to 45 days of the sale's closing, you can file a dispute outlining the situation and send eBay into action. (You can immediately do this after a sale if the buyer is no longer registered on eBay or if you and the buyer mutually agree to undo the transaction.)

2. eBay notifies the buyer through e-mail and pop-up messages that payment is due or requests confirmation that the buyer agreed to dispute resolution as outlined to eBay by the seller.

Continued . . .

Submit and Review Unpaid Item Disputes

An Unpaid Item Dispute starts the process of resolving issues with buyers who do not pay for delivered items (see the QuickFacts "Understanding the Unpaid Item Dispute Process").

1. Click **My eBay** on the eBay header.

2. In the My eBay Views sidebar on the left, scroll down and click **Dispute Console**.

   > Dispute Console

3. Under the As A Seller You Can, click **Report An Unpaid Item** to start the process. The Report An Unpaid Item Dispute page will be displayed.

4. Enter the **Item Number** in the text box, and click **Continue**.

5. On the next page, indicate why you're reporting the problem and its status. Click **Continue** and finalize the steps that are presented, which are dependent on the reason you're reporting and the status you chose.

Mediate Feedback with NetNeutrals

In eBay Motors, if you have a dispute with a buyer over a transaction for a vehicle, you can get negative feedback evaluated by a third party, NetNeutrals. This can be useful in certain cases if you feel there was significant reason why the negative rating was unreasonable. There is no equivalent mediation process in eBay's other selling arenas.

1. To begin the process, go to www.netneutrals. com. The page shown in Figure 5-22 is displayed.

2. Type in the Item Number and your eBay User ID, and click **Continue**.

3. You will be led through the process of appealing negative feedback that you think is unfair.

CAUTION

Try to avoid resolving disputes in such a way that the buyer is totally ticked off. Although you might be in the right (for example, you stipulated UPS ground shipping and the buyer wants a relatively modest monetary recourse because the item didn't arrive before he left for the south of France), the buyer can retaliate with negative feedback and tales of woe in the discussion boards, and can disparage your business reputation elsewhere. All it takes is for one potential buyer or bidder to avoid one of your sales for you to lose.

TIP

Click **Unpaid Item Process** on the left sidebar on the Dispute Console Overview page to find out about the process.

UICKSTEPS

UNDERSTANDING THE UNPAID
ITEM DISPUTE PROCESS (Continued)

3. eBay fosters communication between you and the buyer by providing scripted responses so the buyer can pay you or acknowledge payment owed to you. eBay also provides a message facility where you and the buyer can communicate without using your e-mail systems.

4. The dispute is closed by eBay after 60 days, if you don't close the dispute beforehand. You can close the dispute by indicating that you and the buyer completed the transaction (no credits to you and no strike to the buyer), you and the buyer agreed to not complete the transaction (you are eligible to receive credits and the buyer doesn't receive a strike), or you give up on the buyer (you are eligible to receive credits and the buyer receives a strike). If eBay closes the dispute, you will not receive a Final Value credit and the buyer will not receive a strike.

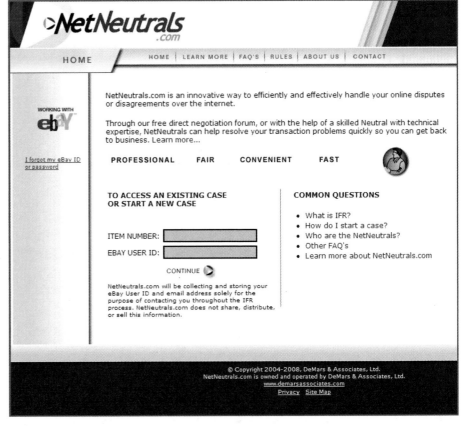

Figure 5-22: *Using NetNeutrals is the only way you can have negative feedback withdrawn if you are a seller in eBay Motors.*

NOTE

Only buyers can leave negative feedback—sellers may only leave positive feedback. For PowerSellers who have been with eBay at least a year, disgruntled buyers must wait for seven days before leaving negative feedback. There is no wait for customers of smaller eBay sellers. The only seller recourse for buyer negative feedback is to block suspected nonpaying buyers from bidding on their site. If a buyer's account is suspended, negative feedback will be removed.

TIP

To view the status of your Unpaid Item Disputes, click **Dispute Console** at the bottom of the My eBay Views sidebar. Any disputes within the last 90 days are listed.

Chapter 6
Setting Up an eBay Store

Beyond your listings, the eBay marketing machine provides a great avenue you can use to supercharge your business's presence on eBay: eBay Stores. An eBay Store allows the beginning eBay businessperson a quick, inexpensive, and effective way to sell merchandise online. You can do this without having to commit resources for new technologies or learn new procedures beyond the eBay basics you are already using. eBay Stores are an online storefront, providing a permanent location within eBay to help you sell your Store Inventory and eBay items, and to develop and grow a customer base. eBay Stores allow you a wide range of creativity and flexibility, including adding custom pages, highlighting promotions, and setting up categories. The basics of setting up an eBay store, along with these features, are described in this chapter (marketing tools and cross-promotional options, such as offering sales and sending e-mails to interested buyers, are covered in Chapter 10).

UNDERSTANDING THE FEATURES AND BENEFITS OF AN eBAY STORE

Some of the basic benefits and features of opening an eBay Store include:

- **Create eBay Store Inventory listings** (Buy It Now format) that run for greater lengths of time than standard listings (30 days or Good 'Til Canceled) to help minimize relisting headaches. No minimum number of listings required.

- **Save money** on eBay Store Inventory listings—for example, the insertion fee for a 30-day listing for an item that sells for under $25 is only $0.03. Though the insertion fees increase for items selling for more money ($0.05 for items selling between $25 and $199 and $0.10 for items selling for $200 and greater), they are still less much less than other listing types. Of course, a final value fee and listing upgrade fees, such as bolding, also apply.

- **Display standard auction and fixed-price listings within your Store** along with your Store Inventory listings (Figure 6-1 shows auction and Store Inventory listings). Your Store acts as an aggregator for all your eBay listings, while the reverse isn't true. That is, your Store Inventory fixed-price items don't show up in non-Store eBay category pages or searches, except when there is a lack of standard auction and fixed-price listings to display that meet the search criteria.

- **Organize your Store items** in up to 300 custom categories and sub-categories.

- **Obtain your own Uniform Resource Locator (URL)**, such as http://stores.ebay.com/all-things-paper, that you can provide to potential buyers, both in and out of eBay.

Continued . . .

Start an eBay Store

An eBay Store (or just *Store*) is designed for you to display quantities of merchandise for longer durations and in a less costly manner than with a traditional eBay listing. Creating the Store is a simple online process of choosing a layout; providing basic Store information, such as a description and logo; and selecting a level of service. The low overhead of $15.95 per month for "rent" to eBay should be easily covered with sales if you are determined to see your eBay activities as a real business.

Professor Polly says: "Control your expenses and work with the Basic Store (the basis for discussion in this chapter) until you see your volume has the potential to increase. At that point, consider the more advanced Store subscription levels and auction-management programs."

Store Inventory fixed-price listings, as opposed to standard fixed-price listings, typically don't show ending dates/times and can include sale prices.

Auction listings

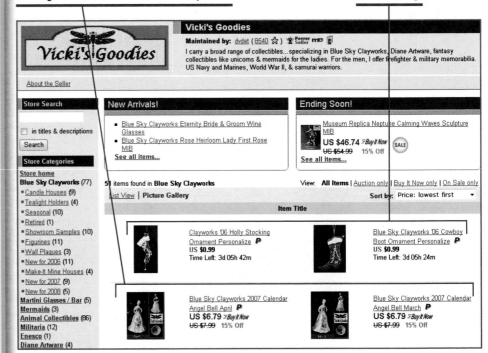

Figure 6-1: **Your auction listings also appear in your eBay Store.**

Open an eBay Store

1. To open an eBay Store , first ensure you meet the minimum requirements. You must maintain a seller's account with a credit card on file. Also, you must have a feedback rating of 20 or higher

   –Or–

   Be ID Verified

   –Or–

   Have a PayPal account in good standing

2. On an eBay page, click **Stores** on the eBay header.

3. On the eBay Stores home page, click **Open A Store** on the right sidebar.

4. On the Stores page, review the informational links on the sidebar. When you are ready to begin building your Store, under the eBay Stores Login sidebar, click the link next to **Open A Store**. Log in if prompted.

Select a Subscription Level and Name Your Store

1. On the Subscribe To eBay Stores: Choose Your Subscription Level page, select the Store subscription you want. Unless you have experience running an eBay Store, it is best to start with the Basic Store. You can always upgrade your subscription to a Premium or Anchor Store (see Figure 6-2) when your sales volume justifies the increase in the monthly cost.

2. Review eBay's opinion of the key benefits each subscription level provides.

3. In the Choose A Store Name text box, type the name you want for your Store. Besides the Don'ts listed in the accompanying Caution, *do* choose a name that is easy for

	Basic Store	Premium Store	Anchor Store
Monthly Subscription Fee	$15.95	$49.95	$299.95
Dedicated Customer Support	6am - 6pm PST	24/7 Access	24/7 Access
Build Your Store	Basic	Premium	Anchor
Store Home Page and Unlimited Product Pages *A single, branded place on the web where all your listings live.*	•	•	•
Custom Pages *Use customizable pages to boost your brand, communicate store policies, and connect with customers.*	5 pages	10 pages	15 pages
Customized Web Address *Get your very own URL (www.stores.ebay.com/yourstorename) so you can drive buyers directly to your Store.*	•	•	•
Promotion Boxes *Highlight premium merchandise in your Store to trigger sales.*	•	•	•
Store Categories *Help buyers browse your Store with up to 300 custom categories.*	300	300	300
Custom Store Header *Create a customized, branded header with merchandising and premium product links.*	•	•	•
eBay Header Reduction *Minimize the size of the eBay header and emphasize your own logo and branding.*		•	•

*Figure 6-2: **Choose from three Store plans with progressively increased costs and features.***

NOTE

Don't get too hung up on the name you initially choose for your Store. You can easily change it, but just do so before you develop a dedicated client base.

Choose a Store Name

Books Booklets Etc

17 characters remaining.

CAUTION

You need to abide by several rules when naming a Store. For example, it cannot contain several characters (<, >, or @) or sequences of characters (cannot start with more than three consecutive letter A's or start with the letter *e* followed by a number); it cannot contain an eBay User ID other than your own; and it cannot contain "www" or anything similar to a trademarked company name (for example, eBay or PayPal).

customers to remember, easy for them to type, as your Store's name becomes part of its Web address (or *URL*), such as http://stores.ebay.com/mikes-books (blanks are hyphenated), and describes what you sell.

4. When ready, click **Continue**. Sign in if prompted.

5. When you have successfully named your Store (if you didn't abide by eBay's rules, you will be notified how to correct your mistake), review discounted features available to you based on the subscription level, and click **Continue**.

Choose a Store Name

All Things Paper

⚠ Name cannot be the same as another user's name on eBay. To see all the requirements for a Store name, please click or the "Learn more about naming your Store" link below.

Subscribe to eBay Stores: Review & Submit

You have selected: **Basic Store and Selling Manager ($15.95 per month)**

Basic Store	$15.95
Selling Manager	4.99
Basic Store subscriber discount for Selling Manager	-4.99
Total	**$15.95**

Before using this software, you must read and agree to these license
terms and conditions. If you do not agree with any of the
provisions you must not accept this agreement.

License Grant:

eBay Inc. ("eBay") hereby grants you the right to use the software

☑ I accept the User Agreement.

Please tell us how you heard about this product: Promotional link on eBay ▾

Subscribe   Back | Cancel

Figure 6-3: *A few administrative actions and review is all that separates you from opening your eBay Store.*

NOTE

If you've opened an eBay Store previously, there is a good chance that eBay will "remember" many of your settings, which is fine if your new Store is similar to your old Store. However, if you are now selling different items under a new name/logo and so forth, you will have to modify many legacy settings to make the changeover complete.

6. On the Subscribe To eBay Stores: Review & Submit page, shown in Figure 6-3, look over the monthly cost, review the terms and conditions, and click the **I Accept The User Agreement** check box. Provide eBay a little marketing feedback by selecting the means by which you heard of eBay Stores.

7. When finished, click **Subscribe** to finalize your application. If you develop a severe case of post-decisional dissonance (also known as buyer's remorse)—not to worry, eBay provides the first 30 days free for Basic and Premium Stores for first-time Store owners, so you can cancel either Store without incurring a subscription fee (listing and final value fees will still apply).

Choose the right subscription package for you.

Open a Store now!

Try it FREE for 30 Days
Basic or Premium Store.
First-time subscribers only*

Your Store is immediately created, and you're provided a unique URL that takes you directly to your Store.

Subscribe to eBay Stores: Congratulations

 You have successfully subscribed to Basic Store and Selling Manager.

You'll receive confirmation emails shortly. All of your active listings will appear in your new eBay Store.

Your Store URL is: http://stores.ebay.com/

8. If you want to get a basic look-and-feel Store set up quickly, click **Start Quick Store Tuneup** (see the "Setting Up a Store Quickly" QuickSteps).

stores 🏪 Quick Store Setup
Take a few seconds to use Quick Store Setup to customize your Store and create a unique shopping experience for your buyers

[Start Quick Store Setup >]

–Or–

You can customize your Store's layout and design from Manage Your Store links on several Store and eBay pages (see "Modify Store Settings" in the next section). Several Store features you can set up or change to customize your Store are covered in "Customize Your Store" later in this chapter.

Browser Earl says: "View your eBay Store at http:// stores.ebay.com/<your-store-name> (add a hyphen between words in your Store name when typing the URL in your browser's address bar)."

QUICKSTEPS

SETTING UP A STORE QUICKLY

When you first subscribe to a Store, you can choose to have eBay provide you a generic Store to get yourself up and running in short order (of course, you will need to add inventory to stock your Store).

1. After clicking **Start Quick Store Setup** (see "Select a Subscription Level and Name Your Store"), the Quick Store Setup page opens. To create a Store with all the recommended settings, simply click **Apply Settings** at the top of the page (at a minimum, you will want to create your own Store description, either now or later in the "Modify Store Settings" section).

[Apply Settings]

2. To use the recommended settings as a baseline from which to modify, scroll down the page, click **Edit** in the area you want to modify, and make any changes, as shown in Figure 6-4. When satisfied, click **Preview Settings** beneath the store design mini-mockup to see how your changes will look.

3. When ready, click **Apply Settings** to have your Store accept the changes.

   –Or–

   Click **Restore Defaults** at the bottom of the page to return to eBay's initial recommendation and continue working on your design.

TIP

You will get toll-free phone support as part of your eBay Store subscription. Phone support for Basic Stores is available Monday through Friday, 6:00 A.M. to 6:00 P.M. Pacific Time (Premium and Anchor Stores are provided 24/7 access). To access the toll-free number, click **Manage Your Store** in My eBay or from the Store's home page.

My Subscriptions
Manage My Store
Sales Reports

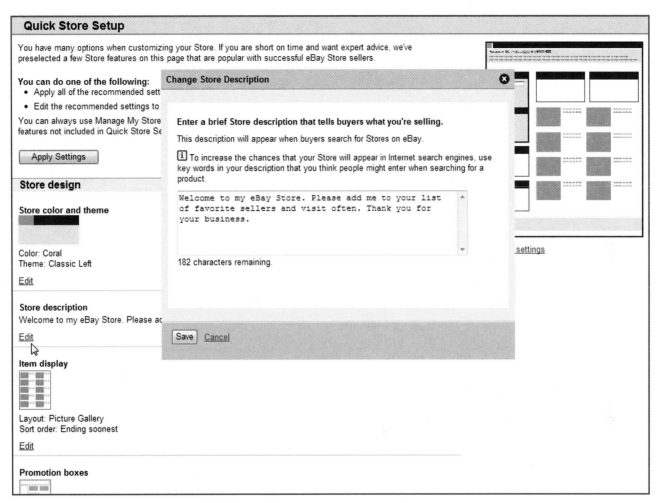

Quick Store Setup

You have many options when customizing your Store. If you are short on time and want expert advice, we've preselected a few Store features on this page that are popular with successful eBay Store sellers.

You can do one of the following:
- Apply all of the recommended sett
- Edit the recommended settings to

You can always use Manage My Store features not included in Quick Store Se

[Apply Settings]

Store design

Store color and theme

Color: Coral
Theme: Classic Left

Edit

Store description
Welcome to my eBay Store. Please a

Edit

Item display

Layout: Picture Gallery
Sort order: Ending soonest

Edit

Promotion boxes

Change Store Description

Enter a brief Store description that tells buyers what you're selling.

This description will appear when buyers search for Stores on eBay.

ⓘ To increase the chances that your Store will appear in Internet search engines, use key words in your description that you think people might enter when searching for a product.

> Welcome to my eBay Store. Please add me to your list
> of favorite sellers and visit often. Thank you for
> your business.

182 characters remaining.

settings

[Save] Cancel

Figure 6-4: **You can easily modify the recommended eBay settings in the Quick Store Tuneup, or, just as easily, you can access the same settings at your leisure from the Manage My Store page.**

Modify Store Settings

While there is a plethora of optional things you can do to customize your Store, there is a short list of things that you really need to do to get maximum exposure from prospective buyers. The tools to make these changes, as well as to modify and customize your other Store features, are conveniently located on the Manage My Store page, shown in Figure 6-5. You can open this page from a link on your Store's home page or from other pages in eBay.

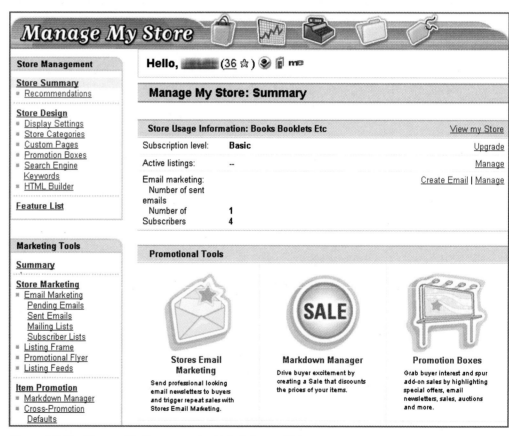

Figure 6-5: *The Manage My Store page is the hub from which you can customize all aspects of your eBay Store.*

OPEN THE MANAGE MY STORE PAGE

1. Display your Store's home page by typing its URL in your browser's address bar and pressing **ENTER** (type the URL in the form http://stores.ebay.com/*your-store-name*).

   –Or–

   Clicking the Store icon  displayed next to your User ID and feedback score displayed on various eBay pages.

   In either case, your Store's home page will display.

2. Scroll down the page, and to the right of the An eBay Store Maintained By heading and your User ID, click **Seller, Manage Store**.

An eBay Store maintained by: ___ (36 ☆) **me** 🗐	Seller, manage Store

3. Alternatively, you can open the Manage My Store page by clicking links of the same name from My eBay (under the My Subscriptions sidebar), the eBay Stores home page (the right sidebar), eBay e-mails, and several other eBay pages.

ESTABLISH BASIC STORE INFORMATION

1. On your Manage My Store page, click **Display Settings** on the sidebar. The first section, Basic Information, contains the current key information about your Store. Click **Change** to the right of the section header.

PowerSeller Sally says: "Give your description some serious consideration. This is your first impression with potential buyers. You need to concisely let them know who you are and what you have for sale."

2. On the Edit Basic Information page, you can modify your Store name, its description, and add a logo using one of several methods, as shown in Figure 6-6. You can select a predesigned logo from one of several categories.

   –Or–

   Upload and select a picture file from your local computer to eBay Picture Manager (free).

   –Or–

Provide a URL to a picture file hosted outside of eBay.

–Or–

If you don't find a logo you like, you can omit it.

3. Select the method of adding a logo (or not adding one), and when finished, click **Save Settings**. If you don't have a logo available, you can always come back and add one later.

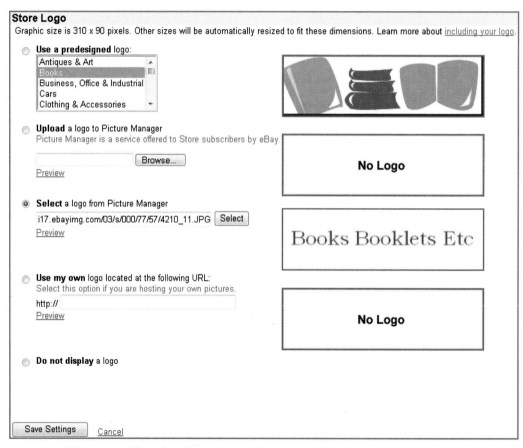

Figure 6-6: **A logo can add a unique flavor to your Store, separating you from the rest of the crowd and reminding customers of the types of items you have for sale.**

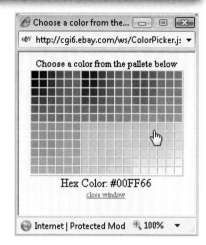

CHOOSE A THEME

Themes provide a unified appearance to all the pages in your eBay Store.

1. On your Manage My Store page, click **Display Settings** on the sidebar. The second section on the Display Settings page, Theme And Display, allows you to change a current theme or switch to a new theme. To change your current theme, click **Edit Current Theme** next to the Store Theme mini-mockup. You can change color and fonts for several of the themes' attributes by selecting colors from a color swatch or by choosing font attributes from drop-down lists. As you make changes, the sample page reflects the changes you are applying.

   –Or–

   To change to a new theme, on the Display Settings page, click **Change To Another Theme** next to the Store Theme mini-mockup. Select one of the four categories of themes from the left sidebar, as shown in Figure 6-7. Click the sample theme thumbnails to see a larger version and a description of how the pages are laid out. Click the option button next to the name of the theme you want, and select a color if choosing one of the Classic/Easily Customizable themes.

2. In either case, click **Save Settings** at the bottom of their respective pages to change your Store's theme.

CHANGE YOUR STORE'S LAYOUT

There are several display features in your Store that you can choose to show or not and modify how some of them appear.

1. On your Manage My Store page, click **Display Settings** on the sidebar. The lower part of the second section on the Display Settings page, Theme And Display, allows you to change settings for the left navigation bar, whether to add additional material to your Store header and how to display the eBay header (Premium or Anchor subscription required), and whether to display items for sale by default in Gallery or List View, as well as how to sort them.

2. Click **Change** to the right of the settings you want to view or change. Unless you have a specific reason to make a change, the eBay default settings work just fine. The setting you might consider changing sooner rather than later is the Store Page Header. You can include more information about your Store or highlight listings by adding to the standard Store header viewed on each page in your Store, as shown in Figure 6-8 and described in the "Adding to Your Store Header" QuickSteps.

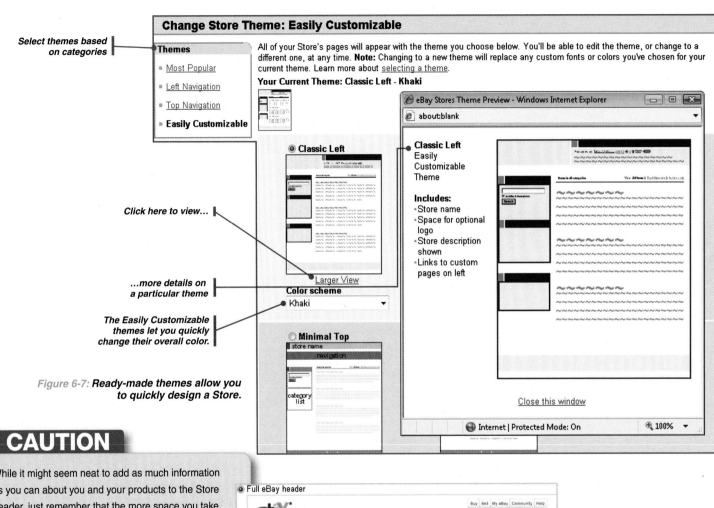

Select themes based on categories

Change Store Theme: Easily Customizable

Themes

- Most Popular
- Left Navigation
- Top Navigation
- **Easily Customizable**

All of your Store's pages will appear with the theme you choose below. You'll be able to edit the theme, or change to a different one, at any time. **Note:** Changing to a new theme will replace any custom fonts or colors you've chosen for your current theme. Learn more about selecting a theme.

Your Current Theme: Classic Left - Khaki

Classic Left

Click here to view...

...more details on a particular theme

Larger View

Color scheme

Khaki

The Easily Customizable themes let you quickly change their overall color.

Minimal Top

store name

navigation

category list

eBay Stores Theme Preview - Windows Internet Explorer

about:blank

Classic Left Easily Customizable Theme

Includes:
- Store name
- Space for optional logo
- Store description shown
- Links to custom pages on left

Close this window

Internet | Protected Mode: On   100%

Figure 6-7: **Ready-made themes allow you to quickly design a Store.**

CAUTION

While it might seem neat to add as much information as you can about you and your products to the Store header, just remember that the more space you take up toward the top of the Store's page with tourist information, the more you detract potential customers from seeing your listings, which is the whole point of having a Store. You can mitigate the issue by using the space to highlight listings (see Figure 6-8) and choosing to minimize the eBay header (if you have a Premium or Anchor Store).

Full eBay header

Minimal eBay header
This setting is unavailable for your current subscription level. Consider upgrading your subscription to get even more flexibility in customizing your Store. Upgrade your subscription.

Figure 6-8: *You can modify your default Store header to accentuate aspects of your Store.*

QUICKSTEPS

ADDING TO YOUR STORE HEADER

You can add text, pictures, or links to listings and Store pages to the bottom of your current Store header.

1. From the Manage Your Store page, click **Display Settings** on the sidebar. Scroll down to the Store Header Display setting, and click **Change**.

2. On the Edit Store Header Display page, click **Yes, Include Additional Information In The Header**, and then click one of the three links to add text, pictures through Picture Manager, or links to listings or Store pages.

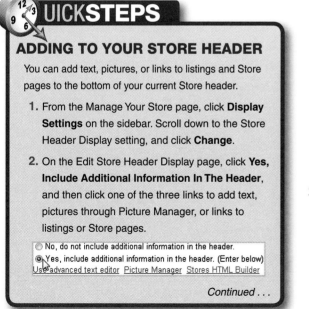

Continued . . .

Customize Your Store

If you look at several eBay Stores, you will quickly notice an uncanny similarity among many of them. These Stores have accepted eBay's defaults, which are not all that bad, but you can achieve a high degree of differentiation from the crowd by creating Store categories, promotion boxes, and custom pages. The small amount of time you will invest will give your Store the personal look and feel you could accomplish in your own physical storefront.

Set Up Store Categories

You can organize your listings by placing them in up to 300 "departments," or *categories,* within your Store. This is a way for visitors to your Store to find products that appeal to them. When you put your Store items in categories, you create a path to the items that are of interest to them. If you are unsure of the categories to create, take a look at eBay Stores that are selling similar material.

UICKSTEPS

ADDING TO YOUR STORE HEADER
(Continued)

3. For example, to add links to your listings, click **Stores HTML Builder**. In the HTML Builder window, under Advanced Link Builder, click **Build Links To Items**:

- In the Build Links To Items window, add a title if you want, select colors, and add up to 20 item numbers and associated link data: the item number, text that will become the link buyers click, a hosted or Picture Manager picture, and a description. Click **Continue**.

- On the Preview Links To Items page, look over your links. When finished, click **Insert HTML** to add the code to the text box on the Edit Store Header Display page (see Step 2).

4. Click **Save Settings**.

```
<table cellspacing="0" cellpadding="0"
border="0"><tr><td><table cellspacing="0"
cellpadding="0" border="0" width="100%"><tr
bgcolor="#333300"><td width="14" nowrap
valign="middle"></td><td height="24" nowrap
colspan="3" valign="middle"><font
face="Arial" size="4" color="#F6F6C9">Check
out our Paper!!!</font></td><td width="14"
nowrap
valign="middle"></td></tr></table><table
cellspacing="0" cellpadding="0" border="0"
width="100%"><tr><td height="1" nowrap
bgcolor="#ffffff" colspan="4"
width="100%"></td></tr><tr><td height="7"
nowrap bgcolor="#999966" colspan="4"
```

NOTE

eBay Store categories do not need to match the eBay categories assigned to an item's listing. When you list a Store Inventory item, you will have the opportunity to choose four level 1 categories: an eBay main and secondary category (for display in certain eBay searches), a main Store category, and a second Store category. If you don't choose a Store category, the item is listed in the Store's default Other Items category.

CREATE CATEGORIES

The first categories you create are level 1 categories, and each can have up to two levels of sub-categories created below them in a hierarchical order.

1. Display your eBay Store's home page. (Type the Store's URL into your browser's address bar, or go to My eBay and click the eBay Store icon next to your User ID.)

2. On your Store's home page, scroll down and click **Seller**, **Manage Store**.

3. On the Manage My Store page, click **Store Categories** on the sidebar.

4. On the Manage Store Categories page, click **Add Category**.

Manage Store Categories

Use Store categories to organize your listings. Category names appear in the left-hand navigation bar of your Store. Review the Store category guidelines for tips on creating effective Store categories.

Reorder Categories

Category: **All Categories**　　　　Add Category

Category (level 1)	# of Subcategories	# of Listings
Other items	--	0

All Categories: **0** of **300** created

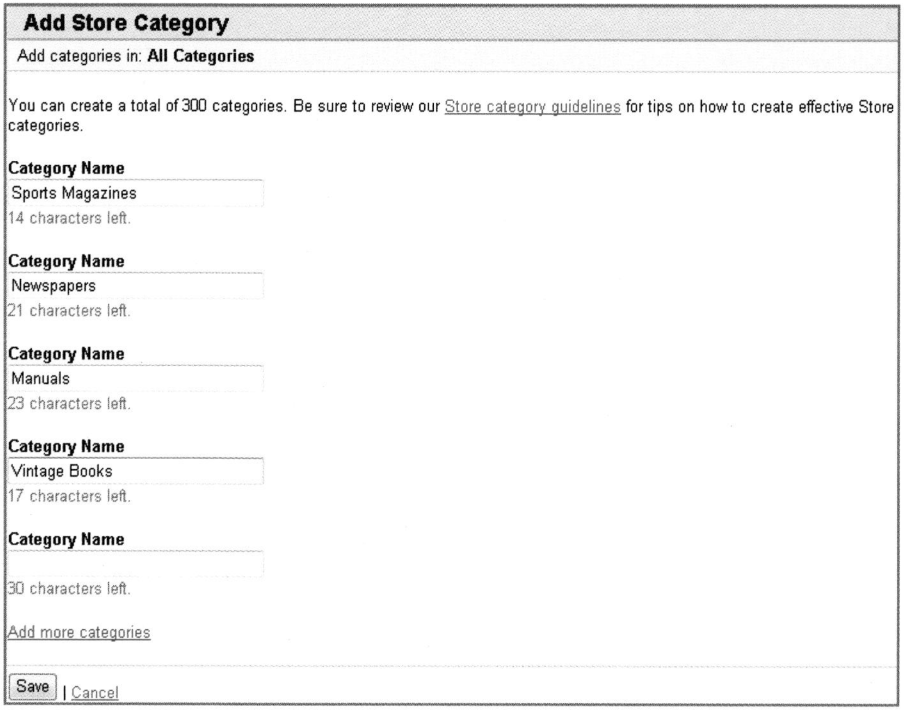

Add Store Category

Add categories in: **All Categories**

You can create a total of 300 categories. Be sure to review our Store category guidelines for tips on how to create effective Store categories.

Category Name

Sports Magazines

14 characters left.

Category Name

Newspapers

21 characters left.

Category Name

Manuals

23 characters left.

Category Name

Vintage Books

17 characters left.

Category Name

30 characters left.

Add more categories

Save | Cancel

*Figure 6-9: **You can add categories by simply typing the name you want for each.***

5. On the Add Store Category page (see Figure 6-9), starting with the first Category Name box, type the text of the first category you want. Continue adding categories as needed. If you need more than the list on the page, click **Add More Categories**. Don't be concerned about the order in which they appear, as you can easily move them (see "Change the Order of Categories" next).

6. Click **Save** when finished. eBay will acknowledge the creation of your categories and let you know they will be available for viewing in your Store shortly (which can be quite a while).

Manage Store Categories

You've successfully created Store categories.
Note: Your changes will appear within a few minutes.

CHANGE THE ORDER OF CATEGORIES

You can change how categories are listed as they appear in your Store.

1. On the Manage Store Categories page, click **Reorder Categories**. On the Reorder Store Categories page, shown in Figure 6-10, choose to reorder alphabetically, by quantity of listings in each category, or by manually setting the order.

Reorder Categories

Add Category

# of Listings

11

TIP

To create sub-categories, simply click the link of an existing category name on the Manage Store Categories page. A new page is displayed as before. Click **Add Category**. An Add Store Category page appears where you can add level 2 subcategory names as you did for level 1 categories. Continue the same logic to add level 3 categories. When you are finished, click **All Categories** in the column heading bar. You will see the # Of Subcategories number increased.

TIP

To rename or delete a category, click the check box to the left of its name on the Manage Store Categories page (if modifying a sub-category, click the category name first to reveal the next level of sub-categories). Click **Rename** or **Delete** below the list of categories/sub-categories. To rename, type a new name, and click **Save**; to delete, confirm the permanent deletion, and click **Delete** a second time.

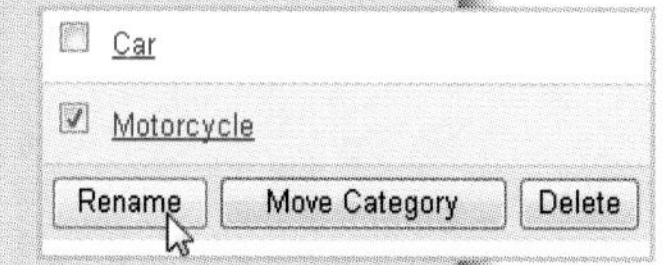

Car

Motorcycle

Rename   Move Category   Delete

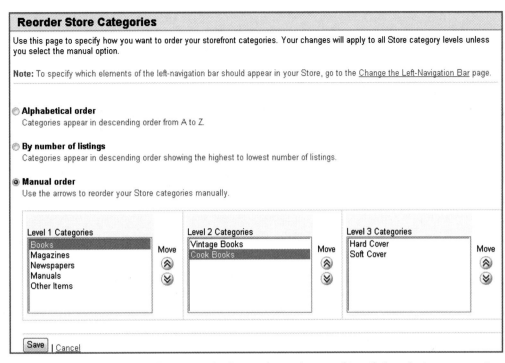

Reorder Store Categories

Use this page to specify how you want to order your storefront categories. Your changes will apply to all Store category levels unless you select the manual option.

Note: To specify which elements of the left-navigation bar should appear in your Store, go to the Change the Left-Navigation Bar page.

○ **Alphabetical order**
Categories appear in descending order from A to Z.

○ **By number of listings**
Categories appear in descending order showing the highest to lowest number of listings.

◉ **Manual order**
Use the arrows to reorder your Store categories manually.

Level 1 Categories	Move	Level 2 Categories	Move	Level 3 Categories	Move
Books		Vintage Books		Hard Cover	
Magazines		Cook Books		Soft Cover	
Newspapers					
Manuals					
Other Items					

[Save] | Cancel

Figure 6-10: **Manually reordering categories lets you organize your Store listings just as you want your customers to see them.**

TIP

Your most popular category should be first in your list of categories.

TIP

To learn more about the Store features described in this and other chapters, as well as additional features, on the Manage My Store page, under the Store Management sidebar, click **Feature List** to view a comprehensive list of links to things you can do with your Store.

2. To manually change the order of categories, click the category you want to move, and then click the **Move** up and down buttons to the right of the category listing to place the category in the order you want. To change the order of sub-categories, first click the higher-level category containing them to expose the next level of sub-categories.

3. Click **Save** when finished.

CHANGE A CATEGORY AFTER SUBMITTING A STORE LISTING

You can change the eBay Store category for a Store item you have for sale.

1. In your My eBay Items I'm Selling view or in your auction-management program, select the revision option for the listing you want to change.

2. At the top of the listing, make changes to the main or second Store category, as shown in Figure 6-11. Save your settings.

Add Promotion Boxes to Your Store

Promotion boxes are defined areas on your Store pages that provide buyers additional information about your items. For example, you can display up to a maximum of four items that are newly listed or ending soon, clickable graphics to other Store pages or items, and links to your Store categories or to custom

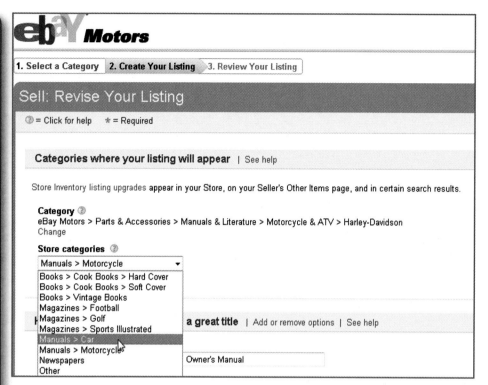

Figure 6-11: *You can easily change the Store category for an active Store Inventory item.*

QUICKSTEPS

CREATING A STORE INVENTORY LISTING

A listing you create for your eBay Store is almost identical to auction or fixed-price listings you create when listing traditionally through eBay.com. When creating a Store Inventory listing:

1. Select the Store Inventory format. Any of your listings using the auction or fixed-price/Buy It Now formats will appear in your Store, but they are not Store Inventory listings. Visually, to the buyer, both formats appear similar, one difference being that non-Store Inventory fixed-price listings have a maximum duration of ten days and typically, Store Inventory listings don't show a listing end time/date. The easiest way to tell the difference between the two fixed-price formats is to view your listings in My eBay and see which listing format icon appears in the Format column.

2. In addition to selecting an eBay category, select a main Store category and an optional (free) second Store category (see "Set Up Store Categories").

3. Enter only a Buy It Now price since there is no bidding on Store Inventory listings (buyers can submit a Best Offer price that you can accept or reject, just as with other formats).

4. Select a listing duration of 30 days or Good 'Til Canceled, which continues to relist every 30 days. You are charged according to duration based on your listing price (see the "Understanding the Features and Benefits of an eBay Store" QuickFacts earlier in the chapter).

pages within your Store and other eBay pages. You can choose where you want the promotion box placed on a Store page from several predefined locations: across the top of the listings area (either as two discrete boxes or one long one) or two custom boxes under the navigation bar on the left side of Store pages. You can create them all at once or, for more flexibility, work through each box location individually (of course, you can always go back and edit each box after you've initially create them).

CREATE PROMOTION BOXES QUICKLY

Using Guided Setup, you can quickly set up promotion boxes and try them out in your Store without having to select numerous options. You can view a

Promotion Boxes

Show: **All Active** | Categories | Custom Pages | Left Navigation | Inactive

Name	Title text	Type	Location ▲	Actions
eBay Guided Setup Position 1		Items	All Items - Top left	Select ▼
eBay Guided Setup Position 2		Items	All Items - Top right	Select ▼
Upper sidebar	Shipping & Payment	Custom	Left navigation - Upper	Select ▼
eBay Guided Setup Position 4	Store Newsletter!	Custom	Left navigation - Lower	Select ▼

| Create New Promotion Box | Guided Setup |

Figure 6-12: **View and manage existing promotion boxes and initiate creating new boxes in one location.**

sample of your Store pages with the boxes in place, and you can change or remove individual boxes.

1. On your Store's home page, scroll down and click **Seller**, **Manage Store**.

2. On the Manage My Store page, under Store Design on the left sidebar, click **Promotion Boxes**.

3. On the Promotion Boxes page, shown in Figure 6-12, you will see a list of any promotion boxes you have already created and the tools to manage them (see "Manage Promotion Boxes" later in the chapter). To create a new box, click **Guided Setup** to create a set of four boxes on the Guided Setup: Create Promotion Boxes In Your Store page, New Arrivals and Ending Soon across the top of your listings, and a custom links box and custom box to communicate to your customers, both under the Store navigation bar.

4. On the Guided Setup page, shown in Figure 6-13, do one or more of the following:

   ● Click **Preview A Sample Page** to see how your Store pages will look with the default promotion box offerings.

   ● Click **Change Promotion Box** or **Remove Promotion Box** under each box location to modify or remove a box from your pages (only available after you have set up a promotion box).

   ● Click **Create Promotion Box** under Promotion Box Location 3 or 4 to create a custom box below your Store's navigation bar.

5. Click **Activate Promotion Boxes** to display your selections on your Store pages. Figure 6-1 shows promotion boxes that appear across the listings area of a Store's pages.

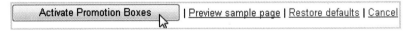
Activate Promotion Boxes | Preview sample page | Restore defaults | Cancel

CREATE CUSTOM PROMOTION BOXES

1. On your Store's home page, scroll down and click **Seller**, **Manage Store**.

2. On the Manage My Store page, click **Promotion Boxes** on the sidebar.

3. On the Promotion Boxes page, click **Create New Promotion Box** (see Figure 6-12).

Guided Setup: Create Promotion Boxes in Your Store

You can create customizable promotion boxes on various pages in your Store. Use them to promote items, help buyers navigate your Store, or give buyers useful information as they shop.

To help you get started, we've provided some promotion boxes you can use right away. Just review them below and click **Activate Promotion Boxes**.

Want to see what your pages will look like? Preview a sample page.

For full customization and control, you can manage your promotion boxes.

All category pages

These promotion boxes will appear at the top of the item list on all of your category pages. Even though the types of promotions will remain the same on each page, the items featured may rotate periodically.

Promotion Box - Location ①
New Arrivals: By default, this promotion box will highlight two items from the page that you have listed recently - helping to keep buyers up to date on the latest developments in your Store.
Change promotion box | Remove promotion box

New Arrivals!

- New York Times Apollo 11 Splash Down Announcement
- 1985 Harley Davidson Sportster 1000cc Owner's Manual

See all items...

Promotion Box - Location ②
Ending Soon: By default, this promotion box will highlight one item from the page that will be ending soon - encouraging your buyers to act quickly.
Change promotion box | Remove promotion box

Ending Soon!

Olympia Challenge Bowl One Program, PAC 8 vs BIG 10
US $10.00
Time Left: 27d 2h 32m 55s
See all items...

*Figure 6-13: **Quickly add promotion boxes by accepting the default choices eBay provides.***

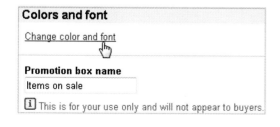

Colors and font

Change color and font

Promotion box name
Items on sale

ⓘ This is for your use only and will not appear to buyers.

4. On the first Create Promotion Box page, select the type of box you want, as shown in Figure 6-14, and click **Continue**. The type of promotion box you select will determine the other available options.

5. On the second page, select the location for the box, and if you have created categories (see "Set Up Store Categories" earlier in the chapter), you can choose to have the box displayed on all category pages, on the All Items page, or on a category page you choose. Click **Continue** when finished.

6. On the last Create Promotion Box page, determine the content of the box. The options you see depend on the type of box you chose in Step 4. For example, you can set up custom links to Store and other Web pages, you can choose how listings appear in the box (Gallery or List View), or you can add a title and text to fully customize a box.

7. In the Colors And Font area of the page, click **Change Color And Font** to make any desired changes to the default colors of your Store. Also, provide a name for the box for your own use.

8. Click **Save** when finished.

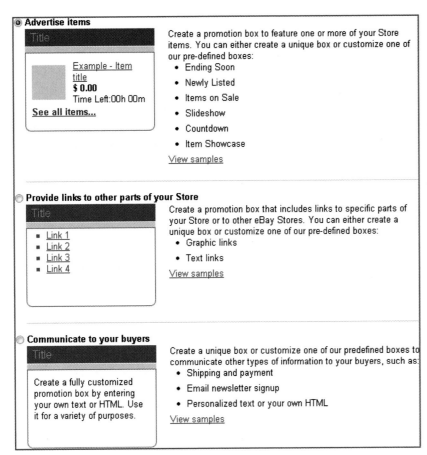

Advertise items

Title

Example - Item
title
$ 0.00
Time Left:00h 00m

See all items...

Create a promotion box to feature one or more of your Store items. You can either create a unique box or customize one of our pre-defined boxes:
• Ending Soon
• Newly Listed
• Items on Sale
• Slideshow
• Countdown
• Item Showcase

View samples

Provide links to other parts of your Store

Title

■ Link 1
■ Link 2
■ Link 3
■ Link 4

Create a promotion box that includes links to specific parts of your Store or to other eBay Stores. You can either create a unique box or customize one of our pre-defined boxes:
• Graphic links
• Text links

View samples

Communicate to your buyers

Title

Create a fully customized promotion box by entering your own text or HTML. Use it for a variety of purposes.

Create a unique box or customize one of our predefined boxes to communicate other types of information to your buyers, such as:
• Shipping and payment
• Email newsletter signup
• Personalized text or your own HTML

View samples

Figure 6-14: **You can choose from three types of promotion boxes.**

MANAGE PROMOTION BOXES

After you create promotion boxes, you can change, duplicate, or remove them from the Promotion Boxes page.

1. On the Manage My Store page, click **Promotion Boxes** on the sidebar. The Promotion Boxes page displays (see Figure 6-12), listing your current promotion boxes.

2. Click the **Actions** down arrow next to the promotion box to which you want to perform an action:

● Click **View** to display promotion boxes on your Store's home page.

● Click **Edit** to open the Edit Promotion Box page, similar to the Create New Promotion Box page described earlier. Make any changes and click **Save**.

● Click **Duplicate** to open the Duplicate Promotion Box page, which basically starts the Create New Promotion Box process, except it skips the first action of selecting a type of box.

● Click **Remove** to no longer display a promotion box on your Store pages. On the Remove Promotion Box page, select whether to make the box *inactive* (available to you but no longer displayed in your Store) or to delete the box permanently. Click **Remove**.

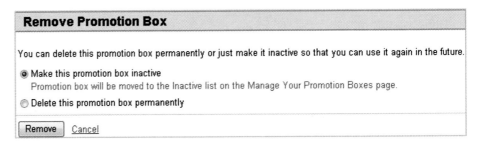

Remove Promotion Box

You can delete this promotion box permanently or just make it inactive so that you can use it again in the future.

● Make this promotion box inactive
  Promotion box will be moved to the Inactive list on the Manage Your Promotion Boxes page.

○ Delete this promotion box permanently

Remove Cancel

Add Custom Pages

You've probably visited eBay Stores that look quite a bit different from your Store when it was first created. The owners of those Stores created custom pages, and so can you. Custom pages allow you to change how your storefront appears and let you provide information to your buyers regarding a myriad of subjects. Custom pages, as the name implies, give you the opportunity to separate your business from those selling similar products—so use them to your advantage! For example, you can create a page and describe your Store policies, provide information about your business, use it to promote items, and just about anything else you want.

CREATE A CUSTOM PAGE

1. On your Store's home page, scroll down and click **Seller**, **Manage Store**.

2. On the Manage My Store page, click **Custom Pages** on the sidebar. The Custom Pages page displays any custom pages you've created and provides a link to create new pages.

3. Under Active Pages, click **Create New Page**. The Create Custom Page: Select Layout page displays the first of three steps used to create the custom page. Read the five definitions at the top of the page to understand the possible elements you can add to a custom page (see "Add Promotion Boxes to Your Store" for more information on the first element). Scroll down the page, and select the layout that best meets your needs, as shown in Figure 6-15, and then click **Continue**.

4. The Create Custom Page: Provide Content page provides tools for you to attach content based on the layout you previously selected. The areas you might encounter include:

   - **Selected Layout** shows the layout you chose on the Select Layout page and describes the elements your layout offers. You can change the layout after you create a page title.

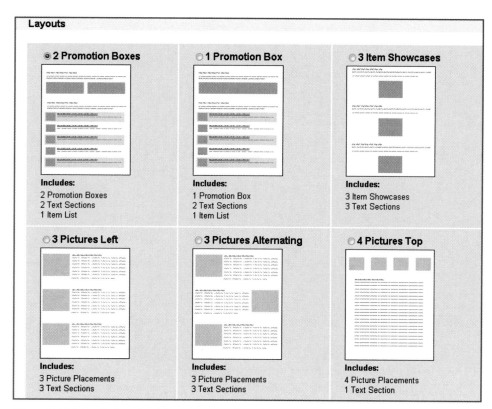

Figure 6-15: *You start customizing your page by selecting a layout from several options.*

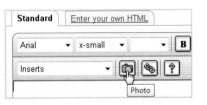

- **Page Title** becomes the label for the link to the custom page. It appears on your Store's left sidebar, under the Store Pages section. Be descriptive in your choice of page title since it is used by search engines, such as Google, to find your page when queried by a buyer.

- **Text Section** contains one or more text boxes that support the typing or pasting of text (if your layout includes multiple text sections, you will see a Text Section for each one). On the Standard tab, you can format text you enter using the tools in the provided toolbars; or, using the **Enter Your Own HTML** tab, you can format your text with Hypertext Markup Language (HTML) tags. The interface is similar to the one used when entering a description in the familiar Sell Your Item form. In addition, you can use Picture Manager to upload pictures you want to display, or you can type the URL for a self-hosted picture.

- **Promotion Box** contains selections regarding the type of promotion box you want, the name for each box you create, and the content that will be in the box. You will have an equal number of Promotion Box sections in the Select Layout page as you do promotion boxes in your layout's design.

- **Item List** contains criteria for the items you want to display and lets you display them in Gallery or List format.

- **Left Navigation Bar** lets you hide or display the list of links that normally appears on the left side of Store pages.

Click **Continue** when finished setting up the content for the page.

5. On the Create Custom Page: Preview & Publish page, preview how your custom page will appear. Click **Back** to make any changes. Click **Save And Publish** when finished. The page, an example of which is shown in Figure 6-16, is added to your list of active custom pages, and its title will appear under Store Pages in the left navigation bar of your Store pages (only the Store pages you have designated to display in the left navigation bar will list your custom pages).

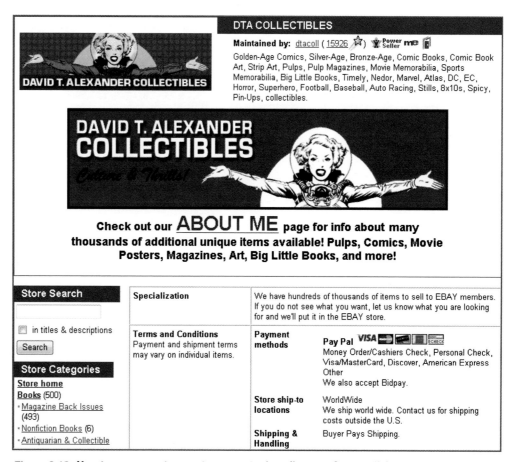

Figure 6-16: *You, too, can create a custom page to describe your Store policies.*

MANAGE CUSTOM PAGES

1. On your Store's home page, scroll down and click **Seller**, **Manage Store**.

2. On the Manage My Store page, click **Custom Pages** on the sidebar. The Custom Pages page displays your active pages (pages currently seen by buyers), inactive pages (pages you created but that are hidden to buyers), and the home page, as shown in Figure 6-17.

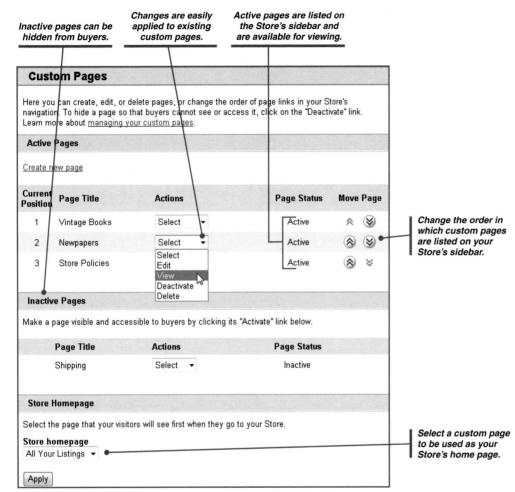

Inactive pages can be hidden from buyers.

Changes are easily applied to existing custom pages.

Active pages are listed on the Store's sidebar and are available for viewing.

Custom Pages

Here you can create, edit, or delete pages, or change the order of page links in your Store's navigation. To hide a page so that buyers cannot see or access it, click on the "Deactivate" link. Learn more about managing your custom pages.

Active Pages

Create new page

Current Position	Page Title	Actions	Page Status	Move Page
1	Vintage Books	Select ▾	Active	⌃ ⌄
2	Newpapers	Select ▾	Active	⌃ ⌄
		Select		
		Edit		
		View		
		Deactivate		
3	Store Policies	Delete	Active	⌃ ⌄

Change the order in which custom pages are listed on your Store's sidebar.

Inactive Pages

Make a page visible and accessible to buyers by clicking its "Activate" link below.

Page Title	Actions	Page Status
Shipping	Select ▾	Inactive

Store Homepage

Select the page that your visitors will see first when they go to your Store.

Store homepage
All Your Listings ▾

Select a custom page to be used as your Store's home page.

Apply

Figure 6-17: *Custom pages can be easily modified, displayed, hidden, or selected to be your Store's home page.*

3. Click the **Actions** down arrow next to the custom page on which you want to perform an action:

- Click **Edit** to make changes in a format similar to the Create Custom Page: Provide Content page described earlier.

- Click **View** to display the custom page.

- Click **Deactivate** to move a custom page from active to inactive status, or click **Activate** to move a custom page from inactive to active status.

- Click **Delete** to permanently remove a custom page from your inventory. Confirm that you want to delete the page by clicking **Delete Now** on the Confirmation page that appears.

4. Click the **Move Page** arrows to the right of each page to change the order in which pages appear in the Store Pages section of the left navigation bar on all Store pages.

5. Click the **Store Homepage** down arrow, and click the custom page you want to first display when a buyer opens your Store. The All Your Listings page is the default page that displays unless you make a change to a custom page.

6. Click **Apply** when finished.

Chapter 7
Selling for Others

As an experienced seller on eBay, you're probably always bombarded with questions from friends, relatives, and cocktail party acquaintances about how they, too, can join in on your eBay success. One option is to spend hours with them, teaching them the ins and outs of your business. Alternatively, you could buy them a copy of this book. Your best option in terms of continuing to be a profitable eBay business is to offer to sell their items on eBay for them. Selling for others on eBay as a business, or *consignment selling,* can be as simple as selling items for friends out of your home, or it can be as involved as opening a brick-and-mortar storefront location. You can wing it, using the same tools you do for your current eBay business, or you can add software, join affiliations, and open a franchise. This chapter explores the avenues you can take to add to your bottom line using this selling opportunity.

UNDERSTANDING EBAY TRADING ASSISTANTS

At first glance, most people seem to think eBay trading assistants are a highly select group of PowerSellers who have warehouses, super auction-management programs, and other top-tier business characteristics. Although some do match those qualifications, the truth of the matter is that virtually any eBay seller with moderate feedback can offer to sell for others. How each trading assistant does it, however, is another matter. Trading assistants differ in:

- What they charge
- What items they will sell (in addition to standard eBay guidelines)
- What drop-off/pick-up conditions they offer
- How they want to be contacted
- How they market themselves

eBay sellers become trading assistants for a variety of reasons:

- Friends, relatives, and neighbors ask them to sell items for them
- They've run out of inventory and need to look for other sources
- They enjoy the mechanics of selling but don't have the time or interest to search for items to sell
- They want to add another sales channel to their overall eBay business plan

Continued . . .

NOTE

eBay trading assistants are independent sellers, not employees or contractors of eBay, Inc.

PowerSeller Sally says: "If you have a specialty in one or more areas, this should be the beginning focus of your TA campaign. Promote what you already know and to those with whom you have already established relationships. This is particularly relevant if you are involved in any of the hobby or collectible fields that derive much of their energy from eBay transactions."

Become an eBay Trading Assistant

eBay provides a program whereby sellers who meet minimum qualifications and express an interest to sell items for others can list their profile in a Trading Assistant Directory. eBay users can search the list and find trading assistants in their locale. Although there's nothing to stop you from selling on eBay for others without becoming an *eBay trading assistant* (or *TA*), there's really no good reason not to become one. As with other eBay-structured programs, the eBay marketing wizards circle around you, help you generate sales, and expand the symbiotic relationship that benefits eBay along with your business.

Apply to Be a Trading Assistant

You must meet certain qualifications to be accepted as an eBay trading assistant. These qualifications ensure that you have demonstrated maintaining a certain level of eBay values and experience:

- **Recent sales experience.** You must have sold at least ten items in the past three months and maintain that rate of sales of ten items each three-month period.
- **eBay buying or selling track record.** Your feedback score must be at least 50.
- **Good customer relations.** Your feedback rating must be 100 percent, maintaining at least 98 percent positive comments.
- **Financial responsibility.** Your eBay account must be in good standing.
- **Maintain eBay values.** You must agree and abide by the Trading Assistant Style Guide, which provides detailed instructions on using the eBay trading assistant logos, the required disclaimer on any TA materials you produce, authorized taglines, and proper identification of yourself, that is, "Trading Assistant on eBay."

UNDERSTANDING EBAY TRADING ASSISTANTS *(Continued)*

If you want to explore this rapidly growing aspect of eBay, give it a shot. Anyone with an eBay seller's account can sell an item for someone else, but if you want to be listed in the Trading Assistant Directory so that buyers can easily find you and have eBay provide other marketing assistance, become an eBay trading assistant (TA). (See "Apply to Be a Trading Assistant" later in the chapter.) If you have a physical storefront and want to provide walk-in services, become a registered eBay drop-off location (see "Open a Drop-Off Store" later in the chapter).

CAUTION

In early 2008, eBay revamped the Trading Assistant program. If you were familiar with the old program, you will want to review the new changes, as some significant differences exist. For example, "Trading Posts" are out, "Registered eBay Drop-Off Locations," or REDOLs, are in; you can now create only one TA profile for each eBay User ID; and you cannot use the terms "auction" or "auctioneer" in your business name, signage, and marketing materials (unless you are a licensed auctioneer).

NOTE

The more detailed address information you provide in your TA profile, the more specific the search will be for prospective clients. However, there are downsides to providing too much address information. See "Apply Trading Assistant Profile Strategies" later in the chapter for more information.

To apply to become a TA:

1. Click **Site Map** on the eBay header.

2. Under Selling Resources, click **Trading Assistant Program**.

3. On the eBay Trading Assistant Program page, click **Trading Assistant Requirements And Sign-Up** on the left sidebar.

> Trading Assistant Program
>
> Sign up
>
> Already a TA? Sign In
>
> Trading Assistant Terms & Conditions

4. On the Sign Up page, click **Trading Assistant Terms And Conditions** on the left sidebar to review the terms of the program.

5. Back on the Sign Up page, click **Sign Up** on the left sidebar.

If you are lacking in qualifications, eBay will quickly let you know, as shown in Figure 7-1. If you do qualify, you will continue to set up the profile page that displays in the Trading Assistant Directory and advertises your services.

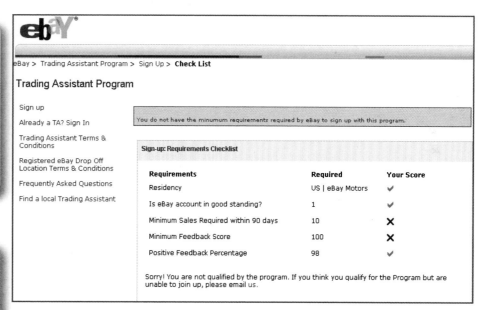

eBay > Trading Assistant Program > Sign Up > **Check List**

Trading Assistant Program

Sign up

Already a TA? Sign In

Trading Assistant Terms & Conditions

Registered eBay Drop Off Location Terms & Conditions

Frequently Asked Questions

Find a local Trading Assistant

> You do not have the minumum requirements required by eBay to sign up with this program.

Sign-up: Requirements Checklist

Requirements	Required	Your Score
Residency	US | eBay Motors	✔
Is eBay account in good standing?	1	✔
Minimum Sales Required within 90 days	10	✗
Minimum Feedback Score	100	✗
Positive Feedback Percentage	98	✔

> Sorry! You are not qualified by the program. If you think you qualify for the Program but are unable to join up, please email us.

*Figure 7-1: **eBay wastes no time in letting you know you are not qualified to become a trading assistant.***

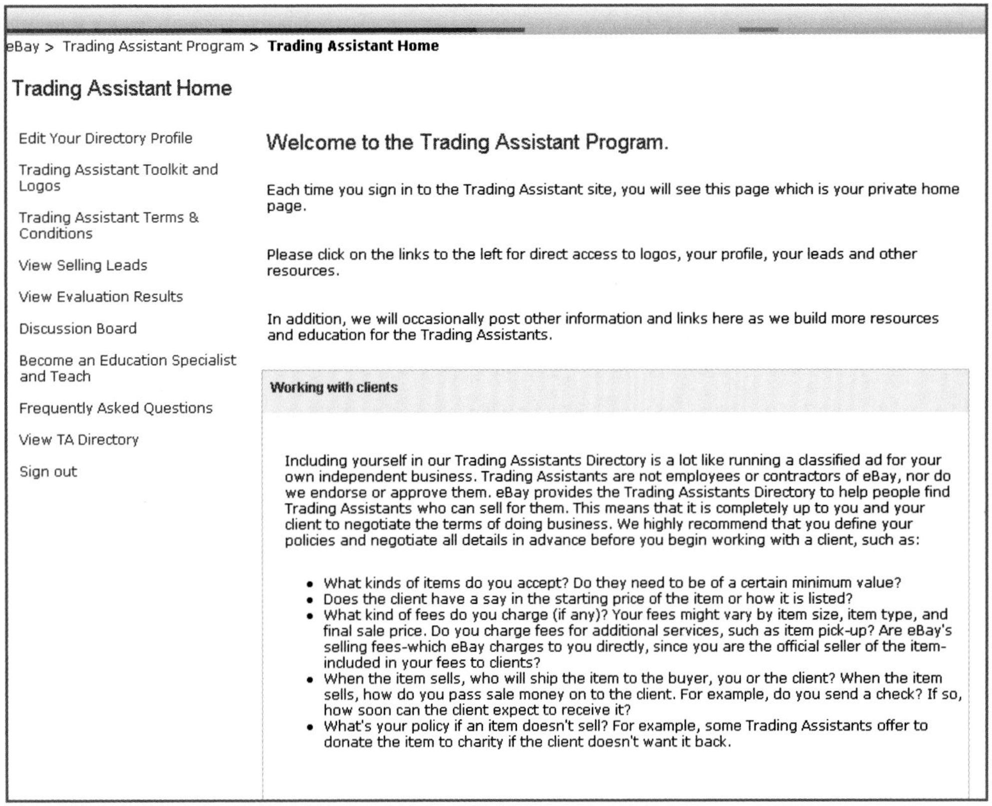

eBay > Trading Assistant Program > **Trading Assistant Home**

Trading Assistant Home

Edit Your Directory Profile

Trading Assistant Toolkit and Logos

Trading Assistant Terms & Conditions

View Selling Leads

View Evaluation Results

Discussion Board

Become an Education Specialist and Teach

Frequently Asked Questions

View TA Directory

Sign out

Welcome to the Trading Assistant Program.

Each time you sign in to the Trading Assistant site, you will see this page which is your private home page.

Please click on the links to the left for direct access to logos, your profile, your leads and other resources.

In addition, we will occasionally post other information and links here as we build more resources and education for the Trading Assistants.

Working with clients

Including yourself in our Trading Assistants Directory is a lot like running a classified ad for your own independent business. Trading Assistants are not employees or contractors of eBay, nor do we endorse or approve them. eBay provides the Trading Assistants Directory to help people find Trading Assistants who can sell for them. This means that it is completely up to you and your client to negotiate the terms of doing business. We highly recommend that you define your policies and negotiate all details in advance before you begin working with a client, such as:

- What kinds of items do you accept? Do they need to be of a certain minimum value?
- Does the client have a say in the starting price of the item or how it is listed?
- What kind of fees do you charge (if any)? Your fees might vary by item size, item type, and final sale price. Do you charge fees for additional services, such as item pick-up? Are eBay's selling fees-which eBay charges to you directly, since you are the official seller of the item-included in your fees to clients?
- When the item sells, who will ship the item to the buyer, you or the client? When the item sells, how do you pass sale money on to the client? For example, do you send a check? If so, how soon can the client expect to receive it?
- What's your policy if an item doesn't sell? For example, some Trading Assistants offer to donate the item to charity if the client doesn't want it back.

Figure 7-2: **The Trading Assistant Home page is your hub for working with your profile and accessing related material.**

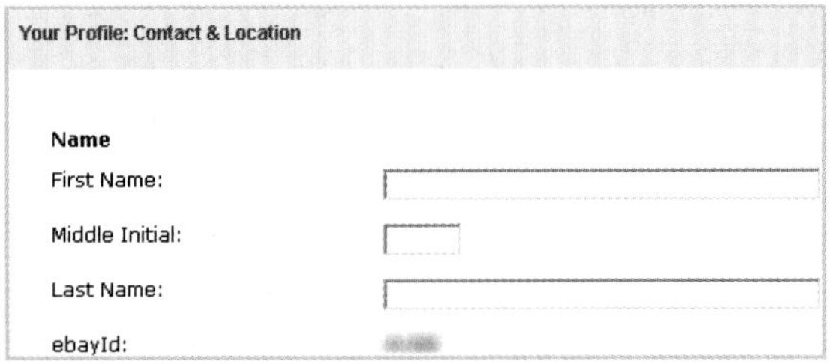

Your Profile: Contact & Location

Name

First Name:

Middle Initial:

Last Name:

ebayId:

Complete a Trading Assistant Profile

You advertise your TA services on eBay by being listed in the Trading Assistant Directory, a searchable listing of all registered eBay TAs. Since the profile in the TA Directory might be the only information a potential customer has when deciding to choose you from a crowd of other TAs, it's imperative that you present your services effectively. To simplify the process, eBay collects most of the information by having you select options from prepared lists (see "Apply Trading Assistant Profile Strategies" for more information on setting up your profile).

1. Continue from the previous section when first setting up a TA account (see "Apply to Be a Trading Assistant").

   –Or–

   Log in to your TA account.

   In either case, the Trading Assistant Home page displays, as shown in Figure 7-2.

2. Click **Edit Your Directory Profile** on the sidebar (you may see Create Your Directory Profile instead). Complete the first page of the form with your contact information. Click **Continue** when finished.

3. On the Your Profile: Services page, select the primary and secondary categories of items you will sell, along with subcategories of items, as shown in Figure 7-3.

Professor Polly says: "Fill out your trading assistant profile using your ABCs: accurately, briefly, and clearly."

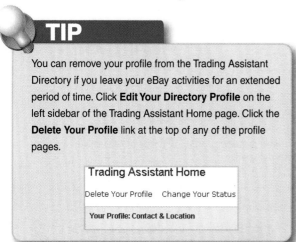

Your Profile: Services

Category Specialities

Primary Speciality:
Collectibles

Secondary Speciality:
Pottery & Glass

Other Speciality:
Entertainment Memorabilia

Sub Categories:
Advertising
Comics
Sewing
Paper
Disneyana
Science Fiction
Clocks
Science, Medical
Transportation
Breweriana, Beer

Sub Categories:
Pottery & China
Glass

Sub Categories:
Autographs-Original
Movie Memorabilia
Television Memorabilia
Other Memorabilia
Music Memorabilia
Theater Memorabilia
Video Game Memorabilia
Autographs-Reprints

*Figure 7-3: **Choose carefully the categories of items you offer as a TA, since customers can define their searches by them.***

TIP

You can remove your profile from the Trading Assistant Directory if you leave your eBay activities for an extended period of time. Click **Edit Your Directory Profile** on the left sidebar of the Trading Assistant Home page. Click the **Delete Your Profile** link at the top of any of the profile pages.

Trading Assistant Home

Delete Your Profile   Change Your Status

Your Profile: Contact & Location

Professor Polly says: "As an eBay trading assistant, you cannot list automobiles or real estate for sale for others unless you have a motor vehicle dealer's license or you are a licensed real estate agent, respectively."

4. Identify the drop-off hours you will be available, if offered, and the pick-up range you will travel to collect items, if offered.

Services Offered

Drop-off and pick-up
☐ I have a Drop-off location with regular business hours. (This means clients can visit your location without calling ahead.)

☑ I offer item pick-ups

Pick-up Distance: 50 miles.

5. Identify your trading specialties, for example, consumer/household goods, charitable donations, and auto parts and accessories. In the Languages Spoken area, indicate the languages you speak.

6. Type a description of your services, your fee arrangement, and your terms and conditions. Click **Continue** when finished.

7. On the final page of the profile, preview your selections and click **Save** when completed. Your profile will be added to the Trading Assistant Directory and will appear to potential clients, similar to the profile shown in Figure 7-4.

LOCATING TRADING ASSISTANTS

It helps to see how potential eBay customers will try and search for you so you can better set up your TA profile to match the techniques they'll use. Also, you can provide these steps to anyone who expresses an interest in your services.

1. Click **Site Map** on the eBay header.

2. Under Selling Resources, click **Trading Assistant Program**.

3. Click **Find A Trading Assistant** on the sidebar.

4. On the Find A Trading Assistant To Sell For You page, click **Find A Personal Trading Assistant** on the sidebar.

   –Or–

   Click one of the selling categories beneath that link to filter the search to only those TAs that have identified in their profile that they sell in a particular category.

Continued . . .

> Find a Registered eBay Drop Off Location
> Find a Personal Trading Assistant
> Sell my consumer/household goods
> Sell my government surplus
> Sell charitable donations

Trading Assistant Profile

Contact Information

(7207 ☆)

Feedback Score: 7207
Positive Feedback: 99.9%
eBay member since 1999 in US

[Contact Assistant]

Items for Sale | Member Profile

Services

Name:

BusinessName:
Vicki's Goodies

Address:

Contact:
(Withheld)

Drop-off Location:
Not Available.

Pickup:
🚚 50 miles.

Will come to your home and assess sales viability between Mt. Vernon and Everett WA.

Specialties:
▪ Collectibles (Primary):
  ▪ *Decorative Collectibles*

▪ Pottery & Glass (Secondary):
  ▪ *Pottery & China*

▪ Entertainment Memorabilia (Other):
  ▪ *Movie Memorabilia*

*Figure 7-4: **A well thought-out and defined profile, along with PowerSeller status, will help drive customers to you.***

Though not an eBay requirement for TAs (it is a requirement for Registered eBay Drop-Off Locations (REDOLs), see the "Becoming Bonded" QuickFacts later in the chapter), consider getting yourself bonded to provide assurance to your clients that their money and items are safe. eBay offers a convenient and affordable means to become bonded **buySafe**, backed by a recognized insurance company.

Apply Trading Assistant Profile Strategies

You can probably complete a TA profile form in less than five minutes, but as with most things, you'll get out of it what you put into it. There are many subtleties embedded in the selections you make and in the text you provide. Consider the following points when setting up or changing your profile:

- **Numbers count** when it comes to your eBay feedback score. Boost your score (and the attention you garner in search results) by buying or selling several cheap items (a recent change to eBay policy provides positive feedback credit for each positive comment, regardless if it's from the same buyer or seller that submits one for you).

UICKSTEPS

LOCATING TRADING ASSISTANTS
(Continued)

5. Type in your ZIP code and filter the search by choosing only the services you offer, that is, drop off and/or pick up of items. Click **Search**. A list of TAs within the default 25-mile radius of the ZIP code is displayed, as shown in Figure 7-5.

Find A Trading Assistant

Enter your zip code to find a Trading Assistant near you.

Zip Code: 98201

Show only Trading Assistants who offer
☐ A drop off service
☐ A pick up service

Search   Advanced Search

6. Click your own eBay User ID or the User ID of any TA whose profile you want to view (see Figure 7-4).

7. To search using additional options, use the criteria in the Search Option sidebar. Click **Show Results**.

   –Or–

   Click the **Advanced Search** link to set up additional search criteria, such as a TA's last name or User ID. Click **Search** when finished.

Refine a search by selecting items you are looking to sell, distance from city or ZIP code, or by specific services offered.

Click to display a TA's profile.

Sort the list of TAs in ascending or descending order by clicking a column header.

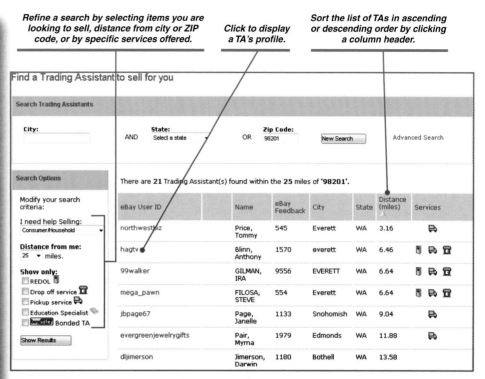

Figure 7-5: *Trading assistant searches are based on several criteria you select in your profile.*

- **Be careful** when selling from your home. Divulging personal details, such as your house number in the Address field, is like offering potential malfeasants a flashing sign that says, "Large inventory of valuable items for grabs—and I'll provide a map for you!"

- **Offer a drop-off service judiciously** to avoid problems at your home. For much of the same reasoning as the previous point, you should prescreen prospective clients at a neutral location or over the phone before inviting them to your home. Of course, if you have a place of business, such as a drop-off store, whether or not you are a registered eBay drop-off location (see "Open a Drop-Off Store" later in the chapter), you'll want to encourage across-the-counter traffic.

TIP

A quick "second opinion" source when estimating the value of items your clients provide for selling on eBay is ItsDeductible (www.itsdeductible.com), a free software program for many versions of TurboTax (an Intuit product, also the maker of QuickBooks). The program's main emphasis is to help you organize and track charitable and other deductible expenses (eBay businesses usually have no shortage of items headed for donation), but it also provides access to the fair-market valuation for thousands of items.

Figure 7-6: ***Don't put off prospective clients with a sense you are more interested in protecting yourself from them than selling their items.***

- **Toot your horn** in the Service Description area. Much of the information in a TA profile is limited to choices provided by eBay. The Service Description area is the one place you have to distinguish your service from others. Emphasize experience, due diligence, and extra services you offer (research and estimates of value, on-site consignment sales, and other value-added opportunities for your clients).
- **Simplify your fee structure** to make it easy for clients to understand. Try and structure your costs in as streamlined a manner as possible to avoid listing a string of seemingly endless fees your clients need to pay. It might all work out the same mathematically, but first impressions count. For example:
  - Charge a modest flat fee upon receipt of an item to cover your research and listing costs in case the item doesn't sell. Average item-receipt fees are in the $15 to $20 range.
  - Add a commission percentage based on the final value fee. A decreasing commission percentage based on a higher final value fee is fair but adds more complexity to the fee structure. By streamlining your fees, you make it easier for the consignor to make a decision.
  - Charge the buyer actual shipping costs plus a small amount to cover your time. This part of the transaction is between you and the buyer, and is transparent to the consignor.
  - Absorb eBay fees into your commission rate so you don't have to list another set of fees to the client.
- **Keep your terms and conditions brief.** State a few relevant points to protect yourself against 99 percent of potential problems. For example, include a statement that you have the right to refuse any item, and declare the limits to your responsibility (you're not liable for shipping problems). Don't try to cover every possible scenario or you'll turn off potential clients with your overzealous legalese (see Figure 7-6).

NOTE

Be certain to accurately determine your costs before quoting a fee to a consignor. You need to consider the listing and final value fees, the credit card or PayPal fee, and the fees of any third-party listing service, such as MarketplaceAdvisor, one of ChannelAdvisor's products.

Market Your Trading Assistant Business

eBay provides a tremendous amount of marketing materials, information, and education to assist TAs. The central repository for links to all things TA is the Trading Assistant Home page (only available for current TAs who have logged in).

1. Click **Site Map** on the eBay header.

2. Under Selling Resources, click **Trading Assistant Program**.

3. On the Trading Assistant Program page, click **Trading Assistant Log-In** on the left sidebar. Sign in with your normal eBay User ID and password.

4. On the Trading Assistant Home page, on the left sidebar, view a list of topics covering various aspects of being a TA. The following sections describe some of these resources in more detail.

Learn the eBay Trading Assistant Business Cycle

eBay provides information in a five-step process to help you develop a selling strategy, find and retain clients, and sell items.

1. From the Trading Assistant Home page for current TAs, click **Trading Assistant Toolkit And Logos**.

QUICKSTEPS

USING THE TRADING ASSISTANT TOOLKIT

eBay has assembled a collection of marketing information, templates, and other examples of marketing deliverables and organized them in a convenient "toolkit" that you can use to find what you want.

1. From the Trading Assistant Home page, click **Trading Assistant Toolkit And Logos**.

2. On the Toolkit page, shown in Figure 7-7, review the list of resources that describe best practices, tools, and ancillary information. Click the links to the information you want. Many documents are in PDF format so you can save them to your local computer system and start building your own business library.

Trading Assistant Home

Edit Your Directory Profile

Trading Assistant Toolkit and Logos

Trading Assistant Terms & Conditions

View Selling Leads

View Evaluation Results

Discussion Board

Become an Education Specialist and Teach

Frequently Asked Questions

View TA Directory

Sign out

Trading Assistant Toolkit and Logos

There are **13** Resource(s) found.

Title ⋀	Summary
Trading Assistant Logo For Screen: RGB (JPG)	Logo for Trading Assistant on eBay for Screen: RGB (JPG)
Trading Assistant Logo For Screen: RGB Black (JPG)	Logo for Trading Assistant on eBay for Screen: RGB Black (JPG)
Trading Assitant on eBay Zip file for the logos	All the file types for the images in the zip file.
Trading Assistant on eBay Business Card	Business Card template for a Trading Assistant on eBay.
Flyer for Trading Assistant on eBay	Flyer PDF file for a Trading Assistant on eBay.
Account Transfers of Ownership	Great Resource
Safe Trading Manual	Great Resource
Customized Mailer Instructions	Use with Mailer Templates
HTML Code for Logo & Link	You can put this code into your listings to link to your TA profile. Recommend you test it first.
Special TA Bond Information from buySAFE	REDOLs are required to get a $25,000 bond, but this is available to all TAs that want to offer an added level of protection to their customers. Very reasonable at only $250/yr.
Customizable Mailer in MS Word	Customize and mail
Customizable Mailer in PDF format	Customize and mail
Trading Assistant Tutorial	Get to know how the Trading Assistant sales cycle works and the marketing and research opportunities to make your

Figure 7-7: **When you become a TA, eBay throws its training, education, and marketing muscle behind you.**

Figure 7-8: **The TA Business Cycle provides a road map for your TA business.**

2. From the list of TA resources (see Figure 7-7), click **Trading Assistant Tutorial**. A PDF document will open (assuming you have Adobe Reader, Adobe Acrobat, or a third-party PDF viewer program).

3. Click a step on the TA Business Cycle graphic, as shown in Figure 7-8.

The five steps are as follows:

1. Plan TA Strategy provides information on foundation business practices, such as developing business and marketing plans (see Chapter 1), tracking sales and accounting data, and branding and integrating your TA business with other eBay and off-eBay selling channels (see Chapter 6 for information on eBay Stores; see Chapter 10 for information on promoting and marketing your business and Store).

2. Generate Client Leads helps you develop traditional marketing materials and techniques, such as flyers, press releases, and phoning, as well as Internet-age avenues, such as e-mail, using keywords effectively, and enhancing your eBay listings, eBay Store, and About Me and My World pages. Chapter 10 describes several of these marketing and promotional tools.

3. Qualify And Close Leads offers pointers to quickly assess prospective clients and determine if they are a good match for you. Sales techniques to help you expand your relationship with clients and to finalize transactions are described. Also covered are ways to protect your business from items that might be counterfeit or copyright-protected, as well as setting up contracts.

GAUGING HOW TO MARKET YOUR TRADING ASSISTANT SERVICES

eBay conducted a survey a few years ago to gauge what marketing techniques TAs used to attract customers and how customers actually learned about the TA marketing efforts.

FOCUS YOUR MARKETING EFFORTS

Thirty-one percent of TAs use other sources of marketing besides their TA profile page to make potential clients aware of their services. The top marketing techniques used include:

- Flyers and other offline marketing materials (54 percent)
- E-mails to friends and family (42 percent)
- TA logo in listings (39 percent)
- Newspapers (28 percent)
- Online advertising and keywords (18 percent)
- Social networks (9 percent)

ENABLE CLIENTS TO FIND YOU

The most effective way to attract clients is to provide superior service to existing clients and let *them* market your business. The top means of finding a TA are:

- Word of mouth (66 percent)
- Flyers and other offline marketing materials (27 percent)
- TA logo in listings (19 percent)
- E-mails from friends and family (19 percent)
- Newspapers (17 percent)
- Online advertising and keywords (6 percent)

4. **Sell Client Product** reviews information on running a conventional eBay business. Best practices on finding the best selling categories, listing techniques, shipping information, and managing the business are also covered.

5. **Retain Clients** provides tips on how to keep your clients returning after you've completed a sale for them.

Add the Trading Assistant Logo to Your Listings

It's a snap to add Hypertext Markup Language (HTML) code to your listings descriptions, advertising to buyers and bidders that you are a TA. eBay will display the TA logo as well as a link to your TA directory profile.

1. From the Trading Assistant Home page for current TAs, click **Trading Assistant Toolkit And Logos**.

2. From the list of TA resources, click **HTML Code For Logo And Link**. A TXT document will open.

3. Copy and paste the code at the end of your item description in your selling form.

   –Or–

   If you cannot access the TXT document, type the following HTML code at the end of your item description:

```
<p align="center">
<img src="http://pics.ebaystatic.com/aw/pics/logos/logoUS_R_TA_RGB_
141x106.jpg" alt="I am a Trading Assistant on eBay" width="141"
height="106" border="0" longdesc="TA Logo" /></a></p>
<p align="center" class="style3">
<aref="http://ebaytradingassistant.com/directory/index.php?page=pro
file&ebayID=XXXX" target="_blank">I am a Trading Assistant - I can
sell your stuff on eBay!</a></p>
```

4. Substitute your eBay User ID for *XXXX*.

5. Preview the listing to ensure the logo and link appear correctly and that clicking the link displays your TA profile. Submit the listing. The link to your profile and eBay's official TA logo are displayed in your listing.

Interact with Other Trading Assistants

As with all aspects of eBay, there is a plethora of support available from other members who operate TA businesses.

JOIN A TA GROUP

eBay *groups* are forums for members who share a common interest to exchange information and experiences. The Trading Assistant groups cover the business of selling for others based on several interest areas, such as geographic location, types of items sold, and experience level.

To access the TA groups:

1. Point to **Community** on the eBay header, and click **Groups** from the drop-down menu.

2. On the eBay Groups page, under **Groups**, click **Seller Groups**.

3. On the Seller Groups page, scroll down to the Trading Assistants area. The first three of the several TA groups are shown. Click **More In Trading Assistant** to access the full list of groups and click any that interest you. The group's home page, as shown in Figure 7-9, will tell you more about the focus of its membership.

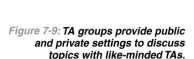

*Figure 7-9: **TA groups provide public and private settings to discuss topics with like-minded TAs.***

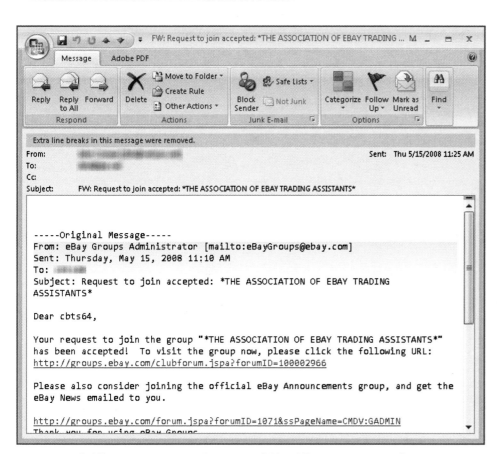

NOTE

Many TA groups are private and require you to contact the group leader and request to join, or you need to be invited to join. Public groups are open to all eBay members.

4. Click **Join Group** to join a particular group and have access to the group's activities and its members. If you haven't already, you will need to sign in. If the group is private, you will also need to request membership to the group by sending a message to the group leader and providing a reason why you want to join the group. Once accepted to a group, you will receive an e-mail confirming your acceptance and providing links for other group-related announcements, as shown in Figure 7-10.

REVIEW THE TA DISCUSSION BOARD

A great place to review comments and questions by both TAs and eBay members who are interested in using TA services is the Trading Assistant Discussion Board.

1. From the Trading Assistant Home page, click **Discussion Board** on the left sidebar.

Click to provide direct access to the Trading Assistant discussion board.

–Or–

Point to **Community** on the eBay header, and click **Workshops/Discussion Forums**. Under Community Help Boards, click **Trading Assistant**.

2. On the Trading Assistant page, scroll through the list of discussions, as shown in Figure 7-11, and click the topic that interests you. Sign in if you want to submit a topic.

Figure 7-10: Public group acceptance happens quickly, while acceptance to private groups depends on how quickly the group leader responds to your request.

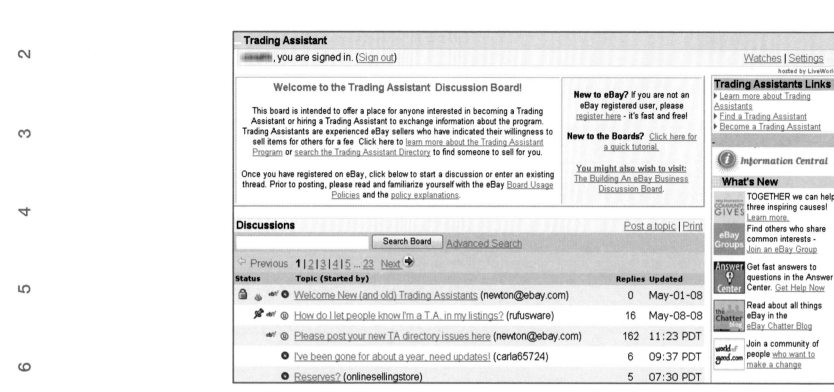

Trading Assistant

██████, you are signed in. (Sign out)   Watches | Settings

                                                                                                  hosted by LiveWorld

Welcome to the Trading Assistant Discussion Board!	**New to eBay?** If you are not an eBay registered user, please register here - it's fast and free!	**Trading Assistants Links**

Figure 7-11: The Trading Assistant Discussion Board allows you to interact with others to answer your questions and gain insight in how others are doing.

Welcome to the Trading Assistant Discussion Board!

This board is intended to offer a place for anyone interested in becoming a Trading Assistant or hiring a Trading Assistant to exchange information about the program. Trading Assistants are experienced eBay sellers who have indicated their willingness to sell items for others for a fee Click here to learn more about the Trading Assistant Program or search the Trading Assistant Directory to find someone to sell for you.

Once you have registered on eBay, click below to start a discussion or enter an existing thread. Prior to posting, please read and familiarize yourself with the eBay Board Usage Policies and the policy explanations.

New to eBay? If you are not an eBay registered user, please register here - it's fast and free!

New to the Boards? Click here for a quick tutorial.

You might also wish to visit: The Building An eBay Business Discussion Board.

Trading Assistants Links
▶ Learn more about Trading Assistants
▶ Find a Trading Assistant
▶ Become a Trading Assistant

🛈 *Information Central*

What's New

TOGETHER we can help three inspiring causes! Learn more.

Find others who share common interests - Join an eBay Group

Get fast answers to questions in the Answer Center. Get Help Now

Read about all things eBay in the eBay Chatter Blog

Join a community of people who want to make a change

Discussions   Post a topic | Print

[   ] Search Board   Advanced Search

⬅ Previous **1**|2|3|4|5 ... 23 Next ➡

Status	Topic (Started by)	Replies	Updated
🔒 🔨 ebY 🌑	Welcome New (and old) Trading Assistants (newton@ebay.com)	0	May-01-08
📌 ebY ⓤ	How do I let people know I'm a T.A. in my listings? (rufusware)	16	May-08-08
ebY ⓤ	Please post your new TA directory issues here (newton@ebay.com)	162	11:23 PDT
🌑	I've been gone for about a year, need updates! (carla65724)	6	09:37 PDT
🌑	Reserves? (onlinesellingstore)	5	07:30 PDT

Figure 7-11: The Trading Assistant Discussion Board allows you to interact with others to answer your questions and gain insight in how others are doing.

ATTEND OR VIEW TA-RELATED WORKSHOPS

eBay workshops allow members to interact online in real time with moderators who present information on various topics. If you cannot make the scheduled workshop, you can view past workshops from the workshop archives.

1. Point to **Community** on the eBay header, and click **Workshops/Discussion Forums**.

2. On the Discussion Boards page, under Workshops, click **Calendar** to review the current calendar for any upcoming or recent workshops that interest you as a TA. Click the link to learn more about the workshop or to review past comments.

Workshops

Workshops
Attend a workshop event hosted by eBay staff or special guest, or get indepth information on interesting topics by reading past workshops. Check our calendar for the latest schedule.

QUICKFACTS

STARTING A DROP-OFF STORE FRANCHISE

eBay drop-off store franchise operations were a hot commodity several years ago, but the intervening years have not been kind to them. One casualty was the national brand, QuikDrop, which went from a high of 95 stores in 2005 to under 30 when it went out of business at the end of 2007 (though individual franchisees can continue using the QuikDrop name). Several reasons have been floated as to the cause for the demise of the individual stores (and the problems experienced by other franchise locations), including eBay policy changes that adversely affected profits, franchise overhead costs, and a tendency to sell used and refurbished items that incurred negative feedback from dissatisfied buyers and subsequent penalties from eBay. Opening any eBay business that requires substantial investment is a risk. Adding costs for a franchise needs to be given a careful cost-benefit analysis.

PowerSeller Sally says: "If your goal is to open a drop-off store and become a Registered eBay Drop Off Location, operate as a TA before incurring the overhead of a physical store. It costs a lot less to start up (and shut down) a TA business operated from your home than a brick-and-mortar operation."

3. To see workshops from past months in the current year, as well as the prior year, click the applicable archive on the left sidebar, and click each month to see a list of the workshops held.

> **April 2007:**
> Member Workshop: 5-Minute Market Research Recipe to Power Up Your Profits - April 02
> Member Workshop: Research 101 - April 06
> eBay Workshop: Listing Items with the Sell Your Item Form - April 09
> Member Workshop: Turn Tire Kickers in to Actual Buyers with Customer Support - April 10
> Member Workshop: The Most Important Question to Ask Your Accountant in 2007 - April 11
> eBay Workshop: Attract Repeat Buyers with New Combined Shipping Discounts - April 13
> Member Workshop: Capturing Shoppers by Fine Tuning Listing Strategies - April 16
> Member Workshop: SKYROCKET Your Spring and Summer Sales - April 17
> Member Workshop: USPS Domestic Rate Changes - April 23
> eBay Workshop: Introduction to the Sell Your Item form - April 24
> Member Workshop: A day is the life of an eBay Trading Assistant! - April 25
> Member Workshop: USPS International Product Redesign and Rate Changes - April 26

Professor Polly says: "The key document that establishes the agreement between you and the franchise company is the Uniform Franchise Offering Circular (UFOC). This states the terms of the franchise agreement, and it should be thoroughly reviewed—and understood—by you before entering into the relationship."

Open a Drop-Off Store

A drop-off store is a physical storefront where customers bring you items they want to have sold on eBay. A drop-off store operates much like a trading assistant who offers drop-off hours at a personal residence, except a drop-off store is in a business or commercial setting and staffed during normal business hours for drop-in customers. While it may seem like an extension of your current trading assistant business, a drop-off store brings you fully into the fold of retail businesses and their associated concerns. As a true brick-and-mortar business, a drop-off store requires a serious look at a number of considerations that go well beyond the plans, models, and experiences you've had with eBay-only selling. However, eBay doesn't leave you completely on your own. You can aspire to become an eBay-sanctioned *Registered eBay Drop Off Location (REDOL)*, a drop-off-store designation for bonded trading assistants with a demonstrated sales record.

Understand Drop-Off Store Considerations

If you are contemplating opening a drop-off store, you need to consider all aspects of running a retail business in addition to those that are more closely related to running an eBay business. A few of the more salient issues you will need to think about include:

- **Location, location, location** is critical, perhaps not in the classic sense of real estate investment value, but in the site's ability to attract and retain a customer base. Does its size meet your needs? Is there adequate parking? Can customers easily transport larger items from their parked location? Will the square footage of the building provide enough room to store inventory (see Chapter 2) and set up processing centers to handle a steady and voluminous stream of merchandise (see Chapter 3)?

- **Zoning, business restrictions, and other governmental influences** come into play. Is the site properly zoned for the business classification under which you'll be licensed? Some municipalities place restrictions on businesses considered "secondhand stores" by placing holding periods on items you sell and requiring documentation of sales. Are you willing to put a public face on your eBay business and incur the exposure, and perhaps scrutiny, that your eBay User ID has shielded you from?

- **Build your own store or work with a franchise.** A few national franchises (see the "Starting a Drop-Off Store Franchise" QuickFacts) can deliver everything you need to get you started and help you build the business. Do you have the experience, time, and entrepreneurial spirit to bring all the facets of the business together and act as your own general contractor, or do you need to spend the upfront and commission costs for an all-in-one solution? One approach is to diversify your business with a few different product lines to spread the risk. For example, Figure 7-12 illustrates how one business combines espresso/ice cream shop retail sales with consignment transactions, both onsite and online.

Figure 7-12: *Before committing to the expense and "all eggs in one basket" approach to a dedicated drop-off location, consider combining it with other selling opportunities.*

Professor Polly says: "Before entering into any franchise agreement, it is prudent to have an attorney examine all contracts and agreements before they are executed and inform you as to the legal requirements of such an enterprise."

BECOMING BONDED

In typical eBay fashion, when they impose a restriction or condition on you, they also provide a convenient and reasonably affordable means to satisfy their demands. One major change to the TA and Registered eBay Drop-Off Location (REDOL) programs enacted in early 2008 was the requirement for REDOLs to obtain a $25,000 bond to guarantee consignees that they will either receive payment for their items or the unsold item will be returned. (Not a bad idea for PowerSellers and TAs as well!) To obtain a buySAFE Trading Assistant Bond, you must first pass a buySAFE Business Inspection and become a buySAFE Bonded Merchant. The bond provides $25,000 total coverage for all your consignees, for all their claims, and costs $250 for a year of coverage. To apply for a bond, visit www.buysafe.com.

NOTE

Visit this Web site to find a complete understanding of the license agreement you'll need to have with eBay to be a REDOL: http://ebaytradingassistant.com/index.php?page=userAgreement&type=redol.

Start and Maintain a Registered eBay Drop-Off Location

A Registered eBay Drop-Off Location (REDOL) is to trading assistants as PowerSellers are to other eBay sellers—they represent the top-tier businesses that maintain drop-off locations. The registered designation provides two major benefits:

- Your profile is highlighted with the REDOL logo when potential clients search the Trading Assistant Directory for TAs with drop-off locations.

- The REDOL logo can be used on the physical storefront (certain restrictions apply, as noted next).

To qualify to become a REDOL, you must first be a TA and adhere to the requirements to be TA (see "Apply to Be a Trading Assistant" earlier in the chapter). Additionally, you will need to abide by a separate user agreement specific to REDOLs (see Note). Some of the requirements include:

- Minimum general liability insurance of $1,000,000
- A $25,000 bond to ensure seller payments (see the "Becoming Bonded" QuickFacts)
- Adherence to the REDOL Style Guide (access the guide from a link in the REDOL user agreement)
- Maintaining entry requirements and being subject to eBay scrutiny through review by customer-satisfaction surveys.

To apply to be a REDOL:

1. From the Trading Assistant Program page (Site Map | Trading Assistant Program), click **Trading Assistant Requirement And Sign-Up** on the left sidebar.

2. On the next Trading Assistant Program page, click **Registered eBay Drop-Off Location Terms And Conditions** on the left sidebar.

3. Review the terms of the user agreement, and click the embedded link to also review the style guide.

4. When you are ready to apply, log in to your TA account, and click **Edit Your Directory Profile** on the sidebar of the Trading Assistant Home page.

5. Click **Change Status** at the top of any of the directory pages.

eBay > Trading Assistant Program > Trading Assistant Home > **Edit Your Directory Profile**

Trading Assistant Home

Delete Your Profile   Change Your Status

Your Profile: Contact & Location

Browser Earl

Browser Earl says: "If you open an independent drop-off store, you will need software to help you track customers, create invoices, and produce reports. Three popular consignment programs are Visual Horizons Software's ConsignPro (www.consignpro.com) and Resaleworld.com's Liberty4 Trading Assistants and Liberty 2002 (www.resaleworld.com). Auctiva, described in Chapter 5, also has a consignment selling segment."

Chapter 8
Using eBay Sales Outlets

eBay.com provides many ways for you to sell your inventory. This chapter discusses three more sites within the eBay empire: eBay Motors, Half.com, and Kijiji. eBay Motors provides a platform for selling motor-driven vehicles and parts. This includes cars, motorcycles, boats, power-sport vehicles (such as ATVs, go-karts, scooters, and snowmobiles), and even airplanes and buses. Half.com provides a venue for selling books, CDs, videos, video games, and game systems at great discounts. Kijiji allows you to place ads for items you want to buy or sell in your particular city or state (similar to Craigslist).

Use eBay Motors

eBay Motors is where you can sell any motorized item, part or accessories. It is the world's largest online market, attracting over 11 million viewers a month.

Over 2 million vehicles have been sold to date. Cars, common vehicles—not the collectible or expensive specialties—make up 70 percent of the cars auctioned. To list a car on eBay Motors, you must have an eBay account and must register with eBay Motors.

On the eBay home page, under the eBay header, click **Motors**. The eBay Motors home page, shown in Figure 8-1, will be displayed.

There are advantages to selling on the Internet:

- There is a huge customer base.
- eBay offers ways to protect both buyers and sellers, making it a safe environment.
- eBay provides links to lenders who can arrange financing for buyers.
- Sellers can expect to get more for a car selling it on eBay than they would get for a trade-in on a new car.
- Sellers can be a vehicle dealer, a dealer assistant, or a trading assistant selling other people's cars.

But using eBay Motors has some drawbacks as well. Sellers have to consider legal issues and a state's rules and regulations, and deal with problems associated with higher prices (such as the buyer's need for escrow and financing). Buying a car online is complex with regards to inspecting and verifying the purchase, handling the shipping, and clearing the title process.

Getting ready to sell has two important stages: gathering information and putting it into eBay Motors.

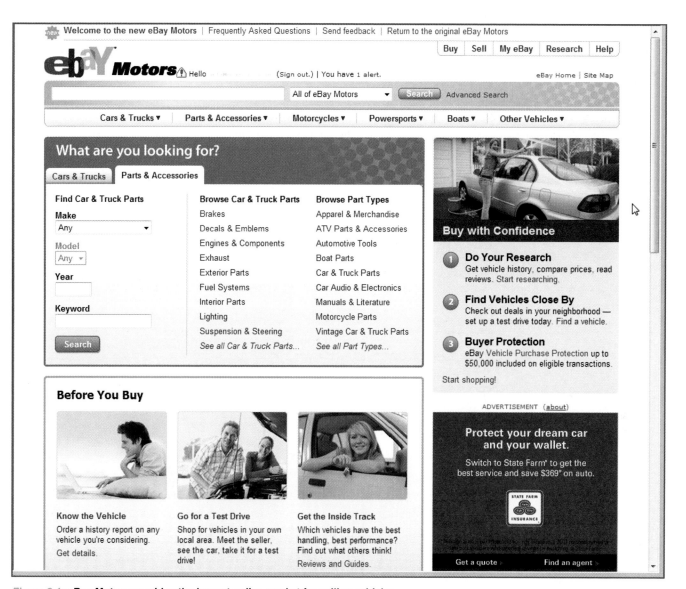

Figure 8-1: *eBay Motors provides the largest online market for selling vehicles.*

QUICKFACTS

RETRACTING A BID OR BEST OFFER

If you have an eBay business, it's almost a certainty you will need a vehicle to acquire merchandise, go to the post office, meet with clients and suppliers, and everything else that goes with running a business. Why not use your knowledge of eBay to help find yourself a great deal on eBay Motors? Just be careful in your exuberance in that you realize this is not the same type of transaction as buying a used CD on Half.com. We're talking big money here (at least to us!) and there can be consequences if you get cold feet.

Retracting a bid is considered an exception and is generally not permitted.

CONSEQUENCES OF RETRACTING A BID OR BEST OFFER

Retracting bids is a serious matter, and eBay may investigate if a bidder has had several retractions within the last six months, if bids are continuously retracted during the last 24 hours (could be *bid shilling*, which is an attempt to raise the bid amount), or if a seller has complained. If a buyer is found guilty of misusing the retraction feature, he or she can be suspended and the number of bid retractions over the past 12 months will be displayed with his or her feedback.

TIMING CONSIDERATIONS

- A buyer can retract a bid if there are more than 12 hours until the auction ends. In this case, all bids made by the bidder for the listing are retracted.
- With less than 12 hours in the auction and without the seller's okay, a buyer cannot retract a bid.

Continued . . .

Figure 8-2: eBay Motors offers a comprehensive checklist for you to use to gather information needed to sell a vehicle.

Organize to Sell Vehicles

To sell vehicles on eBay Motors, you will need to organize your resources.

1. Create both an eBay account and a seller's account. If you already are registered with eBay and have an eBay seller's account, you are good to go. If you do need to create the seller's account, you will need to provide credit card and bank account information so that eBay Motors can verify that you are who you say you are and also determine how you will pay fees.

2. Organize information about the item(s) to be sold:
   - Complete the Sell Your Vehicle Checklist, as seen in Figure 8-2. Get as much information as you can about the history and condition of the car or vehicle, tires, and so on. The more information you have, the more comfortable the buyer will feel about making a purchase from you. Itemize all damages, dents, and dings.

eBay Motors

Sell Your Vehicle Checklist

Print this checklist: Gather the information needed to list your vehicle

1 GATHER YOUR PAPERWORK*:

We recommend finding your vehicle registration insurance card or your title/pink slip, since they contain important information (example: make, model, year, VIN) that you will need to complete your eBay vehicle listing.

2 VEHICLE INFORMATION:

- ☐ Year, Make, Model   Examples: 2003 Toyota Solara, 2001 BMW 3 series _____
- ☐ VIN   (17-digits if 1981 or later) _ _ _ _ _ _ _ _ _ _ _ _ _ _ _ _ _
  Tip: You can find your VIN in one or more of the following places:
  Driver's side dashboard, driver's side door jamb, vehicle registration, title, or your insurance card
- ☐ Sub Model (not all vehicles have Sub Models) Example: SE, LS, LX, Limited Edition, GT, 328 _____
- ☐ Mileage _ _ _ , _ _ _

Options / Additional equipment
- ☐ Sunroof   ☐ Cassette Player   ☐ CD Player
- ☐ 4-wheel drive   ☐ Leather Seats   ☐ Convertible
  (4x4 or AWD)

Safety Features
- ☐ Anti-Lock Brakes   ☐ Driver Airbag   ☐ Passenger Airbag   ☐ Side Airbags

Power Options
- ☐ Air Conditioning   ☐ Cruise Control   ☐ Power Windows   ☐ Power Locks   ☐ Power Seats
  Tip: If you have additional equipment on you car that you want people to know about, be sure to write about it in the section called "Describe your vehicle"

Transmission
- ☐ Manual   ☐ Automatic

|◀ ◀   1 of 2   ▶ ▶| ⊙ ⊙

TIP

Your buyers can also get car history reports and use Kelley blue book pricing. So assume that the buyers will have much the same information you have.

TIP

Reserve-payment listings can reduce a buyer's interest in your car if the reserve is too high. So if you choose to sell with a reserve, make it the lowest price you will accept for the car. This can be true of a Buy It Now listing as well. If it is too high, you may not get any bidders.

- Have the descriptive and legal information you need, such as the make, model, year, engine details, standard and optional features, vehicle identification number (VIN) number for cars after 1981 (and for some cars before 1981), and the mileage.

- Do you have a clear title? Disclose any liens against the vehicle. What are the requirements in your state for transferring the title to a car? Will you have to pay taxes or obtain a smog/emissions check before selling the vehicle? Find out your requirements from the department of motor vehicles for your state.

- Get a vehicle history report for the car that provides a detailed history of the vehicle. You enter the VIN and pay a fee, depending on whether this is a one-time report or one for multiple vehicles. eBay offers a history source: AutoCheck Vehicle History Reports by Experian Automotive. The fee is about $8 for one vehicle report and about $15 for up to ten reports.

- Is there a manufacturer's warranty on the vehicle? Does it qualify for comprehensive warranty protection?

3. Research the prices:

- Use Search in the eBay Motors header to research vehicles similar to the one you are selling that have recently sold. What was the price range? How did the condition of the car resemble yours?

- Do research with Kelley Blue Book (www.kbb.com), Edmunds.com (www.edmunds.com), or National Automobile Dealers Association (NADA) Guides (www.nada.com) to know what buyers will be expecting to pay for a similar car.

4. Determine pricing and strategy for your vehicle:

- What is the lowest price you will accept for the vehicle?

- Will you require a reserve minimum payment, no reserve, fixed price, or best offer?

5. Take photos of the vehicle. Use at least a dozen photos in a listing. Use them to:

- Show various angles of the car, inside and out.

- Show the engine, tires, interior, odometer, and inside the trunk. Let the buyer see everything he or she would want to look at if inspecting the car in person.

- Highlight defects clearly in the photos so the buyer won't be surprised.

QUICKFACTS

PROTECTING THE BUYER

eBay provides several programs for protecting the buyer and thereby encouraging confidence in bidding for a vehicle on eBay.

PUBLICIZE THE VEHICLE PURCHASE PROTECTION (VPP) PROGRAM

eBay offers a free and automatic program to all buyers for vehicles purchased on eBay Motors. The transaction is protected for up to $50,000 or the purchase price, whichever is lower (to include up to $800 in transportation expenses for the buyer to get to the vehicle). This protects the buyer against fraud and, for some vehicles, against misrepresentation by the seller. There is a deductible ranging from $100 to $500. It is not insurance or a way to get out of a sale you no longer want.

1. Click **Vehicle Purchase Protection** on the eBay Motors home page under 3. Buyer Protection.

> **3 Buyer Protection**
> eBay Vehicle Purchase Protection up to $50,000 included on eligible transactions.

OFFER A CONDITION GUARANTEE

Sellers can also offer a Condition Guarantee to buyers, guaranteeing that the vehicle will be as they described and that they will work to solve any disputes and make right any misrepresentations or misunderstandings. This reassures buyers that the sellers are reputable and that they have the buyers' interests at heart. This is not a means by which buyer's remorse can undo a commitment to buy a vehicle.

To find a description, click **Site Map** on the home page, and then click **Condition Guarantee By Seller** under Buyer Services & Protection.

6. Determine what your terms of sale will be: payment procedure and timing, vehicle inspection, vehicle pickup or delivery, and title transfer:

- Examine how other dealers handle the terms of sale, and decide what works for you.

- Will you ship worldwide?

- What is your price? Are state taxes required? Will you charge a "prep fee" to perform final preparations to the car before shipping? How can payments be made? Do you require a deposit? How much? How soon must payment be made? Do you provide financing, or will you help the buyer get financing? What will be your refund policy if the buyer feels the car is not what he or she expected?

- If the buyer wants a vehicle inspection, how will you help that happen? Will you suggest eBay's recommended services by SGS Vehicle Inspections or Pep Boys, as many buyers prefer?

- What are your options regarding shipping or delivery of the vehicle? Will you get an auto-shipping specialist like DAS (Dependable Auto Shippers) to deliver the vehicle? Do you require the buyer to handle shipping?

Browser Earl says: "Although it is not perfect, a history of the car can be obtained from AutoCheck Assured Reports for about $8, or CarFax (www.carfax.com) for $24.99 for a single report, or $29.99 for unlimited reports in a 30-day period. Find out how to get a passenger car's history at http://pages.motors.ebay.com/buy/vehicle-history-report/index.html."

Professor Polly says: "eBay is particularly suitable for selling specialty vehicles, offering unusual choices for collectors. Other possibilities are older but popular models, hard-to-find vehicles, or those with unusual features."

Professor Polly says: "It is a common procedure for the buyer to pay for shipping. If the buyer is going to pick up the car, then the buyer generally pays for transportation to where the car is being stored for him or her."

Enter Information into eBay Motors

After you have accumulated all the information needed for listing the vehicle, you enter it into the Sell Your Item form for eBay Motors.

1. From the eBay Motors home page, under Sell on the eBay Motors header, click **Sell Your Item**.

Buy	Sell	My eBay	Research
	How to Sell a Vehicle		
	Sell Your Item	Home	S
dvance	Dealer Center		

2. On the Sell page, click **Sell Your Item**. You may want to check the reminders about the listing checklist or the tips about selling a part. You may have to sign in.

3. On the Select Category page, you will specify the category path that someone will follow to find your item. Click the category your vehicle is in: Cars and Trucks, Motorcycles, Other Vehicles and Trailers, Powersports, or Parts & Accessories.

4. Continue to select categories until you reach the last possibility, such as seen in Figure 8-3. Click **Save and Continue**.

5. On the Sell: Select Your Market and Format page, click whether you want to sell the vehicle at an online auction or at a fixed price. With an online auction, you may get more than you expect or less. With a fixed-price format, you only get paid what you ask, and it must be a competitive price for the car to sell at all.

Click **Save and Continue** to go from page to page.

Sell: Select Your Market and Format

To begin, select a format and click the "Save and continue" button.

◉ **Sell using the auction-style format**
The auction-style format enables bidding on your items. This format is recommended for vehicles and parts. You may choose to include a Buy It Now option in your auction listing. Learn more

○ **Sell at a Fixed Price**
Allow buyers to purchase your items at a price you set. You can also choose to accept a Best Offer from your buyers in the Fixed Price format. Learn more

[Save and continue]

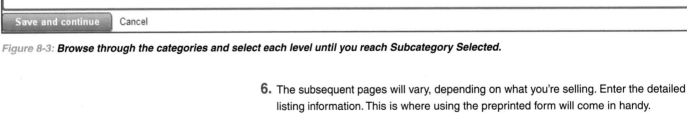

Sell: Choose a Category

Help buyers find your listing

- Select the category that best describes your item.
- If you are selling parts or accessories, reach more buyers by selecting two categories (additional fees apply)

| Browse categories | Recently used categories |

Having trouble with this feature? Try the basic version

Categories

& Trucks >	Chrysler >	Avenger	You have finished selecting a category.
cycles >	Citroen	Caliber	
Vehicles & Trailers >	Cord	Caravan	Click the **Save and continue** button below.
sports >	Daewoo >	Challenger	
& Accessories >	Datsun >	Charger	
	DeLorean	Coronet	
	DeSoto	Dakota	
	Dodge >	Dart	
	Eagle	Durango	
	Edsel	Grand Caravan	
	Ferrari >	Intrepid	
	Fiat	Journey	

Categories you have selected

- Cars & Trucks > Dodge > Caravan | See sample listings | Remove

Category number: 6193

| Save and continue | Cancel |

*Figure 8-3: **Browse through the categories and select each level until you reach Subcategory Selected.***

6. The subsequent pages will vary, depending on what you're selling. Enter the detailed listing information. This is where using the preprinted form will come in handy.

- Enter the VIN for newer vehicles to get pre-filled information about your vehicle.

  –Or–

  For older vehicles, click **Let Me Specify The Details Myself**. You can then manually enter detailed information about the item being sold.

  In either case, then enter Title and Description information.

- Set your price requirements: your starting price, reserve price, or Buy It Now price and auction duration and item location.

- Identify and download photos to be used. Make sure your photos are clear, with adequate lighting, and of all parts of the car (see Figure 8-4).

- Choose a theme, layout, and upgrades, such as bolding, highlighting, or Featured Plus!, or a listing icon.

- Enter your payment and shipping requirements and terms. Enter any terms, such as a required deposit, whether you accept only PayPal or checks, and so on. Identify how you want to communicate with the buyer, who is responsible for the pickup and shipping, and whether you want to block any particular buyers, for example those who live in foreign countries.

7. Review what you have entered, make any changes if necessary, and then click **Submit Listing**.

Figure 8-4: *Taking a complete set of photos that displays all parts of your car, including defects, will give your buyers confidence.*

Polly Professor says: "Use special listing-management tools, such as CARad, for professional listings. It costs about $10 for a single listing, or up to about $300 for unlimited listings for 30 days. Check it out at www.CARad.com."

Professor Polly says: "Often, potential buyers will request additional photos. You can save some time by taking a large number of photos during your initial shooting and choosing the best to display on eBay, keeping the others available if additional photo requests are made."

NOTE

The more like a bargain you can make your vehicle appear, the more activity you will have. In the collectible field, heavy bidding can draw additional attention. Many buyers are looking for a vehicle as an investment, hoping to resell it at some future date. Heavy bidding will often draw the attention of this type of buyer. Sometimes an item looks better if someone else is about to get it, and a no-reserve auction assures bidders that someone will be successful with this auction. If you must start an auction with a reserve, you can ignite a bidding fire when you reduce it or remove it.

Pay eBay Motors Fees

eBay Motors has three basic fees: an insertion fee, a transaction services fee, and feature fees:

- Insertion fees depend on the vehicle's category. The first four listings in a 12 month timeframe have no insertions fees. As of the fifth sales, the fees are $20 for passenger vehicles and other vehicles (which includes a large assortment of vehicles, such as aircraft, commercial trucks, and RVs), $15 for motorcycles and power-sport vehicles.

- Unless your vehicle received no bids or the reserve price was not met, you will be charged a transaction service fee, whether or not the transaction is finalized. The fee for passenger vehicles is $125, for motorcycles and power-sports vehicles is $100.

- Feature fees are ways you can emphasize or enhance the basic listing. They include listing upgrade fees, which vary from $99.95 for listing the vehicle on the eBay Motors home page to $1 for a Buy It Now listing or for a custom scheduled auction. These options include fees for placing the listing for exceptional exposure to enhancing the title and subtitle or the listing itself so that it is more visible in the standard placement. Vehicle reserve fees allow you to list with a reserve. Picture services fees present options for various photo features (ranging from $0.15 after the first photo to $2.00 for Gallery Plus). Fees vary, depending on the item.

Use Half.com

Half.com is where you can sell books, music, movies (DVD or VHS), video games, and game systems. This market is huge, consisting of thousands of used items sold at high discounts. As a seller, you can easily list and sell items here.

This is a fixed-price market. Half.com collects the money and deposits it to your account. A Half.com fee is charged when you make a sale.

From the footer links on the bottom of the eBay home page, click **Half.com**. The screen shown in Figure 8-5 is displayed. Or, as the name implies, type half.com in your browser's address box and press **ENTER**.

Research the Price of Items

Before you sell your books, you will want to research the prices currently offered on the market. If there are not a lot of books already listed, you can charge rates up to 50 to 60 percent of the publisher's price for new, unused, popular books to about 25 to 35 percent for used books. However, if there are books already listed, you'll have to follow their guidance to be competitive.

1. From the Half.com home page, click the **Search All Categories** down arrow, and click the category you want to search. Click **Go** to the right of the Search text box.

TIP

Include the "X" that some International Standard Book Numbers (ISBNs) may have and the small numbers on the right or left that some Universal Product Codes (UPCs) may have.

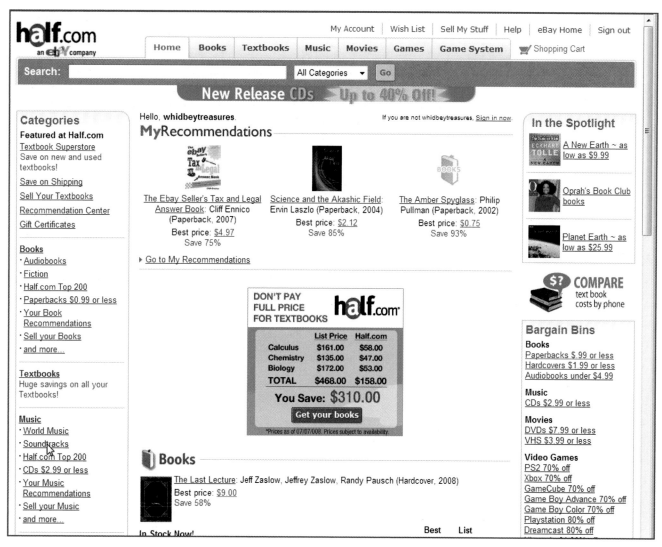

*Figure 8-5: **Half.com is a specialty market within eBay for selling used books, videos, CDs, and games and game systems.***

2. Again, click the **Search** text box and click how you want to search—for instance, by Title, Author, or ISBN.

3. In the text box to the left, type the title, author's name, the ISBN (for books only), or the UPC (for all other products). Click **Go**. A list of items matching your search term listed for sale by all sellers is displayed, as shown in Figure 8-6.

–Or–

To focus a search, click **Advanced Search**, where you can define a search by Title, Author, ISBN, and the type of media.

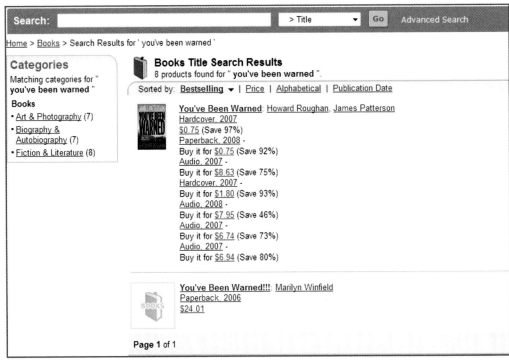

Figure 8-6: *Through searching for copies of a book that are currently for sale, you can see the varying costs for each book and the stated condition each is in.*

QUICKFACTS

DETERMINING CONDITIONS

It is important to be accurate and not try to make your item appear to be in better condition than it is. Your customers may be dissatisfied and leave negative feedback otherwise. If an item cannot meet the "Acceptable" condition, it cannot be sold on Half.com.

DETERMINE CONDITIONS FOR BOOKS

- **Brand New**: Unread, new, in perfect condition.

- **Like New**: No missing or damaged pages, no creases or tears, no underlining or highlighting, binding undamaged, cover undamaged, dust jackets not missing for hardcover books.

- **Very Good**: No blatant damage to the cover, dust jacket not missing for hardcovers, all pages undamaged, no underlining or highlighting, no writing in margins, very minimal wear and tear.

- **Good**: Very minimal damage to the cover, dust jacket may be missing, minimal wear to binding, no highlighting of text, no writing in the margins, no missing pages and most are undamaged.

- **Acceptable**: Some damage to the cover and binding but book still holds together, possible writing in the margins, may have underlining or highlighting, no missing pages. The book has wear but is readable.

Continued . . .

NOTE

If you are selling one item and know your ISBN or UPC or Manufacturing Part Number, you can use the Quick Sell technique. Click **Sell Your Stuff**, type your ISBN or other ID in the Quick Sell text box, and click **Continue**.

List an Item to Sell

There are several paths to getting to the Sell My Item pages. If you have previously searched for an item, you can follow these steps. Use the Note to go directly to how you can sell an individual item without searching for comparative prices first.

1. To list an item to be sold, from the search results page, click the **Sell Your Stuff** link above the title bar in the upper-right area.

2. If this is your first time selling an item through Half.com, you will have to register first.

3. Depending on how you elect to sell your item, you may need to click a category to get to the Describe Your Item page. (If so, enter the identifying information (ISBN, UPC, product name) your category requires and click **Continue**.) You may be already there if you first searched for the item. On the Sell Your Item | Describe Your Item page:

   - Click the **Condition** down arrow, and choose an option. (See the "Determining Conditions" QuickFacts.)

   - Under Comments, type up to 500 characters describing your item. You may not use this area to advertise or type other information, such as directions to your other items for sale or to your Web site.

   - You may also enter an expanded description of the item. Click **Preview Your Description** to see what it will look like.

   - Click **Continue**.

4. You now set the price for the item and formally list it. On the Sell Your Item | Price And List Your Item page:

   - A Pricing Information table is displayed next to the pricing text box. The Average Sell Price and Last Sold Price are displayed. Under Your Price, type the price you want for your book. It should be consistent with the other books being sold.

DETERMINING CONDITIONS *(Continued)*

DETERMINE CONDITIONS FOR CDS

- **Brand New**: Unread, unused, unopened, and undamaged CD, video, or game in perfect condition.

- **Like New**: Item still in shrink-wrap or looks as if it is just taken out of it, all components present, no missing parts, no damage.

- **Very Good**: No damage to the case or item cover, all parts present, no scratching on CDs or DVDs or fuzzy frames on VHS tapes.

- **Good**: May have some damage to the case or cover, instructions still included, no scratches on a CD or DVD or fuzzy VHS frames, cover art and liner notes are included.

- **Acceptable**: May have a tear or hole in the cover or box, video game instructions may not be present, still usable.

NOTE

You will be asked to register as a seller on Half.com. You must provide your credit card number and address. These will not be used to charge any costs against your account. Rather, the card and address are used to verify your identity. You will be asked for your bank name, bank routing number, and checking account number. This is used to deposit money from your sales directly into your banking account. Click **Register**.

- Type the quantity you have if it is different from the default of 1.

Your Price * Required	Pricing Information		
$ 0.75		Like New Condition	All Conditions
	Average Sell Price	$0.75	$0.94
Quantity * Required	Last Sold Price	$0.75	$0.75
1	Current Price Range	$0.95 - $10.61	$0.75 - $25.56
Maximum of 1000	Number of items listed	0	0

5. Click **List Item**. The Congratulations, Your Item Has Been Listed message is displayed.

6. At this point, you can list another item, list multiple items (only used if you are entering books by ISBN or other items using UPC numbers), manage your inventory, or continue shopping.

List Multiple Items

If you are listing several books, CDs, or other items and you can identify the item using an ISBN or UPC number, you can quickly and easily enter several at a time. If you have material that was produced prior to the use of the UPC or ISBN, you probably should list them on the eBay site instead of the Half.com site.

Professor Polly says: "Believe it or not, it generally pays to downgrade your condition descriptions. If the book is not absolutely new, try to be as critical as possible when grading your merchandise. Look at it through the eyes of the buyer when she opens your package. If the buyer thinks it is actually nicer than described, you are on your way to repeat sales."

1. On the Half.com home page title bar, click **Sell Your Stuff**.

2. Click **Multiple Item Listing**; or, on the last page of listing a single item, click **List Multiple Items**. The page shown in Figure 8-7 is displayed.

> **Multiple Item Listing**
> To list in bulk with ISBN's or UPC's use the Multiple Item Listing page to list up to ten items at one time.

- Type the ISBN or UPC codes.

- Click the **Condition** down arrow, and click an option.

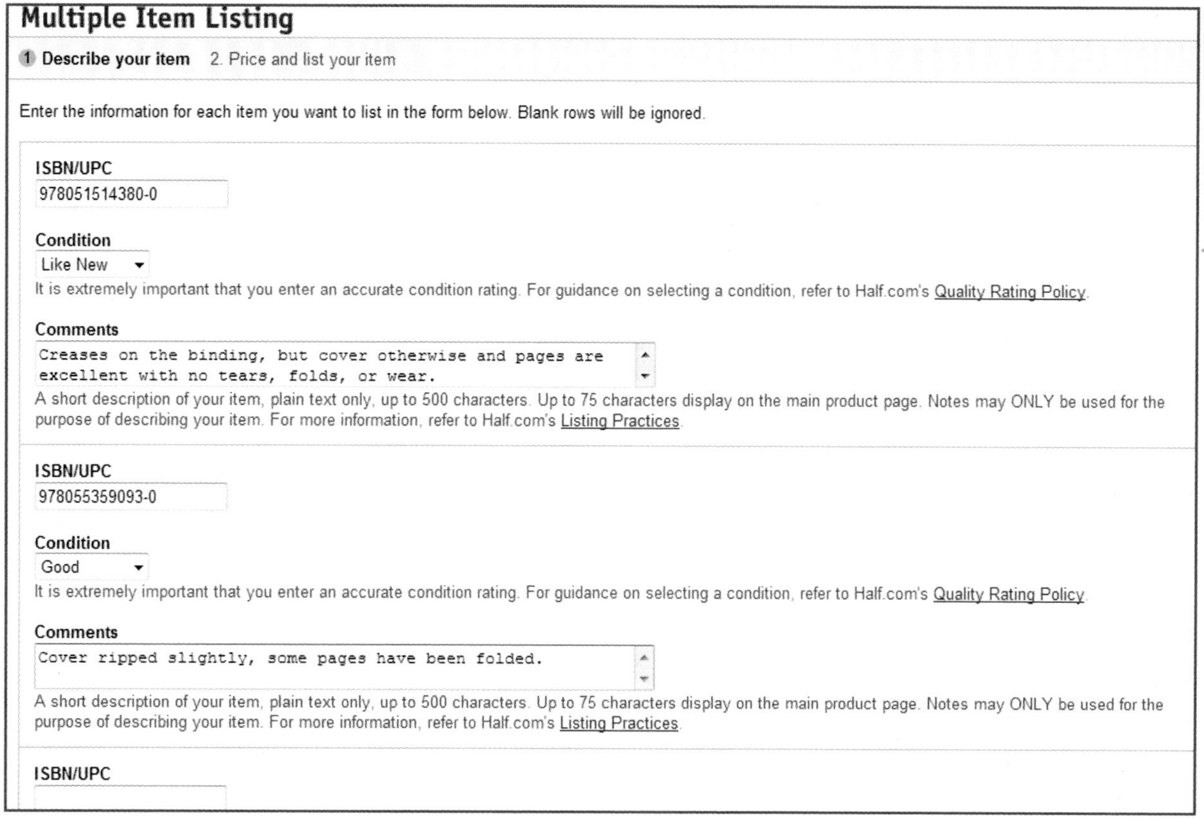

Multiple Item Listing

① **Describe your item**   2. Price and list your item

Enter the information for each item you want to list in the form below. Blank rows will be ignored.

ISBN/UPC

> 978051514380-0

Condition

> Like New   ▼

It is extremely important that you enter an accurate condition rating. For guidance on selecting a condition, refer to Half.com's <u>Quality Rating Policy</u>.

Comments

> Creases on the binding, but cover otherwise and pages are
> excellent with no tears, folds, or wear.

A short description of your item, plain text only, up to 500 characters. Up to 75 characters display on the main product page. Notes may ONLY be used for the purpose of describing your item. For more information, refer to Half.com's <u>Listing Practices</u>.

ISBN/UPC

> 978055359093-0

Condition

> Good   ▼

It is extremely important that you enter an accurate condition rating. For guidance on selecting a condition, refer to Half.com's <u>Quality Rating Policy</u>.

Comments

> Cover ripped slightly, some pages have been folded.

A short description of your item, plain text only, up to 500 characters. Up to 75 characters display on the main product page. Notes may ONLY be used for the purpose of describing your item. For more information, refer to Half.com's <u>Listing Practices</u>.

ISBN/UPC

*Figure 8-7: **You can quickly enter information about multiple items if you use the ISBN or UPC numbers to identify them.***

- Type any comments that go with the item.
- Continue with these steps until all your items are entered.
- Click **Continue**.

3. Each item will be displayed on the Multiple Item Listing | Price And List Your Item page. Review your shipping information. Verify that the default price in the Your Price text box is correct; change it if you want. You can check the current pricing by clicking the ISBN in the book information.

4. After verifying each item, click **List Item**. The Congratulations, Your Page Has Been Listed message is displayed.

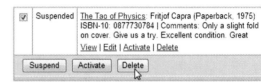
Manage Your Inventory

Half.com contains an inventory-management page where you can edit, delete, or suspend items or make other changes. You can list up to 100 items per page.

1. From the Half.com home page, click **My Account** in the Half.com header. You'll have to sign in. On the My Account sidebar, under Selling, click **Manage Inventory**. You will see a summary of the categories of inventory you have listed.

2. Click the category you want to see. You'll see a page similar to that shown in Figure 8-8:

- To delete items, place a check mark in the leftmost check box next to the item's name, and click **Delete**. You can also click Delete beneath the item's name.

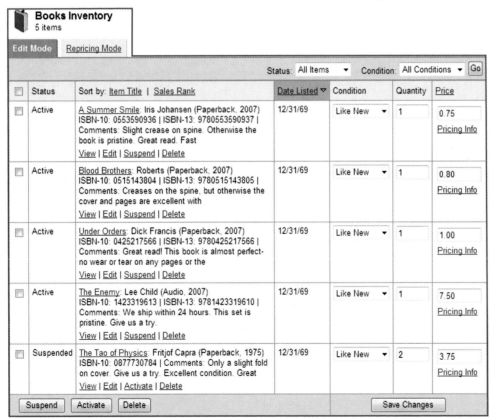

☑	Suspended	The Tao of Physics: Fritjof Capra (Paperback, 1975) ISBN-10: 0877730784 | Comments: Only a slight fold on cover. Give us a try. Excellent condition. Great View | Edit | Activate | Delete

[Suspend] [Activate] [Delete]

- To suspend items, place a check mark in the check box next to the item's name, and click **Suspend**. You can also click **Suspend** beneath the item's name.

- To reactivate suspended items, place a check mark in the check box next to the suspended item's name, and click **Activate**. You can also click **Activate** beneath the item's name for previously suspended items.

- To view the item as it is listed, click **View** beneath the item's name and description.

- To sort the display by item name, sales rank, date listed, or price, click the relevant column heading.

Revise Prices

You will want to review your prices periodically to see how your prices compare to what is being

Figure 8-8: **Edit Mode allows you to manage your inventory by deleting items, suspending them, repricing them, or editing their descriptions.**

Books Inventory (from Figure 8-8)

Books Inventory
5 items

Edit Mode | Repricing Mode

Status: All Items ▼   Condition: All Conditions ▼ [Go]

	Status	Sort by: Item Title | Sales Rank	Date Listed ▽	Condition	Quantity	Price
☐	Active	A Summer Smile: Iris Johansen (Paperback, 2007) ISBN-10: 0553590936 | ISBN-13: 9780553590937 | Comments: Slight crease on spine. Otherwise the book is pristine. Great read. Fast View | Edit | Suspend | Delete	12/31/69	Like New ▼	1	0.75 Pricing Info
☐	Active	Blood Brothers: Roberts (Paperback, 2007) ISBN-10: 0515143804 | ISBN-13: 9780515143805 | Comments: Creases on the spine, but otherwise the cover and pages are excellent with View | Edit | Suspend | Delete	12/31/69	Like New ▼	1	0.80 Pricing Info
☐	Active	Under Orders: Dick Francis (Paperback, 2007) ISBN-10: 0425217566 | ISBN-13: 9780425217566 | Comments: Great read! This book is almost perfect- no wear or tear on any pages or the View | Edit | Suspend | Delete	12/31/69	Like New ▼	1	1.00 Pricing Info
☐	Active	The Enemy: Lee Child (Audio, 2007) ISBN-10: 1423319613 | ISBN-13: 9781423319610 | Comments: We ship within 24 hours. This set is pristine. Give us a try. View | Edit | Suspend | Delete	12/31/69	Like New ▼	1	7.50 Pricing Info
☐	Suspended	The Tao of Physics: Fritjof Capra (Paperback, 1975) ISBN-10: 0877730784 | Comments: Only a slight fold on cover. Give us a try. Excellent condition. Great View | Edit | Activate | Delete	12/31/69	Like New ▼	2	3.75 Pricing Info

[Suspend] [Activate] [Delete]   [Save Changes]

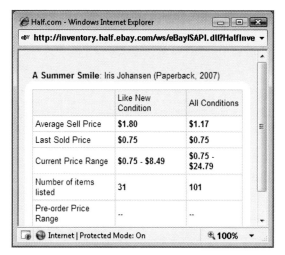

Figure 8-9: **The Pricing Info table reveals competitive pricing information, such as the last price sold, the average sell price, and more.**

currently asked/paid. If you have slow-to-sell items, reevaluate whether your prices are still competitive.

1. On the Books Inventory page (see previous section), click the **Pricing Info** link to the right of a book to see the pricing information, as shown in Figure 8-9.
2. To change prices, click **Edit** beneath the item title and description, and type a new price. You can also change the Condition, Quantity, or Comments boxes.
3. Click **Save Changes** to make them final.

Use Kijiji to Post Ads

Kijiji is where you can post an online ad for the city closest to you. It is similar to Craigslist, and is another way to sell your items. Posting an ad is free, and there are no fees if you sell or buy an item. You can post up to 25 ads per day. But if you want to post more than 25 ads, you can contact Kijiji and get permission. Kijiji is simply a way to exchange information about what is for sale or available.

Post an Ad

To post an ad for an item:

1. On the eBay home page, on the second links bar at the bottom of the page, click **Kijiji**.

2. Before posting or viewing an ad for the first time, you will have to select a state on the map, and select a city or enter a ZIP code (see Figure 8-10). Click a state on the map and then a city, or click the **Select A State** down arrow and click your selection, or click a city link beneath the map.
3. On the Kijiji home page header, click **Post Ad**.
4. Click a category on the Select A Category page, shown in Figure 8-11.

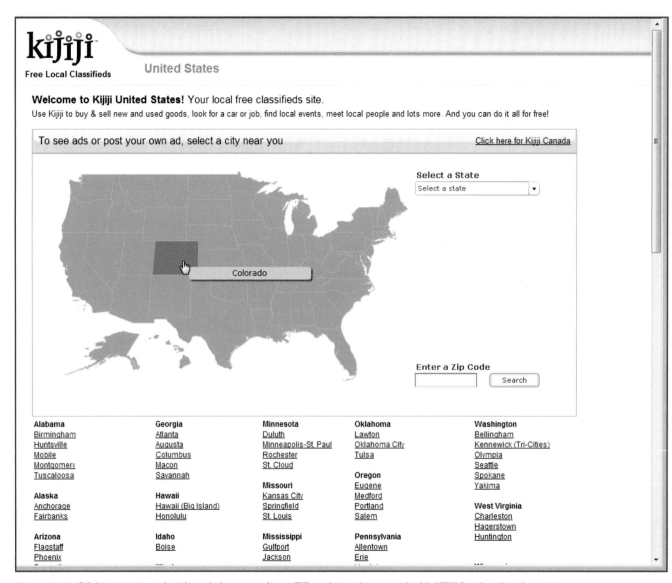

Figure 8-10: *Click a state to select it and choose a city or ZIP code to place an ad with Kijiji for the city closest to you.*

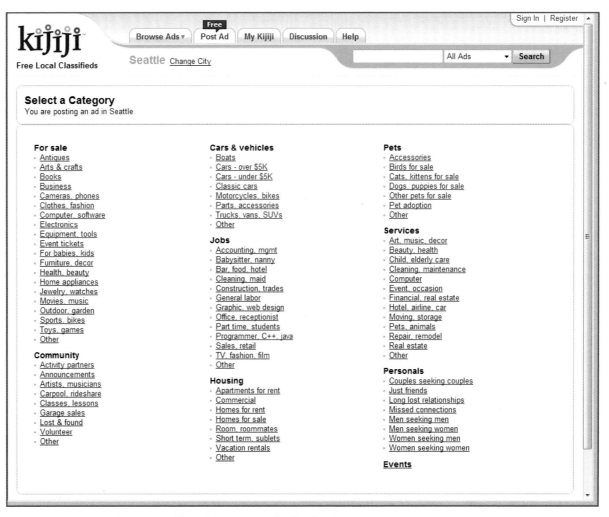

Figure 8-11: You can place a classified ad by category for the city closest to you.

5. Complete the form, as shown in Figure 8-12:

- Click whether you are selling or seeking the item.

- Give your item a short title.

- Type the price or click the down arrow, and select another way to offer the item.

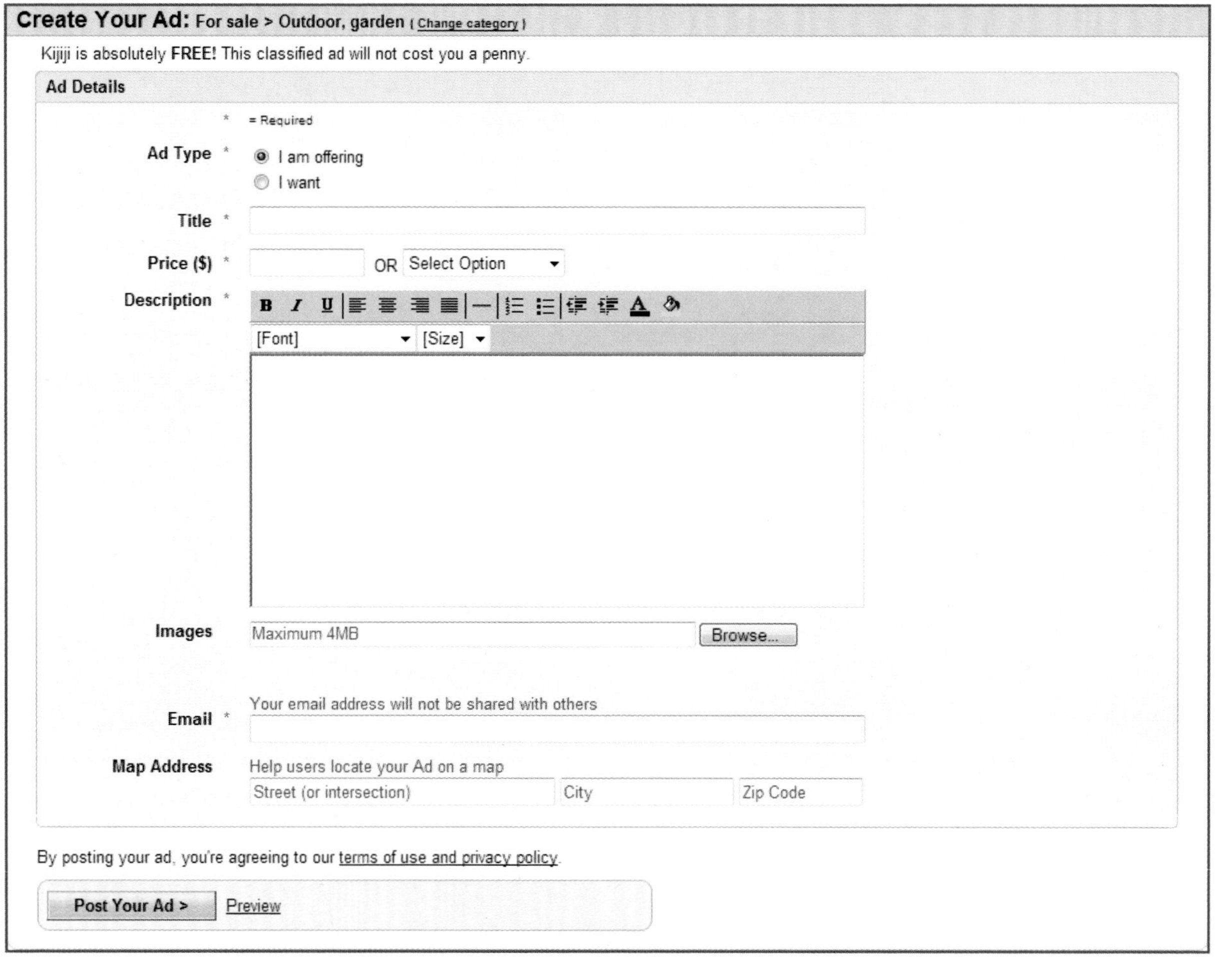

Create Your Ad: For sale > Outdoor, garden (Change category)

Kijiji is absolutely **FREE!** This classified ad will not cost you a penny.

Ad Details

* = Required

Ad Type *	◉ I am offering
	○ I want
Title *	
Price ($) *	OR Select Option ▾
Description *	**B** *I* U ⊫ ≡ ≡ ≣ — ⁝≡ ⁝≡ ⫤ ⫥ A ⬥
	[Font] ▾ [Size] ▾

Images	Maximum 4MB Browse...
Email *	Your email address will not be shared with others
Map Address	Help users locate your Ad on a map
	Street (or intersection) City Zip Code

By posting your ad, you're agreeing to our terms of use and privacy policy.

Post Your Ad >   Preview

Figure 8-12: *After selecting a category, you will see the form where you define your ad in Kijiji.*

- Type a description.
- If you want to add images, click **Browse** and find and select the file image.
- Type your e-mail address.
- Type the name of a main street close to you, type the city, and ZIP code.

6. Click **Post Your Ad** when you are ready. You will receive a confirming e-mail.

TIP

To improve your hits on your ads, you should include pictures of the item. Another aid is to offer "Best Offer" to give some flexibility to your pricing. Your description and title should be very clear to enable to the reader to understand exactly what it is you are offering.

NOTE

You cannot post an ad in multiple cities.

CAUTION

There is little redress if a transaction goes badly. If you feel you are defrauded or cheated, you must handle it yourself by going to the police. You should contact Kijiji so they can track and block repeat offenders, but their actions will be limited since they do not get involved in any transactions.

Register with Kijiji

Although you don't have to register with Kijiji to place an ad, there are a few benefits to doing so. You will be able to create ads and then work with them without needing to confirm your actions with Kijiji. You can add your two cents to the Discussion blocks, and you can have a unique nickname all your own.

To register:

1. Click **Register** in the upper-right area of the Kijiji page.

2. Fill in the form as displayed in Figure 8-13, and then click **Register.**

Figure 8-13: **You can register with Kijiji to create your own nickname, participate in discussions, and work with your ads with less effort.**

Chapter 9
Applying eBay to Nonprofits

There are currently around 1.7 million nonprofit organizations in the United States representing over 7 percent of the nation's GNP (gross national product). Nonprofits are a growing and vital part of eBay through Giving Works auctions, its nonprofit face. To date, over 13,000 nonprofits have registered with eBay, and more than $78 million has been raised through eBay sales. Selling on behalf of nonprofits is done in three ways:

- You can register as a *nonprofit* organization and sell items directly to eBay buyers. This is also called being a *direct seller*.

- You can be a *community seller* by registering either as a *casual seller* and contributing a percentage of your sales to a nonprofit of your choice, or as a *professional seller* (where you have an eBay Store and are selling full-time) and donate a percentage of your auction sales to the nonprofit cause of your choice.

UNDERSTANDING MISSIONFISH

MissionFish, a service of the Points of Light Foundation, a 501(c)(3) nonprofit, operates the charity auctions for eBay. The charity auctions are known collectively as eBay Giving Works. eBay Giving Works allows nonprofit organizations to raise money for their charitable causes. Since November 2003, over 13,000 nonprofits have registered with MissionFish, and through it have raised over $78 million. MissionFish does several tasks for eBay:

- It enables sellers to sell in-kind donations to raise funds.

- It provides a directory of nonprofits associated with eBay Giving Works.

- It verifies that the nonprofits are real and valid entities.

- It collects the donations of supportive sellers and distributes them for eBay.

- It handles online contribution tracking and tax receipts for sellers.

A seller registers with eBay Giving Works to sell a product and agrees to give a percentage of the proceeds (from 10 to 100 percent, stated in the item description) to a nonprofit organization that the seller supports. Before they post an item for sale, sellers must register with MissionFish, who then verifies that the recipient of the donation is a valid nonprofit. MissionFish handles the distribution of the money, so you can be assured that the donation goes to the nonprofit organization.

- You can be a *trading assistant/drop-off location/agency* selling items for others, and attracting nonprofits to your own business.

All of these methods present innovative ways to raise funds and to reach out to millions of people, finding fresh sources of funds for your favorite nonprofit and exposing your cause to a whole new group of backers. Offering material on eBay can give your nonprofit a constant presence to a worldwide audience. If your nonprofit organization can continuously keep items for sale on eBay, it will provide additional exposure for your cause. Furthermore, selling goods on eBay offers your volunteers and supporters new and fun avenues to support your cause. Other sellers, in addition to the tax deductions for charitable donations, often find their auctions selling for higher percentages, since people are willing to pay more for charity items, and eBay Giving Works provides more ways to guide buyers to nonprofit auctions.

NOTE

The eBay Foundation in its Community Gives program supports three nonprofits by giving $1 million and then adding one dollar for each donor that chooses that nonprofit. The three nonprofits are *First Books* to provide new books for low-income children, *Best Friends Animal Society* to build and support non-kill animal sanctuaries, and *Oxfam America* to provide clean, safe water to people in Ethiopia and Zambia.

TIP

To find eBay's nonprofit auction pages, click **Giving Works** at the end of the Categories sidebar on the home page.

Video Games
Everything Else
Giving Works

TIP

Direct-seller nonprofits do not use MissionFish to receive and distribute funds; rather, they handle these activities themselves.

Become an eBay Nonprofit Organization

A nonprofit organization is a legal entity. It is governed by strict laws regarding what makes up a nonprofit organization and how it must be registered with the state. This book assumes that you know those rules and have followed legal advice to set it up properly within state and federal laws.

But once you have become a nonprofit, or decided to support one on eBay, you might wonder, "Why use Giving Works?" After all, you can sell items on eBay whether or not you are registered as a nonprofit. When you are a recognized nonprofit on eBay, however, your items sold through eBay Giving Works are identified by an icon 🎗. Your donors can find you on a list of certified nonprofits; you have access to millions of potential donors; and your item will have greater exposure by being listed in four places: in an eBay category, in eBay Giving Works, in your eBay Store, and in your About Me page. The MissionFish home page is shown in Figure 9-1. The percentage being donated to the nonprofit will appear in the description of the item, for most items. It may not appear for items sold by third parties, such as trading assistants.

Browser Earl says: "Find out about the Points of Light Foundation at www. pointsoflight.org, and research MissionFish at www.missionfish.org."

Browser Earl

Browser Earl says: "Look through GuideStar's database of 1.7 million nonprofits for information on tax-exempt nonprofits registered with the IRS at www.guidestar.org."

In order for a nonprofit organization to benefit from Giving Works, it must possess the following characteristics, as determined by eBay, that distinguish the organization from a for-profit or nonqualified nonprofit group:

● The group provides a public service. What determines a public service varies widely. It can be a prosperous multimillion-dollar-based college or a small, struggling childcare facility. Among the organizations that are allowed are 501(c)(3) nonprofits, religious organizations, local chapters of larger nonprofits (such as Lions, Red Cross, or Rotary), small nonprofits (under $5,000 in revenue), and government agencies.

*Figure 9-1: **The MissionFish home page is one place you can register to be certified as a nonprofit.***

RAISING FUNDS

Fundraising consists of establishing relationships with as many people as you can, identifying your donors, planning events, and following up when donations are made with thank-yous and other outreach efforts. Using eBay as a part of your overall fundraising helps to maximize your donor base. To get to Giving Works, click **Giving Works** at the bottom of the Shop Your Favorite Categories list on the home page. Figure 9-2, displayed when you click **Are You A Nonprofit** on the Giving Works header, explains how eBay Giving Works helps.

IDENTIFY DONORS

Fundraising is all about establishing relationships. You need to get and keep donors to ensure your organization's success. The first step is to identify donors. Potential sources include:

- Present and past board members
- Volunteers
- Present and past donors
- Vendors or suppliers
- People responding to the mission or purpose of the nonprofit
- The targeted service group (if feasible—the homeless, for example, would not necessarily be a good donor base)

Continued . . .

- The group is exempt from paying federal taxes.
- The group possesses special status that allows gifts to be tax-deductible.
- The group must not have self-interest or private financial gain.
- The group does not engage in illegal or terrorist activities.
- The group accepts electronic funds transfer (EFTS) payments.

Professor Polly says: "Some organizations do not qualify to be nonprofit organizations. These include political organizations, private foundations, fraternities or sororities, business or homeowner associations, or other organizations with tax-exempt but not tax-deductible status."

Keep Your Nonprofit Viable

A nonprofit corporation has just as much need for planning and managing as does a for-profit corporation. Perhaps there is even a greater need, since nonprofits don't have a built-in requirement to stay solvent—the organization is built around the mission rather than around making money. Planning is essential to keeping a nonprofit viable.

CREATE THE PURPOSE OR MISSION OF THE NONPROFIT

One of the main differences between nonprofit and for-profit organizations has to do with their mission, or purpose for existing. For-profit corporations exist to make money for their owners or investors, while nonprofits raise money for a public purpose. This is a rather significant difference, and some of the potential impacts include the following:

- **There really is no "ownership" in nonprofits.** No one owns the corporation; therefore, no one personally receives the donations. At the same time, a nonprofit can be profitable. Funds go back into the nonprofit corporation's operations rather than to an individual. Nonprofits can be highly innovative, energetic, and entrepreneurial; or they can be conservative and cautious in their fundraising approaches and in fulfilling their mission.

QUICK**FACTS**

RAISING FUNDS *(Continued)*

ESTABLISH RELATIONSHIPS

Establish relationships by keeping in touch with your employees, donors, and volunteer base. Ways to do this include:

- Follow-up with immediate thank-you letters for donations.
- Send regular e-mail notices regarding your organization's activities. Send announcements of related events, introduce new personnel, and announce awards won or pending, or any other news pertaining to the organization.
- Send flyers on new legal challenges or accomplishments.
- Give parties, lunches, or other special events to recognize volunteers or donors.
- Send out press releases to recognize people and announce upcoming events.

Professor Polly says:
"You cannot tell if your nonprofit mission is being met if you do not have goals and objectives that you can track."

TIP

Notice that the goals did not include providing shelter for *all* the homeless on Washington Island. Only 20 persons can be sheltered during the summers, and up to 35 can be sheltered during emergencies. This is an essential part of defining a nonprofit mission: You must provide boundaries or limits to your mission; you can't do it all.

- **It is much easier to tell if a mission is being met for a for-profit than for a nonprofit.** The for-profit has the purpose of supplying something to a market, and if people buy their product or service and the corporation is profitable, then the mission is met. This is not the case with a nonprofit. Here, the success of a mission is often murky or hard to quantify. For example, how easily can you determine if a shelter for the homeless is meeting its mission? Is it by the number of homeless people who stay there? Is it by the numbers of new people who pass through? Is it by the absence of homeless people living on the nearby streets? The measurements of a nonprofit are often intangible and subjective. It has less to do with money raised and more to do with another purpose altogether.

- **Survival of a for-profit is not an issue of controversy.** If the corporation makes money, then the company survives. If it does not make money, then the corporation does not survive (although it may not be obvious for a while that it is not surviving). A nonprofit also has a need to survive, but there is more to it than just meeting the bottom line. There are questions around whether the mission is being met, as well as whether the group is financially viable. A constant pull exists between spending money to preserve the company versus spending money on the mission (that is, spending to keep an accounting employee versus spending to acquire another bed for a homeless person).

For these reasons, it is critical that a nonprofit develop a business plan that contains all the elements of a for-profit plan: a vision statement, a mission statement, and goals and objectives. There needs to be a broad statement of the dream or vision, a concise statement of how the vision will be fulfilled, and details about how the nonprofit will operate. These factors will help you evaluate whether you are meeting your purpose. The following is an example of a nonprofit's mission statement and goals:

- **Mission Statement:** To provide shelter for the homeless on Washington Island
- **Goals:**
  - To provide breakfast and a warm dinner per day for residents
  - To provide safe shelter for up to 20 individuals a night during normal weather
  - To provide emergency shelter for up to 35 individuals a night during severe weather
  - To provide linens and towels, soap and shampoo, tooth care supplies, and showers for residents
  - To provide a network within the community for full-time and part-time jobs for residents

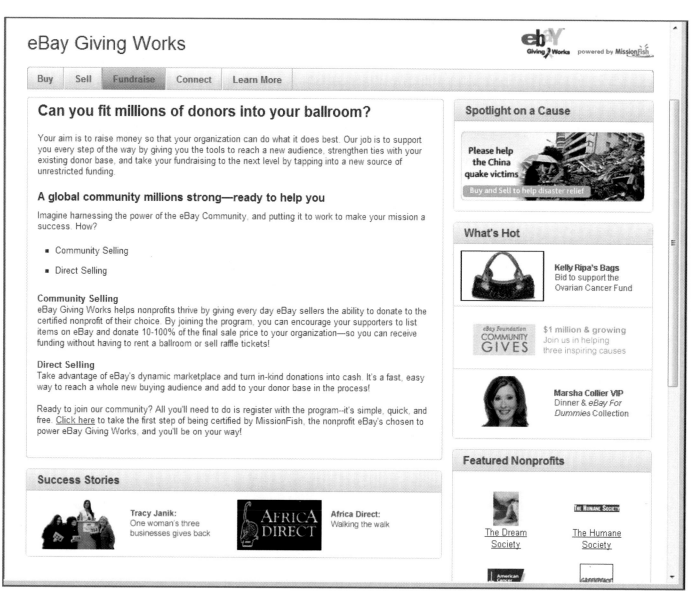

eBay Giving Works

eb**Y** Giving Works powered by MissionFish

| Buy | Sell | Fundraise | Connect | Learn More |

Can you fit millions of donors into your ballroom?

Your aim is to raise money so that your organization can do what it does best. Our job is to support you every step of the way by giving you the tools to reach a new audience, strengthen ties with your existing donor base, and take your fundraising to the next level by tapping into a new source of unrestricted funding.

A global community millions strong—ready to help you

Imagine harnessing the power of the eBay Community, and putting it to work to make your mission a success. How?

- Community Selling
- Direct Selling

Community Selling
eBay Giving Works helps nonprofits thrive by giving every day eBay sellers the ability to donate to the certified nonprofit of their choice. By joining the program, you can encourage your supporters to list items on eBay and donate 10-100% of the final sale price to your organization—so you can receive funding without having to rent a ballroom or sell raffle tickets!

Direct Selling
Take advantage of eBay's dynamic marketplace and turn in-kind donations into cash. It's a fast, easy way to reach a whole new buying audience and add to your donor base in the process!

Ready to join our community? All you'll need to do is register with the program--it's simple, quick, and free. Click here to take the first step of being certified by MissionFish, the nonprofit eBay's chosen to power eBay Giving Works, and you'll be on your way!

Success Stories

Tracy Janik:
One woman's three businesses gives back

Africa Direct:
Walking the walk

Spotlight on a Cause

Please help the China quake victims
Buy and Sell to help disaster relief

What's Hot

Kelly Ripa's Bags
Bid to support the Ovarian Cancer Fund

eBay Foundation COMMUNITY GIVES
$1 million & growing
Join us in helping three inspiring causes

Marsha Collier VIP
Dinner & eBay For Dummies Collection

Featured Nonprofits

The Dream Society

The Humane Society

*Figure 9-2: **Using eBay as a part of your overall fundraising is another way you can maximize your donor base.***

With these goals in mind, you can determine whether you are meeting them. Have residents been able to find jobs through your network? Have you had space for 20 people during the summer nights? How many breakfasts and dinners were you able to serve?

Work with Paid Staff and Volunteers

Many nonprofits have both paid staff and volunteers. Normally, a paid staff tends to the ongoing operations of the organization, while volunteers carry out the mission. One thing to consider is that often volunteers come and go, even when loyal and dedicated to the mission. Volunteers also have a greater need for training and appreciation. While the staff gets paid for their services, volunteers have varying needs and motivations for volunteering. Making sure these needs are satisfied and that the volunteers feel wanted and appreciated is an important part of the organization's success.

Another issue with nonprofits can be choosing the right person for a job. Choosing someone who is passionate about the mission may not be the best choice over someone better suited for the task at hand. Passion is a great thing, but you need people with relevant skills as well.

Build an Image

As with for-profit corporations, nonprofits also need to market themselves to the public. You may not be selling a product, but you are selling an image as a group worthy of providing a service and receiving donations for it. The image to donors, volunteers, and those being served is essential to the success of the organization. If donors do not see the organization as worthy and being something they want to support, donations will not keep the nonprofit viable. If volunteers do not see the organization as being worthy or appreciating their work, they will not support the organization, and a vital part of the organization will wither. Finally, if those being served feel uncomfortable with the nonprofit's image, they will stay away, diminishing the opportunity for the purpose of the organization to be served.

QUICK**FACTS**

USING eBAY FOR FUNDRAISING

Make eBay a part of your overall fundraising plans:

- Be a direct seller on eBay. Organize your volunteers and donors to contribute to a special one-time eBay auction drive. Schedule the week to be used for the auction. Notify everyone and gather donated items. Have volunteers or employees list the donated items on eBay. Send out press notices and e-mails reminding everyone of the auction.

- Open an eBay Store. Use donated goods, consignments, overstocked, or off-season items from manufacturers, vendors, and others.

- Organize your volunteers and donors as community sellers to sell items on behalf of your organization. Plan and promote special auction events.

- Notify everyone on your past and current donor lists about your eBay presence and how they can participate by selling items on behalf of your organization.

- Promote your auctions by arranging to be "In the Spotlight," placing a notice of your event on the Giving Works home page.

Spotlight on a Cause

BID TO HELP ANIMALS

- Use banner advertising for eBay keyword searches.

- Establish partnerships with other nonprofits for higher exposure.

Use the tools within eBay to establish an image. Let donors, volunteers, and others dealing with your organization know who you are by performing the following tasks:

- Create a Web site for your nonprofit that can be linked to from eBay.
- Create an About Me page.
- Create a logo to use on eBay that is easy to read and creative, if you don't already have one.
- Create a statement for eBay that explains your mission and allows your readers to get additional information through a link to your Web site.

Nonprofit Sally says: "You can offer good publicity for your donors by listing them in your auction pages. For example, 'This Arrow shirt was donated to our cause by Big-Mart.' It will help increase donations if you can offer your donors a little additional incentive to help your cause."

Use eBay to Sell Your Nonprofit Items

Where does eBay fit into all this? eBay offers a new way for donors to donate and for volunteers to contribute, and it introduces your service to thousands, perhaps millions, of new people. Many people will donate to you through eBay simply because they like to support nonprofits.

Be a Nonprofit Direct Seller

If you are a direct seller registered as a nonprofit 501(c)(3) corporation, you can sell your items directly on eBay, and eBay will donate some of your costs. In order to accomplish this:

1. Register as a nonprofit with MissionFish. Once they've verified that you meet their requirements to be considered a nonprofit charity, you are entered into the MissionFish database. (See "Register with MissionFish to Sell as a Nonprofit.")

2. Register with eBay for a seller's account.

3. Create your nonprofit listings using the regular Sell Your Item form.

Once you have set up your nonprofit account and seller's account, you can list items for sale. The listings will be identified on eBay with the eBay Giving Works ribbon icon. Item descriptions will contain your logo and mission, and will state that you will be receiving 100 percent of the final sales amount. See "Donate a Percentage of Your Sales to a Nonprofit" later in the chapter.

2 LARGE FISH WATER ANIMAL
Ostlund ART PRINT JAPANESE
$24.99
$28.99 *Buy It Now*
Time Left: 36m

NOTE

eBay Giving Works will donate proportional insertion and final value fees up to a total amount of $2 million annually for all successful sales listed by MissionFish when community sellers donate 10 to 100 percent to listed nonprofits.

Register with MissionFish to Sell as a Nonprofit

To become a nonprofit direct seller on eBay Giving Works, you must first establish a seller's account with eBay and register with MissionFish. As a nonprofit direct seller, you can sell items directly to a buyer within eBay. This book assumes that you have already sold items on eBay and therefore know how to register to sell on eBay. Before registering as a nonprofit with MissionFish, be prepared with the following items:

- Your nonprofit name.

- A mission statement consisting of fewer than 512 characters.

LEARNING ABOUT GIVING
WORKS FEES *(Continued)*

- eBay's insertion fees and final value fees for successful sales are credited to the seller proportional to the amount donated by the seller to the nonprofit. For instance, if the item sells for $50 and the seller donates $10 to a nonprofit organization, the insertion and final value fees would be reduced by 20 percent.

If a listing is unsuccessful, the listing fees are still charged but no final value fees are charged.

FEES FOR TRADING ASSISTANTS/
DROP-OFFS/AGENCIES

A trading assistant can become identified as a direct seller of the nonprofit. To do this, the nonprofit needs to be certified by MissionFish, the trading assistant needs to have an eBay ID for an eBay account, and the nonprofit needs to identify the trading assistant as a direct seller to MissionFish. In this case, the trading assistant would be subject to the same fees as a nonprofit direct seller, as noted previously.

CAUTION

A nonprofit organization cannot promote hate or terrorism or racial intolerance of any type or be engaged in illegal activities. It must not be on any list of terrorist organizations in the United States or in Europe or on any list of such belonging to the United Nations.

- Up to five keywords providing a way for sellers and buyers to find you on eBay searches.
- Up to three mission areas for categorizing your mission.
- A Web site Uniform Resource Locator (URL) (don't enter the "http://" part of the address).
- Your logo in .jpg, .jpeg, or .gif format, no more than 50 kilobytes (KB) in size. The file should be at least 72 dpi (dots per inch) resolution and be 150 pixels wide and not more than 250 pixels tall to be clear and readable.
- Your Employer Identification Number (EIN).
- The type of nonprofit you are: 501(c)(3), religious, a local chapter of a national nonprofit, a small nonprofit (less than $5,000 in income), governmental, or other.
- Your physical address.
- Contact name, phone number, fax number, e-mail address, and a second phone number to be used to notify your organization about a posted listing or with questions. This e-mail address will be used to notify you to complete the registration.
- Your 501(c)(3) verification letter (or other proof that your organization has tax-deductible status). You will have to fax a copy of this to MissionFish.
- Your bank account number and ABA routing number.
- A voided check from your nonprofit organization or a letter (on bank letterhead) from your bank verifying that you have an account there. The letter must give your nonprofit name and address, your bank account number, and the ABA routing code for the bank. You will have to fax a copy of this letter to MissionFish.

Professor Polly says: "You cannot use bank deposit slips, bank e-mail correspondence, or new account checks to verify your bank account."

To register with MissionFish to be a nonprofit direct seller:

1. Sign in to eBay for added security.
2. On the eBay home page, click **Giving Works** under the Shop Your Favorite Categories sidebar. The Giving Works home page is displayed, as shown in Figure 9-3.

Figure 9-3: *The home page of Giving Works displays spotlighted nonprofits and categories available for selling items.*

QUICKSTEPS

CANCELLING A CHARITABLE DONATION

As a nonprofit listed with MissionFish, you will receive donations from sellers who offer part or all of the proceeds from the sale of an item to your organization. Occasionally, an item may be unacceptable to your organization for any reason. You can decline to be part of the sale for this item as soon as it is posted on eBay by cancelling the listing.

When registering with MissionFish, you elect whether to receive e-mail alerts when an item is being sold naming your organization as the beneficiary. If you want to decline to be part of a listing, you request this using tools within your MissionFish account. The auction will be cancelled within 24 hours.

1. In your nonprofit's MyMissionFish account, click **My Open Listings**.

2. Click **Cancel** next to the auction item you want to cancel.

3. Complete the procedure by providing the reason why you want to cancel the sale.

4. Click **Continue**.

An e-mail disclosing your name and e-mail address is sent to the seller of the item, informing him or her of your decision to cancel the sale and why.

All insertion fees are credited to the seller's account, and there are no feedback effects.

3. Click **Sell** on the Giving Works header. Scroll down to Ready To Do Well While Doing Good, and click the **Nonprofit** link.

> **Ready to do well while doing good?** Choose the link below that best describes you:
>
> Are you a: Casual Seller who'd like to support your favorite cause?
>
> Professional Seller who'd like to learn more about how cause marketing can give your business a boost?
>
> Trading Assistant, Registered Drop-Off Location, or Agency who'd like to learn how eBay Giving Works can help you generate new business opportunities?
>
> Nonprofit who'd like to tap into the power of the eBay marketplace to raise funds for your organization?

4. On the Can You Fit Millions Of Donors Into Your Ballroom page, click **Click Here** under Direct Selling. The Register page will be displayed.

5. Follow the instructions on the form, and click **Review Your Information**. If it is as you want, submit it.

6. Check for the confirmation message at your e-mail address. Follow the instructions to continue the process.

7. Enter a password.

8. Fax the proof of tax-deduction status and your voided check.

MissionFish will verify that you are a valid nonprofit charity and will notify you when you can continue.

Browser Earl says: "To read the MissionFish Nonprofit User Agreement, click Help on the www.Missionfish.org web site. Under Policies, click Nonprofit User Agreement."

Browser Earl says: "If you have problems registering as a nonprofit, go to www.missionfish.org and click Help. Under Getting Started, click How To Register With MissionFish."

Search for Your Favorite Nonprofit on Giving Works

To find your favorite nonprofit, or to find any nonprofit, on Giving Works and make a donation:

1. From the eBay home page, click **Giving Works** on the bottom of the Categories sidebar.

2. Scroll towards the bottom of the Giving Works page, and next to Browse, click the letter of the name.

There are over 13,000 nonprofits raising funds on eBay. Meet them by browsing below or searching here.

Browse   # A B C D E F G H I J K L M N O P Q R S T U V W X Y Z

3. The Select A Nonprofit search page is displayed, shown in Figure 9-4. At the top is a form you can complete to search for a specific nonprofit or for a specific type of nonprofit. Beneath the form is the number of nonprofits in the directory for the letter you chose in Step 2 and the complete list alphabetically. You can perform one of the following actions:

- Scroll through the list to search for the name of the nonprofit you are looking for. You may have to click a different page number or type the page number in the Go To Page text box to find your entry.

Page 10 of 406   ← Previous **10** | 11 | 12 | 13 | 14 | 15 | 16 | 17 | 18 | 19 Next →

- Point at a link name to see a pop-up description of the nonprofit, as seen in Figure 9-4.

- Click **View** on the right of the nonprofit name link to see details regarding the organization.

- Fill in the form at the top of the page (see Figure 9-4) to narrow your search. Click the **State** down arrow, and select a state. Type a keyword or name in the Nonprofit Name Or Keyword text box. Click the **Nonprofit Type** down arrow, and select the nonprofit type. Click the **Spotlight On A Cause** down arrow to see a group of causes you might want to support. Click **Search** to initiate the search.

view

Spotlight on a Cause
Select topic
Select topic
Spotlight on the Environment
Saving the Arts
Healthy Hearts
Children in Need
Global Poverty
American Cancer Society
Breast Cancer Awareness
Disaster Relief
Education
Spotlight to support China Earthquake Relief
Support Myanmar Cyclone Relief
Helping Animals

Browser Earl says:
"Find Feature
Nonprofits on the
Giving Works home
page's right sidebar."

Browser
Earl

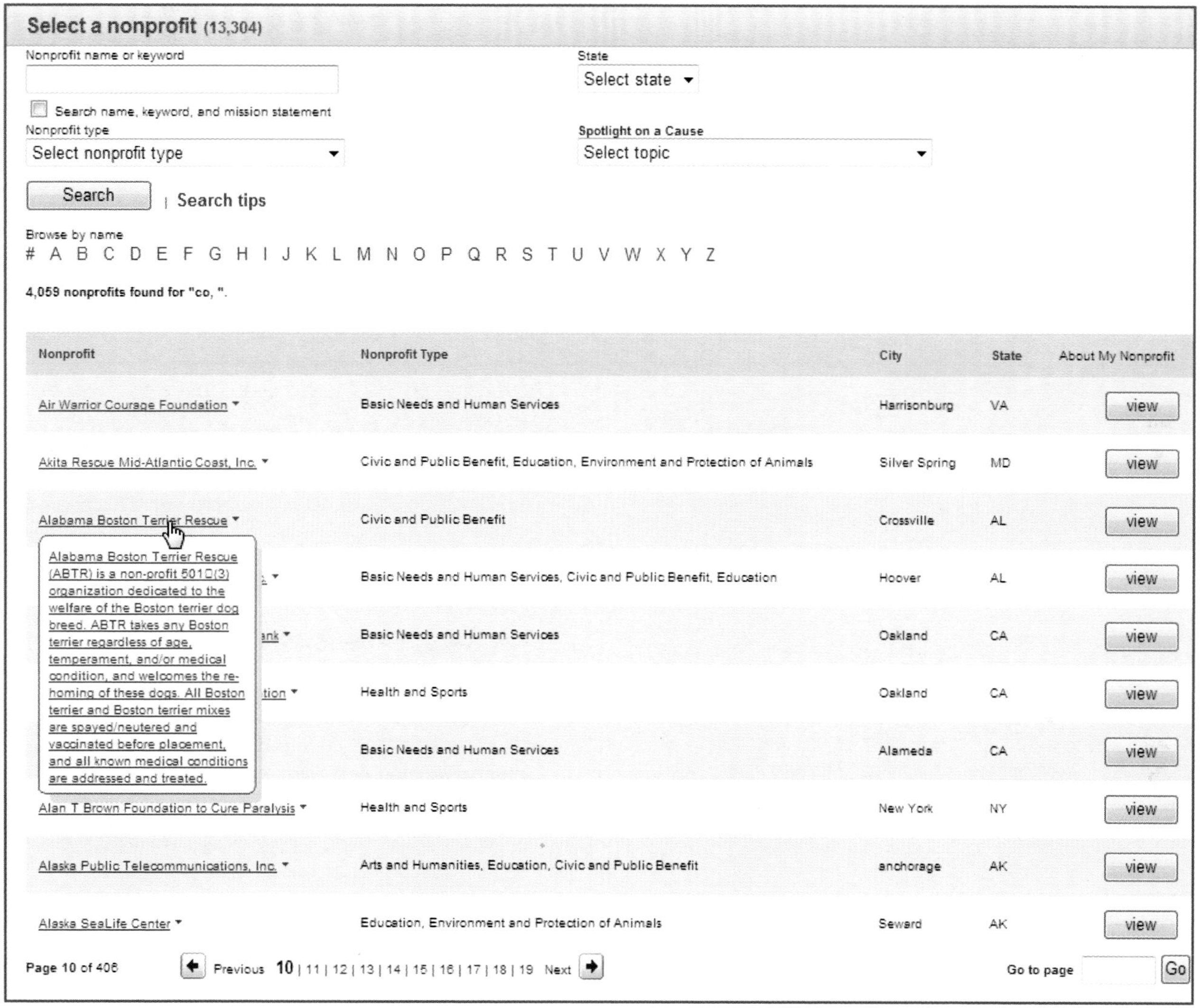

Select a nonprofit (13,304)

Nonprofit name or keyword

[   ]

☐ Search name, keyword, and mission statement

Nonprofit type

[Select nonprofit type   ▼]

State

[Select state ▼]

Spotlight on a Cause

[Select topic   ▼]

[Search] | Search tips

Browse by name

\# A B C D E F G H I J K L M N O P Q R S T U V W X Y Z

4,059 nonprofits found for "co, ".

Nonprofit	Nonprofit Type	City	State	About My Nonprofit
Air Warrior Courage Foundation ▼	Basic Needs and Human Services	Harrisonburg	VA	[view]
Akita Rescue Mid-Atlantic Coast, Inc. ▼	Civic and Public Benefit, Education, Environment and Protection of Animals	Silver Spring	MD	[view]
Alabama Boston Terrier Rescue ▼	Civic and Public Benefit	Crossville	AL	[view]
...▼	Basic Needs and Human Services, Civic and Public Benefit, Education	Hoover	AL	[view]
...nk ▼	Basic Needs and Human Services	Oakland	CA	[view]
...tion ▼	Health and Sports	Oakland	CA	[view]
	Basic Needs and Human Services	Alameda	CA	[view]
Alan T Brown Foundation to Cure Paralysis ▼	Health and Sports	New York	NY	[view]
Alaska Public Telecommunications, Inc. ▼	Arts and Humanities, Education, Civic and Public Benefit	anchorage	AK	[view]
Alaska SeaLife Center ▼	Education, Environment and Protection of Animals	Seward	AK	[view]

> Alabama Boston Terrier Rescue (ABTR) is a non-profit 501©(3) organization dedicated to the welfare of the Boston terrier dog breed. ABTR takes any Boston terrier regardless of age, temperament, and/or medical condition, and welcomes the re-homing of these dogs. All Boston terrier and Boston terrier mixes are spayed/neutered and vaccinated before placement, and all known medical conditions are addressed and treated.

Page 10 of 406   ◀ Previous **10** | 11 | 12 | 13 | 14 | 15 | 16 | 17 | 18 | 19 Next ▶   Go to page [   ] [Go]

*Figure 9-4: **Find the nonprofit you want by scrolling through the alphabetic list or by filling in the search form.***

Donate a Percentage of Your Sales to a Nonprofit

Even if your business does not have nonprofit status, you can donate a percentage of your income from a sale on eBay to your favorite nonprofit charity.

1. You must have an eBay seller's account with a feedback rating of at least 10, or you must complete the ID Verify procedure. You must have a credit card on file associated with the eBay account.

2. Click **Sell** in the eBay menu, and click **Sell An Item** on the drop-down menu. Click **Get Started** in the Sell window. This displays the Sell Your Item window.

3. Under Create Your Listing segment of the form, scroll down to Choose How You'd Like To Sell Your Item to the eBay Giving Works options.

4. You will be able to select the nonprofit you want to donate to from the MissionFish database, as shown in Figure 9-5. You may be prompted to click the **I Accept The Terms And Conditions** check box.

   - Select the name of the nonprofit you want, either by selecting one of the default choices or by clicking **Or, Select Another Nonprofit You Love** to browse for it.

   - Click the **Donation Percentage** down arrow, and click the percentage of the sale that you want the nonprofit to receive. It can be from 10 to 100 percent.

   - In the Updated eBay Giving Works Terms And Conditions area, click **I Accept The eBay Giving Works Terms and Conditions** and, optionally, **I Would Like To Pass My Contact Details Onto My Chosen Nonprofits**.

5. When your item is listed, it will display the eBay Giving Works ribbon icon 🎗. The item description itself will contain the icon, the name of the nonprofit you have selected, and the donation percentage, as well as a short description of the nonprofit that will receive the donation, as shown in Figure 9-6.

6. The nonprofit will be notified about the donation. They have 24 hours to cancel the donation if the item conflicts with their mission or for any other reason. (You will be sent an e-mail explaining the cancellation and why it occurred if that happens.)

🎗 eBay Giving Works ⑦

Donate part of your sale to your favorite nonprofit and eBay will give you a credit on basic selling fees for sold items.

○ I do not wish to donate at this time

◉ 🎗 Coupeville Arts Center

○ ⚕ St. Jude Children's Research Hospital

○ 🐼 World Wildlife Fund

<u>Or, select another nonprofit you love</u>

Donation percentage

| 10% ▼ |

Updated eBay Giving Works Terms and Conditions

- A donation of at least $5.00 is required if your listing sells.
- The donation will be collected from the same method you selected to pay your eBay fees. To pay with a different method, please visit your donation account inside My eBay.
- eBay has chosen MissionFish, a registered nonprofit, to collect and distribute your donation. They retain a small portion of each donation to help cover their costs.

☐ I accept the eBay Giving Works Terms and Conditions.

☐ I would like eBay to pass my contact details onto my chosen nonprofits (Optional - I can change this selection at any time in My eBay).

*Figure 9-5: **When you list an item for sale, you will have an opportunity to donate to the Giving Works nonprofit of your choice.***

TIP

To find the Charity Listing Policy, go to the eBay Giving Works home page. Scroll down to the **At A Glance** links on the lower-right area of the page. Click **Review The Charity Listing Policy**.

Nonprofit Sally says: "The description is particularly important. Provide as much information as possible, including brand name, model number, additional features, and manufacturer's suggested retail price if the item is new. Don't forget—buyers often have an interest in the charity organization and will often bid in excess of the real value. Give them as much help as you can."

7. After the item has been purchased, collect the funds as usual. The procedure by which the nonprofit receives the funds is displayed in Figure 9-7.

8. You will be given an opportunity to pay the fees, including the donation, with a one-time donation. This will shorten the donation time and allow you to waive the right to request a refund. If you don't pay this way, MissionFish will bill you for the amount of the sale on the second Monday after the auction has ended.

9. MissionFish pays the donation to the nonprofit you chose, after deducting the processing fees, and will send you a tax receipt. Donations are paid on the 25th of each month. However, donations are held by MissionFish for 45 days to allow time for sellers to request refunds. After the holding period, the donation will be paid on the next 25th of the month. If you waive your right to request a refund, the donation will be made to the nonprofit as much as 14 days sooner.

Browser Earl says: "To sign in to your MissionFish account, go to www.missionfish.org and click Sign In on the home page."

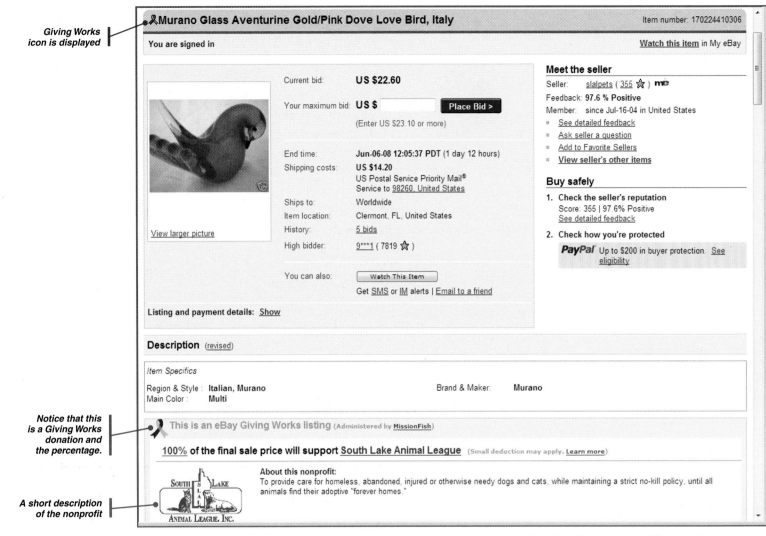

Giving Works icon is displayed

⚘Murano Glass Aventurine Gold/Pink Dove Love Bird, Italy   Item number: 170224410306

You are signed in   Watch this item in My eBay

Current bid:	**US $22.60**
Your maximum bid:	**US $** [ ] **Place Bid >**
	(Enter US $23.10 or more)
End time:	**Jun-06-08 12:05:37 PDT** (1 day 12 hours)
Shipping costs:	**US $14.20**
	US Postal Service Priority Mail®
	Service to 98260, United States
Ships to:	Worldwide
Item location:	Clermont, FL, United States
History:	5 bids
High bidder:	9***1 (7819 ☆)

View larger picture

You can also: **Watch This Item**

Get SMS or IM alerts | Email to a friend

Meet the seller

Seller: slalpets (355 ☆) me
Feedback: **97.6 % Positive**
Member: since Jul-16-04 in United States

- See detailed feedback
- Ask seller a question
- Add to Favorite Sellers
- View seller's other items

Buy safely

1. **Check the seller's reputation**
   Score: 355 | 97.6% Positive
   See detailed feedback

2. **Check how you're protected**

   PayPal Up to $200 in buyer protection. See eligibility

Listing and payment details: Show

Description (revised)

Item Specifics

Region & Style : **Italian, Murano**   Brand & Maker: **Murano**
Main Color :   **Multi**

Notice that this is a Giving Works donation and the percentage.

🎗 This is an eBay Giving Works listing (Administered by MissionFish)

100% of the final sale price will support South Lake Animal League (Small deduction may apply. **Learn more**)

A short description of the nonprofit

About this nonprofit:
To provide care for homeless, abandoned, injured or otherwise needy dogs and cats, while maintaining a strict no-kill policy, until all animals find their adoptive "forever homes."

Figure 9-6: The item description contains the identifying Giving Works icon, a notice that this is a donated item and the percentage donated, and a description of the nonprofit.

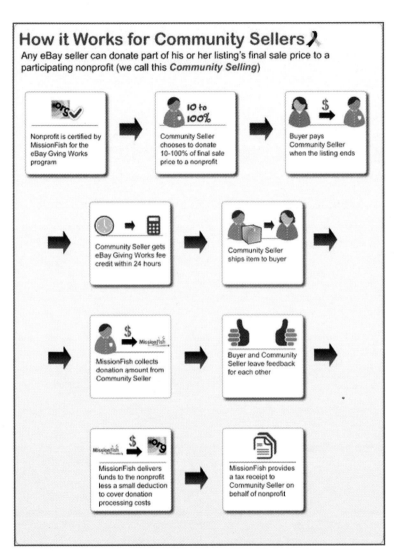

How it Works for Community Sellers

Any eBay seller can donate part of his or her listing's final sale price to a participating nonprofit (we call this *Community Selling*)

Nonprofit is certified by MissionFish for the eBay Gving Works program

Community Seller chooses to donate 10-100% of final sale price to a nonprofit

Buyer pays Community Seller when the listing ends

Community Seller gets eBay Giving Works fee credit within 24 hours

Community Seller ships item to buyer

MissionFish collects donation amount from Community Seller

Buyer and Community Seller leave feedback for each other

MissionFish delivers funds to the nonprofit less a small deduction to cover donation processing costs

MissionFish provides a tax receipt to Community Seller on behalf of nonprofit

*Figure 9-7: **The role of MissionFish is that of background facilitator, as it manages the flow and recording of money in the transaction.***

MissionFish Fees

MissionFish charges a fee for each item that is actually sold using Giving Works. These fees pay for the work required to maintain a database of nonprofits, to certify nonprofits, and to manage the flow of donations from the revenue of the sold item to the nonprofit, as well as the refund of the eBay insertion and final value fees. Here is how the fees are applied:

PERCENTAGE	DOLLAR AMOUNT
20%	From $5 (minimum) to $49
15%	From $50 to $199
10%	From $200 to $999.99
5%	From $1,000 to $4,999
3%	From $5,000 and up

The minimum fee is $1 for $5. The fees tend to average 10 percent over all Giving Works' donations. Your donation is 100 percent tax deductible, including the fee amount that is deducted from the donation amount.

Use Your Donation Account

Your Giving Works account can be found in My eBay, just like the rest of your eBay sales.

My Account
- Personal Information
- Addresses
- Notification Preferences
- Site Preferences
- Feedback
- PayPal Account
- Half.com Account
- Seller Account
- Donation Account
- Subscriptions

1. Click **My eBay** on the eBay header.

2. On the My eBay Views sidebar, under My Account, click **Donation Account**. The Donation Account page displays.

3. Click one of these links in the Donation Account page:

   - **Donations Due** lists the items you have sold and the donations due.

   - **Donation History** lists previous Giving Works donations.

   - **Preferences** allows you to change your My eBay settings.

   - **Donation Payment Method** allows you to specify your credit card, PayPal account, or bank account to be used for donations and fees.

QUICKSTEPS

RECOMMENDING A NONPROFIT TO eBAY

If your favorite nonprofit is not in the MissionFish directory, you can request that it be added. Provide the name to MissionFish, and eBay will send your named nonprofit an e-mail asking if they want to become a nonprofit on eBay. If they do, they will be asked to go through the registration process. MissionFish can then verify them and add their name to their directory.

1. From the eBay home page, click **Giving Works** at the bottom of the Categories sidebar.

2. Scroll to Browse and type a letter. It doesn't matter which one, since you want to display a particular screen, not find a nonprofit, assuming your desired nonprofit is not yet in the directory. (You may want to first verify that they are not already in the directory and then recommend them.)

3. Scroll to the bottom of the Select A Nonprofit page, and click **Recommend A Nonprofit That Is Not Listed**. A form is displayed. Recommend a nonprofit that is not listed

4. Complete the form, displayed in Figure 9-8, with your name and e-mail address, the nonprofit organization name and e-mail address, and a contact name, and click **Invite This Nonprofit**.

MissionFish will contact the organization and arrange for them to be certified so that they can be listed in the eBay Giving Works directory.

NOTE

By recommending your favorite charity to eBay, you could be doing them a big favor. Many charitable causes are unaware of the fundraising opportunities and potential exposure that eBay offers.

Request a Tax Receipt

To request a tax receipt after you have paid one or more donations:

1. On the My eBay listing on the Donations History page, click the boxes for each donation for which you want a tax receipt.

2. Click **Request A Tax Receipt**. Request a Tax Receipt

Receive a Nonpaying Bidder Refund

If you, as a community seller, have donated a percentage of an auction to a nonprofit from a successful sale and the bidder does not pay, you may be able to get a full refund of your donation and fees from the nonprofit organization.

1. Within 45 days of the listing end, you can file an Unpaid Item (UPI) Dispute with eBay (Chapter 5 describes how to initiate a UPI), checking the box, **I Want To Request A Refund For My eBay Giving Works Donation As Well**.

2. After 17 days without payment have elapsed, you can file for an eBay final value fee credit.

3. Request a donation refund from MissionFish (you'll need the date you filed for the final value fee credit):

   - Sign in to your seller's account, and click **Make A Payment**.

   - Fill in the **Refund Request** line on the right of the page.

4. You will get an e-mail approving or denying your refund.

Figure 9-8: **You can invite your favorite nonprofit organization to be included in eBay Giving Works' directory by completing this form.**

How to...

- *Place Items on Sale*
- *Create E-mail Mailings*
- *Understanding E-mail Messaging Fees*
- *Create a Flyer*
- *Understanding Cross-Promotion*
- *Leverage Your Off-eBay Web Sites*
- *Cross-Promote from eBay*
- *Add Search Engine Keywords to Your Store Pages*
- *Create an About Me Page*
- *Use the eBay Affiliate Program*
- *eBay-ing Your Traditional Business*

Chapter 10
Market and Promote Your eBay Business

A key concept of eBay marketing is to help you promote your items across all your eBay content, including listings, Stores, notifications, and even off-eBay locations. The ultimate goal is to drive customers to your eBay presence and keep them in your sphere of auctions, fixed-price listings, and informational pages, such as your About Me page. While all sellers have access to a foundation of promotional tools, it's when you open an eBay Store that eBay really rolls out the red carpet so you can fully take advantage of the concept of cross-promoting your items through sales, flyers, e-mailed newsletters, and more (see Figure 10-1).

This chapter addresses several key promotional considerations you will want to explore to better integrate your business into the overall marketing phenomenon that eBay provides.

10

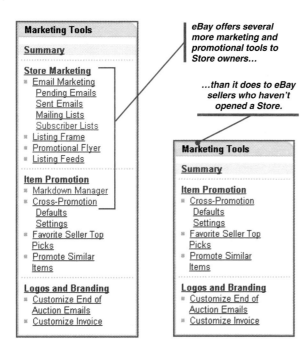

Marketing Tools

Summary

Store Marketing
- Email Marketing
  - Pending Emails
  - Sent Emails
  - Mailing Lists
  - Subscriber Lists
- Listing Frame
- Promotional Flyer
- Listing Feeds

Item Promotion
- Markdown Manager
- Cross-Promotion
  - Defaults
  - Settings
- Favorite Seller Top Picks
- Promote Similar Items

Logos and Branding
- Customize End of Auction Emails
- Customize Invoice

eBay offers several more marketing and promotional tools to Store owners...

...than it does to eBay sellers who haven't opened a Store.

Marketing Tools

Summary

Item Promotion
- Cross-Promotion
  - Defaults
  - Settings
- Favorite Seller Top Picks
- Promote Similar Items

Logos and Branding
- Customize End of Auction Emails
- Customize Invoice

Figure 10-1: To take advantage of eBay's marketing might, you need to open an eBay Store.

NOTE

Purchase-amount sales only apply to fixed-price items. You can apply a sale to auction listings only by offering free shipping. Also, any items currently on sale that are included in a new sale will assume the characteristics of the new sale.

Highlight Your Merchandise

In the first quarter of 2008, eBay sold in the neighborhood of $16 billion of merchandise among 84 million users. So the $64 question is: How do you direct a greater percentage of those users to help you gain a larger piece of that revenue? Since you've created an eBay presence, you've adhered to the adage of location, location, location. What you have to do now is distinguish your items to those millions of buyers from the other sellers and 547,000 eBay Stores. eBay provides several ways you can customize your selling persona to accomplish that goal.

Place Items on Sale

To attract buyers and move inventory in your eBay Store, you can discount items and hold what is analogous to "a sale." You can discount selling prices on your Store Inventory and eBay.com fixed-price items, though items in auctions are not eligible for selling-price discounts. (You can also offer free shipping, a sort of sale). You manage the items you place on sale and the discounts you offer using eBay's Markdown Manager.

1. From My eBay, on the Selling Manager sidebar, click **Marketing Tools**. On the Marketing Tools page, click **Markdown Manager** on the sidebar under Item Promotion.

   –Or–

   From your eBay Store home page, click **Seller, Manage Store**. On the Manage My Store page, click **Markdown Manager** on the sidebar.

   In either case, then click **Create Sale**.

Markdown Manager

Selectively putting items on sale is an excellent way to promote your listings and attract new buyers. Learn more about Markdown Manager.

Create Sale

2. On the Markdown Manager: Create Your Sale page, provide a name for the sale (for your own use), and select start and end times.

10

Choose your discount

☑ Price discount (auctions excluded)

○ Offer a percentage off the original price

　5 ▼ %

◉ Discount the original price by a set amount

　3.00

☐ Free Shipping (applies to the first U.S. shipping service)

3. Under Choose Your Discount, select whether the discount applies to price and/or free shipping. If offering a price discount, choose whether to offer a percentage or set amount from the original selling price. The final discounted price must be at least $1.00.

4. Under Choose Your Listings, select whether you want to include listings by one specific category and/or by listing format, or by selecting individual listings. To select individual listings, click **Select Listings Individually**, and select the listings you want to discount from the Create Sale: Select Listings For Sale page, as shown in Figure 10-2. Use the search functions on the top of the page to locate listings, and then select the check box to the left of each listing you want in the sale. Click **Continue** to return to the Markdown Manager: Create Your Sale page.

☑ Add all listings from a category

Select a category ▼

| Select a category |
| Newspapers |
| Magazines |
| Books |
| Manuals |

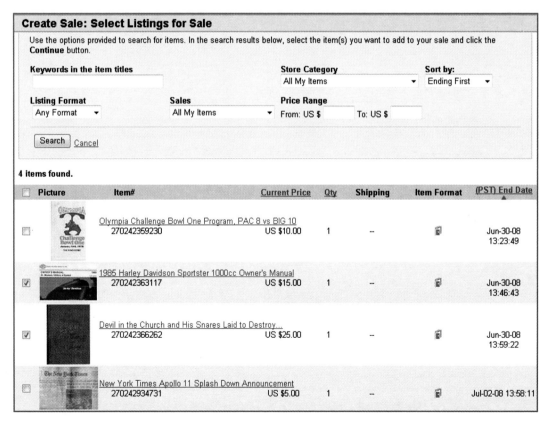

Create Sale: Select Listings for Sale

Use the options provided to search for items. In the search results below, select the item(s) you want to add to your sale and click the **Continue** button.

Keywords in the item titles

Store Category　All My Items ▼

Sort by:　Ending First ▼

Listing Format　Any Format ▼

Sales　All My Items ▼

Price Range　From: US $ 　 To: US $

[Search] Cancel

4 items found.

☐	Picture	Item#	Current Price	Qty	Shipping	Item Format	(PST) End Date
☐		Olympia Challenge Bowl One Program, PAC 8 vs BIG 10 270242359230	US $10.00	1	--	📄	Jun-30-08 13:23:49
☑		1985 Harley Davidson Sportster 1000cc Owner's Manual 270242363117	US $15.00	1	--	📄	Jun-30-08 13:46:43
☑		Devil in the Church and His Snares Laid to Destroy... 270242366262	US $25.00	1	--	📄	Jun-30-08 13:59:22
☐		New York Times Apollo 11 Splash Down Announcement 270242934731	US $5.00	1	--	📄	Jul-02-08 13:58:11

Figure 10-2: You can tag individual listings to be included in a sale.

10

5. Under Promote Your Sale, if you have newsletter subscribers, select which categories of subscribers you want to be notified by e-mail of your sale (see the next section for information on creating marketing e-mails).

6. When finished, click **Create Your Sale** to place your items on sale. The nature of the discount for on-sale items will be identified in listings and in Stores, as shown in Figure 10-3.

Create E-mail Mailings

You can communicate and market your listings to buyers who have expressed an interest in your merchandise line when they add you as a My Favorite Store and subscribe to e-mail newsletters you create. Your mailing lists can promote your more robust-selling Store categories. For example, if you sell electronic entertainment items, you could have a mailing list for DVDs, one for CDs, one for entertainment devices, and so forth.) You can add a message to the e-mail you broadcast, as well as showcase and list your items, similar to the listings buyers see when searching items. An example of an e-mail your subscribers might receive is shown in Figure 10-4.

An item for sale on a listing page.

An item for sale in an eBay Store.

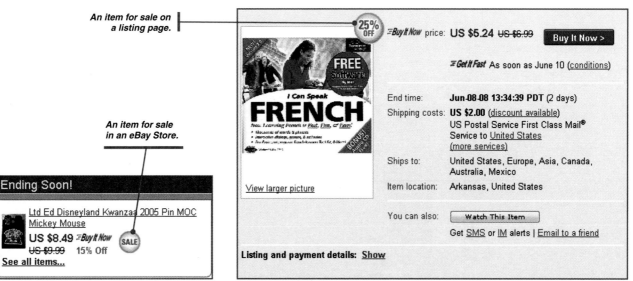

Figure 10-3: Sale items are identified in several places and in different formats.

From: store-newsletter@ebay.com [mailto:store-newsletter@ebay.com]
Sent: Friday, June 06, 2008 11:54 AM
To:
Subject: eBay Seller Email: Check out my Newly Listed Items

 **eBay sent this message to John Cronan** .
Your registered name is included to show this message originated from eBay. Learn more.

 Great news! We have new items in our Store! Take a look at our new inventory and see if you can find some great deals.

New York Times Apollo 11 Splash
Down Announcement

US $5.00 =Buy It Now
Jul-02-08 13:58:11 PDT

See other items in this category:
Newspapers

1985 Harley Davidson Sportster 1000cc
Owner's Manual

US $15.00 =Buy It Now
Jun-30-08 13:46:43 PDT

See other items in this category:
Motorcycle

Figure 10-4: You can easily market your Store to interested buyers by sending them e-mails advertising your merchandise.

CREATE MAILING LISTS

1. From My eBay, on the Selling Manager sidebar, click **Marketing Tools**. On the Marketing Tools page, click **Email Marketing** on the sidebar.

   –Or–

   From your eBay Store home page, click **Seller, Manage Store**. On the Manage My Store page, click **Email Marketing** on the sidebar.

   In either case, the Email Marketing Summary page opens, as shown in Figure 10-5, which lists pending and sent e-mails, and mailing and subscriber lists (whose individual sections can be accessed directly from the Marketing Tools sidebar—see Figure 10-1).

2. In the Mailing Lists section, current mailing lists are displayed along with the number of subscribers in each. Click **Create Mailing List** to create a new mailing list.

   –Or–

   Click the **Action** down arrow, and click **Edit** next to an existing mailing list to change its name.

3. On either the Email Marketing: Create Mailing List or the identical Edit Mailing List page, type a new or revised name. Click **Save**. The change is reflected in the Mailing Lists section. Now you are ready to create the e-mail and distribute it to your mailing lists.

NOTE

You must wait at least six days before sending another e-mail to the same mailing list.

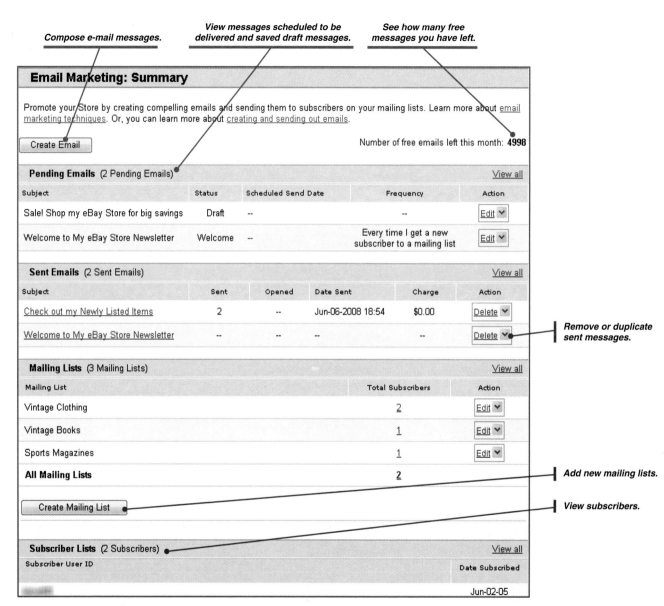

Compose e-mail messages.

View messages scheduled to be delivered and saved draft messages.

See how many free messages you have left.

Email Marketing: Summary

Promote your Store by creating compelling emails and sending them to subscribers on your mailing lists. Learn more about email marketing techniques. Or, you can learn more about creating and sending out emails.

Create Email

Number of free emails left this month: **4998**

Pending Emails (2 Pending Emails)   View all

Subject	Status	Scheduled Send Date	Frequency	Action
Sale! Shop my eBay Store for big savings	Draft	--	--	Edit ✓
Welcome to My eBay Store Newsletter	Welcome	--	Every time I get a new subscriber to a mailing list	Edit ✓

Sent Emails (2 Sent Emails)   View all

Subject	Sent	Opened	Date Sent	Charge	Action
Check out my Newly Listed Items	2	--	Jun-06-2008 18:54	$0.00	Delete ✓
Welcome to My eBay Store Newsletter	--	--	--	--	Delete ✓

Remove or duplicate sent messages.

Mailing Lists (3 Mailing Lists)   View all

Mailing List	Total Subscribers	Action
Vintage Clothing	2	Edit ✓
Vintage Books	1	Edit ✓
Sports Magazines	1	Edit ✓
All Mailing Lists	2	

Create Mailing List

Add new mailing lists.

View subscribers.

Subscriber Lists (2 Subscribers)   View all

Subscriber User ID	Date Subscribed
	Jun-02-05

Figure 10-5: All things promotional e-mail-related can be accessed from in one view.

NOTE

In early 2008, the eBay Store final value fee was changed: 12 percent of the selling price for items up to $25.00; for items $25.00 to $100, $3.00 to cover the first $25.00 plus 8 percent of the selling price for items up to $100; for items $100.01 to $1000, $9.00 to cover the first $100 plus 4 percent of the selling price for items up to $1,000; and for items over $1,000, $45.00 to cover the amount up to $1,000 plus 2 percent of the selling price over $1,000.01

CREATE THE MAILING

1. On the Email Marketing: Summary Page, click **Create Email**.

2. On the Email Marketing: Select A Template page, click the **Type Of Email** down arrow, and select the topic of the e-mail you're sending. Select one of the predesigned layouts or select **Custom** to create your own layout. Click **Continue** when finished.

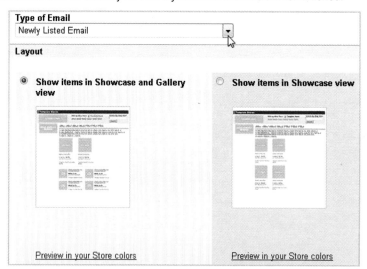

3. On the Email Marketing: Create Email page, you compose your message by selecting options from several sections, as well as composing your text:

- Under **Recipients**, select the mailing lists whose subscribers you want to send the message to. Also choose whether to limit the mailing to those who have made a certain quantity of purchases from you in the last 90 days.

- Under **Send Recurring Email**, choose whether to send e-mails on a recurring frequency and the day of the week to send it. Also, select the **Email Limit** check box to ensure you don't send any message over the free limit set by your Store subscription (see the "Understanding E-mail Messaging Fees" QuickFacts).

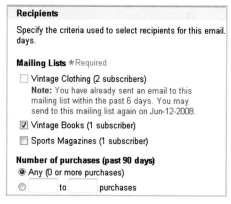

NOTE

For more information on showcasing your items and displaying lists of your items in your eBay content, see "Cross-Promote from eBay" later in the chapter.

- Under **Subject**, which determines the subject line your subscribers will see in their incoming e-mail, accept the default text determined by your choice in Step 2, or edit the text as you want. To avoid any chance of having your message kicked into junk e-mail folders, it's safest to accept the default text.

- Under **Header**, if you have previously created a listing frame, you can have that header also included in the message. (see "Create a Listing Frame" later in the chapter.)

- Under **Personal Message**, type and format the text portion of the e-mail using the text-editing tools on the Standard tab.

  –Or–

  Click the **Enter Your Own HTML** tab, and include text with Hypertext Markup Language (HTML) tags.

Specify Criteria for Automatic Selection

Specify the criteria that will be used to select items automatically for your item list.

Keywords in the item titles	Store Category	Sort by:
sports illustrated swimsuit	All My Items ▾	Ending First ▾

Listing Format	Sales	Price Range
Any Format ▾	Only sale listings ▾	From: US $ 3.00 To: US $ 15.00

[Save Criteria]   Preview search | Cancel

- Under **Item Showcase**, you can select up to four items to highlight in the message or choose to have them displayed based on criteria you establish. Click **Change To Manual Selection** to start adding individual items.

  –Or–

  Click **Change Criteria** to set up display criteria.

  In either case, choose whether to display the items in a horizontal or vertical format.

- Under **Item List**, click **Change Criteria** to modify the default criteria used to set up and display a list of your items at the end of the message, such as those items with certain keywords in the title, certain categories of items, items sorted by ending date or price, and so on. Click **Save Criteria**. Then select a layout and number of items to display, up to a maximum of 50 (more isn't always better, as the e-mail message will, at some point, get too large for many viewers to tolerate).

- Under **Show Your eBay Feedback**, select whether to include your feedback statistics in the message.

4. Click **Preview And Continue**. On the Email Marketing: Preview Email page, review your monthly e-mail account to ensure you have a sufficient number of emails available to be sent and preview how the message will appear. Click **Edit Email** to make changes, and click **Send Email** when done.

   –Or–

   Click **Save Draft** to save your settings and add the draft to your list of pending e-mails displayed in the Pending Emails section (see Figure 10-5).

Books Booklets Etc

Visit my eBay Store: http://stores.ebay.com/Books-Booklets-Etc

Books Booklets Etc

Maintained by: ▓▓▓ (36 ☆) me 📷
Books Booklets Etc specializes in classic, vintage, and antique items. We have a growing selection of printed materials including vehicle manuals, sheet music, magazines, other useful and collectible items.

Thank you for your purchase! Please visit my eBay Store for more great items and friendly, reliable customer service.

New York Times Apollo 11 Splash Down Announcement

US $5.00 *=Buy It Now*
Jul-02-08 13:58:11 PDT

Category: Newspapers

1985 Harley Davidson Sportster 1000cc Owner's Manual

US $15.00 *=Buy It Now*
Jun-30-08 13:46:43 PDT

Category: Motorcycle

Figure 10-6: eBay provides a quick and easy format to create a flyer you can print and use to advertise your eBay Store.

POWER SELLER

Seller Sally

PowerSeller Sally says: "The flyer is a powerful promotional tool that can help keep buyers returning to your eBay Store. To achieve success, you will need repeat buyers, and you need to do everything possible to keep people interested in your Store."

Create a Flyer

Promotional flyers are designed to be printed and distributed to buyers in their packages, posted in areas such as shows and auctions where potential buyers lie, and can used as a type of greeting or business card.

1. From My eBay, on the Selling Manager sidebar, click **Marketing Tools**. On the Marketing Tools page, click **Promotional Flyer** on the sidebar.

   –Or–

   From your eBay Store home page, click **Seller, Manage Store**. On the Manage My Store page, click **Promotional Flyer** on the sidebar.

2. On the Promotional Flyer page, if you are just starting out, click **Create Promotional Flyer** to create a new flyer. If you have already created a flyer, you can view the summary of current settings for a flyer, preview it, and print it. Click **Change** to edit the default flyer that eBay pulls information from your eBay Store to initially set up.

Promotional Flyer		Preview and print	Change
Store header		
Include my Store name:	**Yes**	
Include my Store URL:	**Yes**	
Include my Store logo:	**Yes**	
Include my user ID:	**Yes**	
Include my Store description:	**Yes**	
Page border:	**Yes - Store Colors**	
Custom message:	**Yes**	

3. On the Store Promotional Flyer: Create Flyer page, select the Store components you want to include in your flyer (see "Create the Mailing" earlier in the chapter for an explanation for most of the flyer components). Note that adding more content than what's offered in the default settings may increase the size of the flyer beyond a single 8.5-inch-by-11-inch sheet of paper.

4. Click **Preview Flyer** when finished. Review the flyer and make any changes by clicking the relevant link at the bottom of the preview page.

5. Click **Save Settings And Print Flyer** to retain a copy on eBay and print a copy you can send to purchasers (see Figure 10-6).

QUICK**FACTS**

UNDERSTANDING CROSS-PROMOTION

The idea of leveraging marketing opportunities between different business lines, known in marketing circles as *cross-promoting*, is not a new concept developed by the eBay marketing wizards in San Jose. eBay has refined the cross-promotion concept, however, productized its delivery, and integrated it throughout its business model. eBay cross-promotions are free merchandising ads that display select examples of your other merchandise for sale and that encourage buyers and bidders to check out your other listings, as shown in Figure 10-7. Probably the most successful example of cross-promotion in modern business practice is Harpo Production, Inc., the business end of daytime TV host, author, actress, and magazine producer, Oprah Winfrey. She consistently cross-promotes her various outlets: her magazines advertise her Web site, which heralds her TV show, which highlights her book club, which points to affiliates (for example, Dr. Phil), which in total have enabled Oprah to become one of *TIME Magazine*'s 100 Most Influential People in the World. Now there's a high bar to which you can aspire!

Cross-Promoting Across eBay

Cross-promoting between your eBay listings, eBay Stores, and off-eBay Web sites and traditional businesses allows you to integrate your business outlets and leverage the marketing potential of each selling channel. eBay provides several cross-promoting techniques and tools that help you drive potential buyers to your eBay listings, but, understandably, not much in the opposite direction that encourages off-eBay sales.

Leverage Your Off-eBay Web Sites

If you have a business in the 21st century, you probably have a Web site that supports it. Business Web sites are set up to satisfy two major goals and typically blend the two, as shown in three unique Web sites in Figure 10-8:

- **Informational Web sites** provide details about products, services, contact information, and other details of the business. Informational Web sites are typically the entry-level foray by a new business into setting up an online presence. They don't require a high degree of sophistication with online technology or tools and can be cheaply hosted. Although, as the Internet matures, more and more users expect an increasing level of features and tools to make their online purchasing more robust, safer, and more closely aligned with traditional shopping and buyer experiences.

Figure 10-7: eBay cross-promotions are an outgrowth of accepted business and marketing practices.

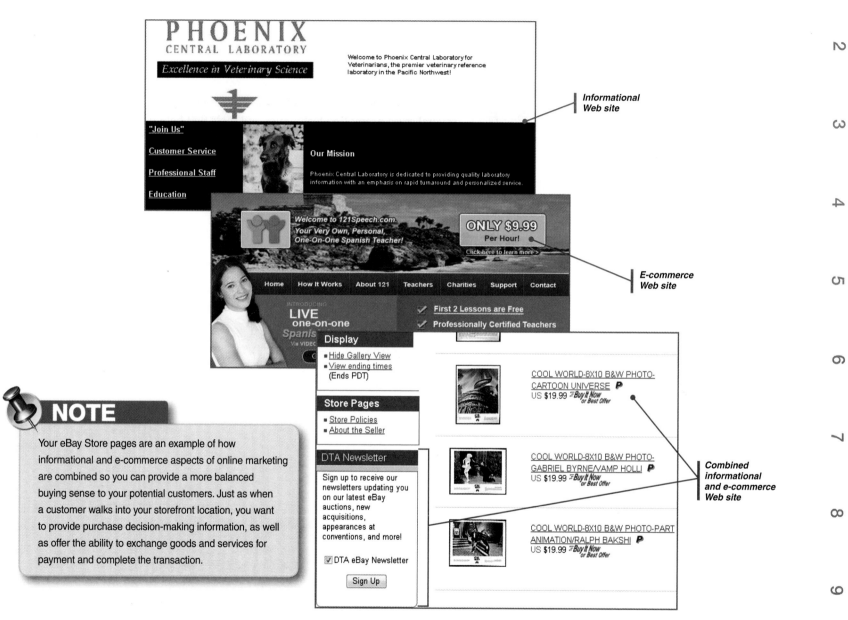

Informational Web site

E-commerce Web site

Combined informational and e-commerce Web site

Figure 10-8: Web sites can cater to specific or combined needs.

- **E-commerce Web sites** provide users with the ability to purchase items online. More than simply listing items for sale, these Web sites typically have shopping basket-type software that allows the user to select and buy items using credit-card and shipping information that was integrated into the purchasing process.

- **Combined Web sites** blend informational and purchasing features. These sites are exemplified by an eBay Store, where you deliver items for sale, but can also provide ancillary information to your buyers through the use of custom pages.

LINK TO eBAY LISTINGS

eBay doesn't go out of its way to encourage links from your listings and other eBay pages to promote off-eBay sites (see "Cross-Promote from eBay" for a few exceptions). However, eBay does encourage you to link to your listings on eBay from whatever external online presence you have.

To drive "outsiders" to your eBay listings, you can use the eBay logo to provide links to the eBay home page and to your listings.

1. Click **Site Map** on the eBay header, and under Sell | Selling Activities, click **Promote Your Listings With Link Buttons**.

2. Select the links that you want on your Web site. You can link to the eBay home page or to a page that displays a list of items you have for sale or bid.

3. Type the Uniform Resource Locators (URLs) of your Web pages that will contain the links.

4. Read the eBay Link License Agreement, and click **I Agree** (if you don't agree, you won't be able to continue).

5. On the Instructions For Installing Buttons On Your Site page, copy the HTML code for the link you want, as shown in Figure 10-9, and paste it onto your Web page.

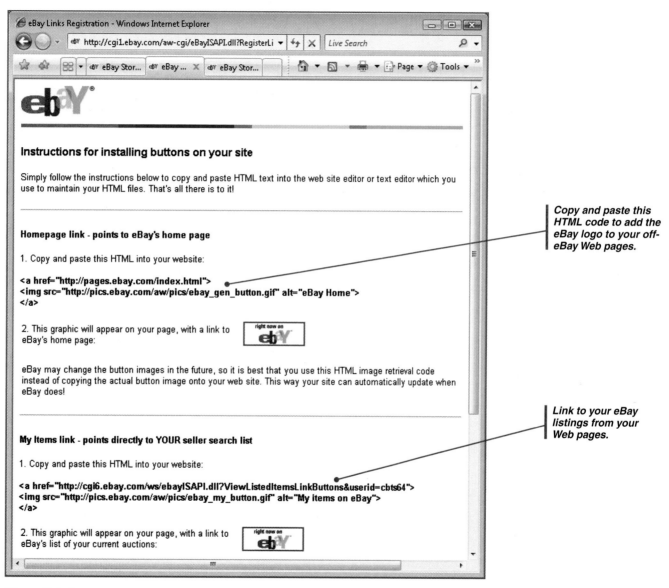

Figure 10-9: On your Web pages, you can place HTML code that displays the eBay logo with a link to your current listings.

Store Categories

Store home
- Golden Age Superhero Comics (743)
- Golden Age Horror/Sci-Fi (297)
- Golden Age Western Comics (568)
- Golden Age Crime Comics (288)
- Golden Age Romance Comics (144)
- Golden Age Other Comics (1074)
- Silver Age Marvel Comics (961)
- Silver Age DC Comics (435)
- Silver Age Other Comics (849)
- CGC Graded Comics (22)

Browse Our Thousands Of Unique Items!

Golden Age Comics:
`Select One` ▾

Silver Age Comics:
`Select One` ▾

Select One
Marvel
DC
Other

Figure 10-10: Duplicate your eBay Store categories on your off-eBay Web site.

LINK TO eBAY STORE CATEGORIES FROM OFF-eBAY

You can link to your eBay Store categories pages from your business Web site and get customers that much closer to viewing your listings.

1. Open the business Web page where you want to create links to your eBay Store in a Web design program, for example, Microsoft Expression, or even in a text editor, such as Notepad.

2. Create a navigation bar or a set of links using labels that closely match the names of the category pages you created for your eBay Store, as shown in Figure 10-10. Leave the design/editor program running.

3. Open your eBay Store, and under Store Categories on the navigation bar, click the first category you want to use.

4. In your browser's address bar, select the URL for the page. Right-click the selection and click **Copy** from the context menu (you don't need to copy the URL beyond your category name).

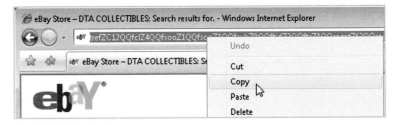

5. Switch to your design/editor program. Create the A HREF hyperlink tag for the link to the category page you just opened by pasting the URL into a Create Hyperlink–type dialog box or directly into the HTML code for the page.

```
10 </p>
11 <a href="http://cgi6.ebay.com/ws/ebayISAPI.dll?ViewListedItemsLinkButtons&userid=      ">
12 <img src="http://pics.ebay.com/aw/pics/ebay_my_button.gif" alt="My items on eBay">
13 </a>
```

6. Repeat Steps 3 through 5 to create links on your business Web page that target each Store category in your eBay Store that you want to display.

7. When finished, save your business Web page, and upload it to the server where your business Web site is hosted. Now, any time a potential customer views your business Web page, he or she will have the opportunity to view the listings you have within your Store category pages.

CREATE AN eBAY STORE MIRROR SITE

One way to work around eBay's listing policy (see the "Reviewing the eBay Links Policy QuickFacts") is to create an off-eBay Web site that contains only eBay listings. While the site itself shows little association with eBay, any item a buyer clicks takes them to eBay and the eBay listing. While this might seem like a duplication of efforts, and it is, it provides several benefits:

- You get another URL that doesn't appear to be associated with eBay. Compare *www. vickisgoodies.com* with *http://stores.ebay.com/Vickis-Goodies.*

- You increase the odds that search engines such as Google will direct searches to your items.

- There are Web sites that offer free tools to set up your mirror site (though they often charge a small fee for the optional domain name registration giving you your unique URL), and they do all the heavy lifting of setting up the Web interface. Figure 10-11 shows one such mirror Web site. (see Chapter 5 for more information on the suite of auction management products offered by Auctiva, www.auctiva.com).

Cross-Promote from eBay

You can use a number of techniques to display your listings and information about your items and eBay business from eBay pages. The most commonly used cross-promotional tool is a display featuring 12 other listings, but you can also link to certain off-site Web sites (see "Create an eBay Store Mirror Site" and the "Reviewing the eBay Links Policy" QuickFacts earlier in the chapter) and to other eBay Stores.

NOTE

Though the cross-promotion feature is available to all sellers, many features are only available to Store owners. For example, the cross-promotion list box also appears to a buyer when he or she *views* a listing page in an eBay Store.

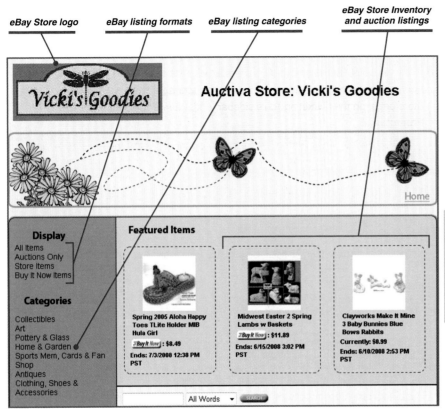

eBay Store logo   eBay listing formats   eBay listing categories   eBay Store Inventory and auction listings

Figure 10-11: A mirror site to your eBay Store listings provides a greater Web presence.

DISPLAY YOUR ITEM LISTINGS

This cross-promotional feature available to eBay Stores allows you to display your listings on your promotional flyer and custom Store pages. You can display as many listings as you have that matches the criteria you establish on custom pages in your Store pages (30 listings per page), but only six listings will show on your flyer. If you don't have enough listings that match your criteria, the list simply doesn't appear. You can choose a List or Gallery View.

Item Title	Price	Bids	End Date PDT
New York Times Apollo 11 Splash Down Announcement	US $5.00	*Buy It Now*	Jul-02-08 13:58:11 PDT
1985 Harley Davidson Sportster 1000cc Owner's Manual	US $15.00	*Buy It Now*	Jun-30-08 13:46:43 PDT
Devil in the Church and His Snares Laid to Destroy...	US $25.00	*Buy It Now*	Jun-30-08 13:59:22 PDT
Olympia Challenge Bowl One Program, PAC 8 vs BIG 10	US $10.00	*Buy It Now*	Jun-30-08 13:23:49 PDT

USE THE eBAY CROSS-PROMOTION FEATURE

This is one eBay marketing feature that is available to all sellers. You can set up rules to establish which eBay categories are searched to find their items to promote. Up to 12 matching items are displayed in a four-at-a-time scrolling list box (see Figure 10-7).

TIP

Cross-promotional notification options are selected on your Site Preferences page (Promote Similar Items area) of your My eBay account settings. See Chapter 2 for information on changing these settings.

1. To set up or change cross-promotion rules, click **Marketing Tools** on the My eBay sidebar, and click **Cross-Promotion** on the Marketing Tools page sidebar under Item Promotion.

   –Or–

   From your eBay Store home page, click **Seller, Manage Store**. On the Manage My Store page, on the Marketing Tools sidebar, under Item Promotion, click **Cross-Promotion**.

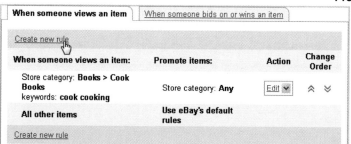

When someone views an item			
When someone bids on or wins an item			
Create new rule			
When someone views an item:	**Promote items:**	**Action**	**Change Order**
Store category: **Books > Cook Books** keywords: **cook cooking**	Store category: **Any**	Edit ▾	≫ ≫
All other items	**Use eBay's default rules**		
Create new rule			

2. On the Cross-Promotion: Summary page, click **Manage** to set up rules for when someone bids or wins one of your items and for all other situations (Store owners can also set up rules for when someone views an item). For each of the choices displayed in the tab, click **Create New Rule** to be led through a series of criteria.

   –Or–

   Click **Edit** under the Action column to modify an existing rule.

3. When finished setting up a rule, click **Save Rule**.

SHOWCASE ITEMS IN A STORE

In addition to the cross-promotional feature available to all eBay sellers, Store owners can further highlight items using a feature called *item showcase*. The items will appear in Store promotional flyers you create and in marketing e-mails you send to subscribers. You can select specific items to display, or you can set criteria that choose which items to use, much like selecting criteria for cross promotions (see the previous section). Information on creating flyers and marketing e-mails in eBay Stores is covered earlier in the chapter.

TIP

To see your current cross-promotion settings for participation and how your items appear, click **Settings** under Cross Promotion on the Marketing Tools sidebar.

TIP

One way to showcase your items beyond what eBay offers is to use third-party features that basically add a showcase to all your listings. Figure 10-12 shows one example you can add for free. Chapter 5 describes how to integrate Auctiva into your eBay arsenal of tools.

Figure 10-12: When eBay doesn't provide what you want, look to third-party companies.

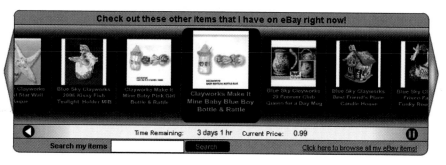

PowerSeller Sally says: "If your eBay Store items complement merchandise sold by other eBay Stores but are not in direct competition with them, consider contacting the Store owners and asking them if they will include a link to your Store on their Store page if you reciprocate with a link to theirs. Just take note that you are limited to ten links on your Store home page, but the sky's the limit on your custom pages."

PowerSeller Sally says: "If your Store Inventory items are not selling at the pace you'd like, experiment with listing them on eBay in either auction or fixed-price formats (and take advantage of reduced fixed price listings fees!). That way, you get the added benefit of eBay listings directing buyers to check your eBay Store."

Figure 10-13: You have several options on which Store elements you want to appear on your listing frame.

CREATE A LISTING FRAME

To more readily expose buyers and bidders to your eBay Store, you can apply layout elements to all your listings in a listing frame. The frame situates your Store header above the item description and can apply your Store navigation bar on the left side of the listing.

1. To set up a listing frame, click **Marketing Tools** on the My eBay sidebar, and click **Listing Frame** on the Marketing Tools page sidebar.

   –Or–

   From your eBay Store home page, click **Seller, Manage Store**. On the Manage My Store page, on the Marketing Tools sidebar, click **Listing Frame**.

2. On the Listing Frame page, select the elements and links you want to appear in your frame. Elements and links are divided between the header and the navigation bar, as shown in Figure 10-13.

3. Make your selection and click **Preview Your Listing Frame** to see how it will look. Click **Apply** when finished.

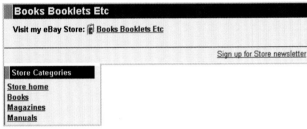

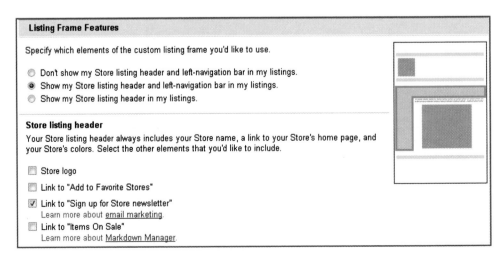

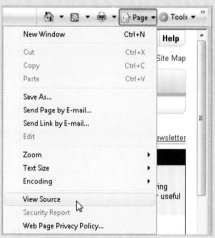

Add Search Engine Keywords to Your Store Pages

More and more people use the Internet to research and locate items they want to buy, typically by typing keywords in search engines, such as Google. You can take advantage of this growing phenomenon by making sure your eBay Store listings have keywords and tags that best describe your Store and products, and that they are readily available to be mined by the search engines' "data crawlers." eBay will display the current keywords found on your Store pages and let you add others.

VIEW YOUR KEYWORDS

1. On your Store's home page, click **Seller, Manage Store**.

2. On the Manage My Store page, click **Search Engine Keywords** on the sidebar. The pages in your Store are listed with primary and secondary keywords.

Search Engine Keywords

Below are keywords currently used on your eBay Store pages. You can customize these keywords to increase your chances of potential buyers finding your store pages when using search engines such as MSN, Google, Yahoo, and so on. eBay uses these keywords to create page Titles and Meta Tags that help search engines better understand and present your eBay store pages.

Category: **All Categories**

Store Page	Current Keywords Used in Your eBay Store		
	Primary keyword(s)	Secondary keyword(s)	
Store Front Page	Books Booklets Etc	Newspapers, Football, Vintage Books, Motorcycle	Edit
Books	Books Booklets Etc, Books	Devil in the Church and His Snares Laid to Destroy...	Edit
Magazines	Books Booklets Etc, Magazines	Olympia Challenge Bowl One Program, PAC 8 vs BIG 10	Edit
Newspapers	Books Booklets Etc, Newspapers	New York Times Apollo 11 Splash Down Announcement	Edit

Professor Polly says: "Search engines look primarily at the data contained in two HTML tags in a Web page. Default and custom keywords are located in the TITLE and META tags, located in the HEAD section."

Keywords found in a Web page title

Keywords found in your Store's description

Custom and default keywords

Books-Booklets-Etc_Manuals_Motorcycle_W0QQfsubZ823156018[1] - Notepad

File   Edit   Format   View   Help

```
<html><head>
<!--eBay V3- msxml 6.0 XXXXXXXXXXXXXXXXXXXXXXXXXXXX-->
<meta http-equiv="Content-Type" content="text/html; charset=UTF-8">
<title>eBay Store - Books Booklets Etc: Motorcycle: 1985 Harley Davidson Sportster 1000cc
Owner's Manual</title>
<meta name="description" content="Books Booklets Etc: Motorcycle - 1985 Harley Davidson
Sportster 1000cc Owner's Manual - all at low prices">
<meta name="keywords" content="motorcycle, 1985 harley davidson sportster 1000cc owner's
manual">
<meta name="XslBuildInfo" content="2008-05-29 20:45:13,,, nu.rusqv651,RcmdId
StoreFront,RlogId p4pqiufvehq%60%3C%3Dkw%2Bppqtt374-11a648daac5"><meta name="Arg1"
content="nu.rusqv651"><link rel="alternate" type="application/rss+xml" title="eBay Store"
href="http://rss.api.ebay.com/ws/rssapi?FeedName=StoreItems&amp;siteId=0&amp;language=en-
US&amp;output=RSS20&amp;storeId=6475168"><script type="text/javascript"
```

Figure 10-14: Keywords found by search engines are primarily found in the TITLE and META tags in a Web page.

	New Custom Keywords	eBay Default
Primary Keyword 1	Books Booklets Etc	Books Booklets Etc
Primary Keyword 2	Magazines	Magazines
Secondary Keyword 1	Olympia Challenge Bowl C	Olympia Challenge Bowl One Program, PAC 8 vs BIG 10
Secondary Keyword 2		
Secondary Keyword 3		

ADD CUSTOM KEYWORDS TO A STORE PAGE

1. On the Search Engine Keywords page, click **Edit** next to the Store page for which you want to add or change keywords.

2. On the Edit Keywords page, change the current keyword or add new keywords in the **New Custom Keywords** text box next to a particular primary or secondary keyword.

3. Click **Save** when finished. Changes will be made to the TITLE and META tags on the Web page, although eBay might not include all keywords you added or changed.

Create an About Me Page

You can create a page about your business (or self), known as an About Me page, that others can reference when researching your eBay activities. If you have an About Me page, a special icon **me** will be displayed next to your User ID and in your eBay Store header.

1. From My eBay, click **Personal Information** on the sidebar. Under Account Information, click **Edit** to the right of About Me Page.

2. The About Me introductory page describes what the page is used for. Click **Create Your Page**.

3. Select how you want to create the page: by using eBay's step-by-step method or by adding your own HTML code. Make your selection and click **Continue**.

Create your About Me page

Begin by clicking the button below.

Create Your Page

10

Browser Earl

4. Add content to your page by using the supplied tools, such as standard eBay text-entry boxes for paragraph text (or copy and paste, or enter you own HTML), eBay Picture Services for adding pictures, and labels and links to Web pages (see the "Reviewing the eBay Links Policy" QuickFacts earlier in the chapter for general linking do's and don'ts). Figure 10-15 shows some of the tools that are available for you to easily add content to the page. Click **Continue** when finished.

Standard	Enter your own HTML

Font Name ▾ Size ▾ Color ▾ **B** *I* U ≡ ≡ ≡ ☰ ☰ ☰ ☰

Preview Paragraph 2

Add pictures
Add your favorite pictures to your About Me page using these tips.

eBay Basic Picture Services	Your Web hosting

Label for Picture 1 **Picture 1** Browse...

Example: The Real Me

Label for Picture 2 **Picture 2** Browse...

Having problems? Learn about eBay Picture Services or get quick troubleshooting tips. Combined picture size cannot exceed 2 MB.

Show Your eBay Activity
You can include your latest listings and feedback information. If you have more than 200 listings or a feedback score greater than 100, eBay will automatically include a link to your Member Profile page.

Show Feedback You've Received:
Show no comments ▾

Label Your Listings: **Show Your Current Listings:**
Show no items ▾

Example: P.G. Wodehouse First Editions

Figure 10-15: You can add text, a picture of yourself, links to Web pages, and your current listings to your About Me page.

Vicki's Goodies

Maintained by: dvdet (8581 ☆) ✦ Power Seller me 🔲

I carry a broad range of collectibles...specializing in Blue Sky Clayworks, Diane Artware, fantasy collectibles like unicorns & mermaids for the ladies. For the men, I offer firefighter & military memorabilia. US Navy and Marines, World War II, & samurai warriors.

About the Seller

← Back to previous page

What You Need to Know About Vicki's Goodies

The Former Suited Me...But Still Bonded!

I am a Bonded Seller

The buySAFE Seal on my listing indicates that:

I have passed the comprehensive buySAFE Business Inspection

Your transaction is protected by a 10-Point Guarantee

buySAFE or not at all

buy safe™

Make sure it's real. Always click on the seal.

Yes, you can do it! You can quit your job as a lawyer to stay home with young children.

The picture up above isn't really me. But I was a lawyer and I did wear a suit...I was just never that tall and thin.

I sometimes say that ebay saved my life. Several years back, I lost a child. I found that being a lawyer after that just wasn't what it used to be. I'd have some whiplash client come in and I'd want to say "Get over it! Stop whining." (Some disgruntled ebayers may report that I still say that.) So when I was pregnant with one of my many boys, I decided to stay home and be a full-time Mom. My little boy who had died actually caught what killed him at a daycare so I vowed to never let any other of my children be raised by someone else and possibly be exposed to anything harmful.

While that is a wonderful sentiment, it is extremely hard for a Type A personality (part Shark)

Listings

To protect bidder privacy, when the price or highest bid on an item reaches or exceeds a certain level, User IDs will be displayed as anonymous names. For auction items, a bold price means at least one bid has been received.

Note: Anonymous names may appear more than once and may represent different bidders.

What's Happening at Vicki's Goodies

Item	Start	End	Price	Title	High Bidder/Status
				White Hand-Beaded	

Figure 10-16: An About Me Page lets you toot your own horn and show your listings and links.

TIP

To change a current About Me page, follow the same steps to create one, and the forms will be prepopulated with your current settings.

5. Choose a layout, preview the page, and click **Submit**. Figure 10-16 shows a sample About Me page. Your About Me page will be available from your profile on your listings and from your Store's pages. Click the **About The Seller** link in the Store Pages area on the left navigation bar.

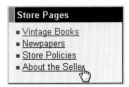

Store Pages
- Vintage Books
- Newpapers
- Store Policies
- About the Seller

Use the eBay Affiliate Program

Ever hear of a fee-less eBay program that not only charges you nothing but also can pay you serious money? No, this is not a lure from an infomercial. The eBay Affiliate program pays you to drive users from your existing Web sites to eBay.com, several of its international sites, and/or Half.com. The payment set up for an eBay site is two-fold. You get paid:

- A percent of revenues on winning bids or purchases by customers who purchase within seven days of clicking your link to the eBay site.

- A fee for each new user who registers on the eBay site within 30 days of clicking your link and who places a bid or makes a Buy It Now purchase. The more users you drive to eBay, the more you are paid for each. For example, if you drive up to 49 users in a month, you get $25 each; increase that to between 50 and under 2,000 users, and you get $28 each.

QUICKFACTS

eBAY-ING YOUR TRADITIONAL BUSINESS

The classic example of a traditional business being overwhelmed by eBay is the local antiques dealer who starts to list items on eBay in addition to operating his or her brick-and-mortar store. For a time, both conventional and eBay sales support the business's bottom line, but over time, the eBay sales start to outshine the across-the-counter transactions. In time, the brick-and-mortar shingle is taken down (and sold on eBay), the overhead costs are recouped, and the proprietor now spends his or her days traveling the globe for new merchandise instead of being chained to a 9-to-5 retail operation. Of course, that's the fairy tale version. Along the way, as with any startup business, there will be despair over the hours you have to spend keeping your Store up and going—that is, no global travel. Not to mention other challenges that the eBayer has no control over, such as eBay fees and new rules, suppliers going dry, and so forth. But there are many success stories of people unchaining themselves from traditional toil and making it with eBay as their partner. "Yes, you can do it! You can quit your job as a lawyer to stay home with your young children." This is the opening line on the About Me page of one of the PowerSellers who contributed to this book (see Figure 10-16).

TIP

If you want to easily create an online storefront with tools to handle Web site hosting, marketing, payment and order management, and inventory and reporting, eBay ProStores might be your answer. ProStores are eBay Stores on steroids and provide eBay integration without being overwhelmed and totally controlled by eBay. You will even receive a 30 percent discount on the subscription fee if you also own an eBay Store. Click **Site Map** on the eBay header, and click **ProStores** under Sell | Web Stores to see if this is something you can use to expand your eBay and online selling business.

The payment for Half.com is based on a percentage of total sales your customers spend within 30 days of clicking your link.

Payment Structure

Time Period	Apr 01, 2008 - Oct 29, 2008 ▼
Payment Structure	Half.com

Monthly total sales

Total sales generated	% of total sales
$0.00 - $499.99	5.00%
$500.00 - $999.99	6.00%
$1,000.00 - $9,999.99	7.00%
$10,000.00 - $49,999.99	8.00%
$50,000.00 - $99,999.99	10.00%
$100,000.00 - $499,999.99	12.00%
$500,000.00 - $1,499,999.99	13.00%
$1,500,000.00+	14.00%

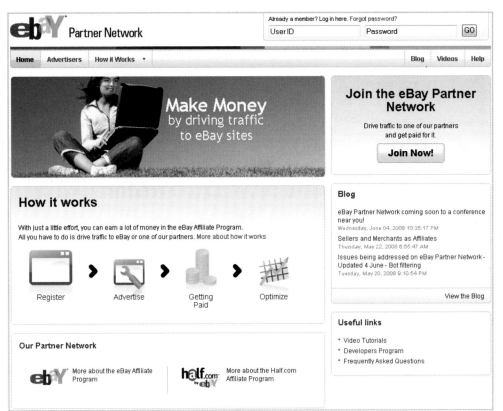

To learn more about the eBay Affiliate program:

1. Click **Site Map** on the eBay header.

2. Under Community | More Community Programs, click **eBay Affiliate Program**.

3. On the Affiliate Program page, shown in Figure 10-17, review the material available from the links on the four-step How It Works section.

4. Click one of the several **Join Now** links.

5. On the Join The eBay Partner Network, accept the eBay Partner Network agreement and privacy policy, and select the programs you want to be affiliated with. Click **Continue**.

6. On the next page, fill out your personal and business contact information, and click **Submit Application** when finished. You will be contacted as to whether you are accepted into the program.

Figure 10-17: eBay provides monetary incentives for you to drive customers to its sites or to Half.com.

Index

customer base
    determining location of, 10
    researching, 7
customer service, providing, 59–60

D

Delete option, using with eBay Stores, 129
demurrage, avoiding in international
    trade, 42
departments. *See* categories
Description Builder, using, 85
desktop, setting up for Listing Central,
    53–55
digital camera, considering for Listing
    Central area, 54
direct sellers. *See also* community sellers;
    sellers
    becoming for nonprofits, 187–188
    defined, 179, 181
    fees for, 188
    registering as on MissionFish,
        189, 191
discounting items, 200–202
discussion boards
    joining, 14–15
    reviewing, 151–152
Display Settings, changing for eBay Stores,
    125–126
disputes, resolving, 113
distribution channel, defined, 38
donation account, using with Giving
    Works, 197
donations, requesting tax receipts for, 198
donors, identifying for fundraising, 183
downloaded data, archiving, 107
drop-off store franchise, starting, 153–156.
    See also eBay Stores
drop-shipping, using, 43–44
DSRs (Detailed Seller Ratings)
    calculating, 108
    checking, 19
duplicate listings, creating in Turbo Lister,
    85–86
Dutch auctions, using, 26–27
duty rates, assignment of, 40–41

E

eBay
    charity auctions on, 180
    getting free packaging material
        from, 65
    nonprofits supported by, 180
eBay Affiliate program, using, 220–222
eBay alerts, receiving, 60
eBay announcements page, checking, 90
eBay brand, establishing, 33–35
eBay businesses
    automating, 103–106
    benefits of, 2
    funding, 16
    outlining, 3–4
    transforming traditional businesses
        to, 221
eBay citizen, being good example of, 5
eBay Giving Works
    accessing, 183
    becoming nonprofit direct seller on,
        188–189, 191
    fees for, 188–189
    locating link to, 181
    searching for nonprofits on, 191–193
    using, 181
    using donation account with, 197
    eBay listings. *See* listings
eBay Live!, attending, 16–17
eBay Motors
    accessing original display of, 158
    advantages and disadvantages
        of, 158
    entering information into, 163–165
    number of cars sold to date on, 158
    paying fees related to, 165–166
    regularity of cars sold on, 158
    selling vehicles on, 163
    using NetNeutrals with, 113–114
eBay ProStores feature, accessing, 221
eBay Radio, listening to, 19–20
eBay services, using, 49–50
eBay sites, adding to Turbo Lister, 84
eBay Stores. *See also* drop-off store franchise
    adding search engine keywords to,
        217–218

advertising, 207
    benefits to marketing, 200
    changing default colors for, 133
    changing layouts of, 125–126
    changing order of categories for,
        129–130
    choosing themes for, 125–126
    creating custom pages for, 135–136
    creating mirror sites for, 213–214
    creating promotion boxes for,
        131–132
    creating store inventory listings
        for, 131
    creating sub-categories for, 129
    customizing promotion boxes for,
        132–133
    displaying, 123
    displaying auction listings in, 116
    establishing basic information for,
        123–124
    features and benefits of, 116–117
    managing custom pages for, 137–138
    modifying settings for, 121–126
    naming, 117–121
    opening, 117
    organizing to sell vehicles on,
        160–162
    receiving toll-free phone support
        for, 120
    renaming and deleting for eBay
        Stores, 129
    selecting subscription level for,
        117–121
    setting up categories for, 127–130
    setting up quickly, 120
    showcasing items in, 215
    using Feature List with, 130
    using logos with, 123–124
eBay tools, using, 49–50
eBay trading assistants (TAs). *See* TAs
    (trading assistants)
eBay training, receiving, 22
eBay transaction data, downloading to
    QuickBooks, 49
eBay University Learning Center, 22
eBay visitors, record-breaking number of, 7
e-commerce Web sites, using, 210

Edit Item window in Turbo Lister, using,
    87–88
EIN (Employer Identification Number),
    obtaining, 13
electronic categories, selecting, 72–73
e-mail, creating for mailings, 205–206
Email Marketing: Summary page, 204
e-mail messaging, fees for, 205
e-mails
    automating, 105
    receiving wireless versions of, 60
employees
    assigning for customer service, 59
    considering for Listing Central
        area, 55
Employer Identification Number (EIN),
    obtaining, 13
entertainment categories, selecting, 72
escalation procedures, developing, 59
escrow service, using, 111
estate sales, finding items at, 37
Excel spreadsheets, using to capture
    purchase data, 47–48
expenses, cutting, 68–69

F

Feature List option, using with eBay
    Stores, 130
Featured Plus! visibility upgrade,
    described, 75
federal Tax ID number, obtaining, 13
FedEx, getting free packaging material
    from, 65
feedback
    leaving automatically, 106–107
    mediating with NetNeutrals, 113–114
    providing, 108
feedback scores, importance to TAs, 144
fee-less program, Affiliate program as,
    220–222
fees, reducing, 68–69, 90
file formats, examples of, 49
final value fee, determining, 205
Financial Data section of business plan,
    described, 6

T

U

V

W